Ezra Pound and *The Cantos*

Ezra Pound and
The Cantos:
A RECORD OF
STRUGGLE

WENDY STALLARD FLORY

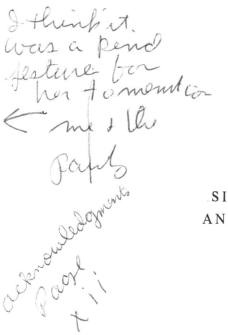

I think it.
was a pend
gesture for
her to mention
← me + the
papers

acknowledgments
page
xiii

SITY PRESS
AND LONDON

Designed by James J. Johnson
and set in IBM Press Roman type.
Printed in the United States of America by
Edwards Brothers, Inc., Ann Arbor, Mich.

Published in Great Britain, Europe, Africa, and
Asia (except Japan) by Yale University Press,
Ltd., London. Distributed in Australia and
New Zealand by Book & Film Services, Artarmon,
N.S.W., Australia; and in Japan by Harper & Row,
Publishers, Tokyo Office.

Library of Congress Cataloging in Publication Data

Flory, Wendy Stallard.
   Ezra Pound and *The Cantos*.

   Bibliography: p.
   Includes index.
    1. Pound, Ezra Loomis, 1885–1972. Cantos.   I. Title
PS3531.082C2935   811'.5'2   79–23904
ISBN 0-300-02392-8

For my mother and father
Ethel Smart Stallard
F. Clifford Stallard

Time that is intolerant
Of the brave and innocent,
And indifferent in a week
To a beautiful physique.

Worships language and forgives
Everyone by whom it lives;

Auden, "In Memory of W. B. Yeats"

Contents

Illustrations

1. *Charon and the Condemned Souls* by William Blake. Watercolor, graphite, and ink on cream colored paper, 37.2 x 52.3 cm. Reproduced by permission of the Fogg Art Museum, Harvard University. Grenville L. Winthrop Bequest. *Page 91*

2. *The Angel Crossing Styx* by William Blake. Illustrations to Dante's *Divine Comedy,* Inferno, Cantos 8 and 10, Roe 19. Pen and watercolor over pencil, 37 x 52.3 cm. Reproduced by permission of the National Gallery of Victoria, Melbourne. Felton Bequest, 1920. *Page 92*

3. *The Circle of the Lustful: Francesca da Rimini* by William Blake, by permission of the Tate Gallery. *Page 134*

4. *Madonna del Roseto* by Stefano da Zevio, by permission of the Director of Museums and Art Galleries of the Commune of Verona. *Page 137*

5. *Guidoriccio da Fogliano victorious over the castles of Montemassi and Sassoforte of Maremma* by Simone Martini, by permission of Aldo Cairola, Director of the Civic Museum of Verona. *Page 159*

6. *Guidoriccio da Fogliano,* detail. *Page 160*

7. *Madonna Enthroned with the Child, Angels, and Saints* by Simone Martini, by permission of Aldo Cairola, Director of the Civic Museum of Verona. *Page 161*

8. *Madonna Enthroned,* detail. *Page 162*

9. *Madonna,* Torcello Cathedral, Venice. Photograph reproduced by permission of Miss Josephine Powell. *Page 273*

Acknowledgments

I should first like to acknowledge my indebtedness to the late Gordon Mills. The quiet subtlety and complexity of his thinking was an incentive to his students always to experiment with new approaches and to test new hypotheses. His example was an inspiration and his unexpected death a great loss. I am particularly grateful to Kathleen Tillotson who, during my undergraduate days, set by her own example a standard of scholarly excellence that continues to be a touchstone. I owe special thanks to A. Walton Litz, whose careful reading and suggestions, both incisive and "excisive," have made this a more informative and less unwieldy book than it would otherwise have been. Clark Emery, whose own book on *The Cantos* is a model of lucid and helpful commentary, was particularly generous with his time and offered many helpful suggestions. To Adrienne Rich who, like Pound, seems tireless in her readiness to help other writers, I am most grateful for her generous encouragement. Mary de Rachewiltz kindly took the time from her very busy schedule of work in the Pound Archive and on her own translation of *The Cantos* into Italian to give the manuscript of the book a very thorough reading, and her unique knowledge of Pound's life and thought made her suggestions especially valuable. Many insights into Pound's poetry have come out of my frequent, provocative, and highly enjoyable discussions with David Anderson and James Wilhelm and also with Richard Reid, Christine Froula, and George Kearns, whose comments on this book at various stages have been very helpful and much appreciated. For their interest in and encouragement of my work

I would like to thank Alice Crozier, Alicia Ostriker, David Kalstone, Adrianne Baytop, and Richard Quaintance; also, for permission to use her powerful portrait of the poet, I am most grateful to Joann Falbo. It has been a pleasure to work with Ellen Graham, my editor, and Sheila Huddleston, my copyeditor. Finally I acknowledge a very special kind of indebtedness—to Quentin and Graham, whose company is a constant education in enthusiasm and new perspectives, and, most of all, for help of all kinds and at all times—to David, "whose firmness makes my circle just . . ."

Quotations from *Charles Olson and Ezra Pound: An Encounter at St. Elizabeths,* edited by Catherine Seelye, are reprinted by permission of Viking Penguin, Inc. Copyright © 1975 by the University of Connecticut.

Quotation from W. H. Auden's "In Memory of W. B. Yeats," from *Collected Poems,* edited by Edward Mendelson, is reprinted by permission of Random House, Inc. Copyright 1940 and renewed 1968 by W. H. Auden.

Quotations from *Time and Western Man,* by Wyndham Lewis, are reprinted by permission of the Executors and Trustees of the estate of Mrs. G. A. Wyndham Lewis. Copyright 1927 by Mrs. G. A. Wyndham Lewis.

Quotations from *The Letters of Ezra Pound, 1907–1941,* edited by D. D. Paige, are reprinted by permission of Russell & Volkening, Inc. Copyright 1950 by Harcourt, Brace & World, Inc.

Quotations from *Discretions,* by Mary de Rachewiltz, are reprinted by permission of Little, Brown and Company, in association with the Atlantic Monthly Press. Copyright © 1971 by Mary de Rachewiltz.

Quotations from the following works are reprinted by permission of New Directions, New York, and Faber and Faber, Ltd., London:

The Cantos, copyright 1934, 1937, 1940, 1948, 1956, 1959, 1962, 1963, 1968, 1972 by Ezra Pound.
Personae, copyright 1926 by Ezra Pound. British title: *The Collected Shorter Poems.*
Collected Early Poems, copyright © 1976 by the Trustees of the Ezra Pound Literary Property Trust. All rights reserved.

A.B.C. of Reading, copyright 1934 by Ezra Pound.

Confucius: The Great Digest, The Unwobbling Pivot, The Analects, copyright 1928 by Glenn Hughes. Copyright 1947, 1950 by Ezra Pound.

Gaudier-Brzeska, copyright © 1970 by Ezra Pound. All rights reserved.

Guide to Kulchur, copyright © 1970 by Ezra Pound. All rights reserved.

The Literary Essays, copyright 1918, 1920, 1935 by Ezra Pound.

Pavannes and Divagations, copyright © 1958 by Ezra Pound.

Pound/Joyce: Letters and Essays, ed. Forrest Read, copyright © 1967 by Ezra Pound.

Selected Prose, 1909–1965, ed. William Cookson, copyright © 1973 by the Trustees of the Ezra Pound Literary Property Trust.

The Spirit of Romance, copyright © 1968 by Ezra Pound. All rights reserved.

Translations, copyright 1926, 1954, © 1963 by Ezra Pound.

Lines from early typescript version of Canto 81, AM 19845, published with permission of Princeton University Library and of New Directions, Agents, copyright © 1980 by the Trustees of the Ezra Pound Literary Property Trust.

The notebook entry for September 28, 1960, is published with permission of the Curator of the Pound Archive at the Beinecke Library and of New Directions, Agents, copyright © 1980 by the Trustees of the Ezra Pound Literary Property Trust.

Abbreviations

L   *The Letters of Ezra Pound.* New York: Harcourt, Brace & World, Inc., 1950.

LE   *Literary Essays.* New York: New Directions, 1968.

PM   *Patria Mia.* Chicago: Ralph Fletcher Seymour, 1950.

PD   *Pavannes and Divagations.* New York: New Directions, 1974.

PDv   *Pavannes and Divisions.* New York: Alfred Knopf, 1918.

P   *Personae: The Collected Shorter Poems of Ezra Pound.* New York: New Directions, 1971.

PE   *Polite Essays.* London: Faber & Faber, 1937.

PJ   *Pound/Joyce.* New York: New Directions, 1970.

SP   *Selected Prose 1909–1965.* New York: New Directions, 1973.

SR   *Spirit of Romance.* New York: New Directions, 1968.

T   *Ezra Pound: Translations.* New York: New Directions, 1963.

WT   *Women of Trachis.* New York: New Directions, 1957.

Secondary Works

Era   Hugh Kenner, *The Pound Era.* Berkeley & Los Angeles: University of California Press, 1971.

Disc.   Mary de Rachewiltz, *Discretions.* Boston: Little, Brown, 1971.

Life   Noel Stock, *The Life of Ezra Pound.* New York: Random House, 1970.

Introduction

Dante's influence on Pound was deep and lasting, yet *The Cantos* clearly does not divide readily into an *Inferno,* a *Purgatorio,* and a *Paradiso,* and the poem differs in some important ways from a traditional epic. *The Cantos* is, as Pound himself described it, "a record of struggle" (*GK,* 135); yet, while he initially chose to commit himself to one kind of struggle, he later found himself involved in a harrowing struggle of a quite different kind. He intended as the central subject of his work the moral struggle between himself (and like-minded men of the past) and the "obstructors of knowledge, / obstructors of distribution" (14/63); yet, as we read the *Pisan Cantos,* we see him involved in an intense personal struggle that cannot have been a part of his original plan for the poem. This personal struggle is ultimately responsible for giving the poem its unity. On one hand it brings the poet himself into his poem, making his role closer to that of the hero of the traditional epic, and, on the other, it makes the poem more directly autobiographical and closer in this way to that Romantic successor to the epic, Wordsworth's *Prelude.*

Pound's poem is an example of an intermediate genre that falls between the *Odyssey* or the *Commedia* and the *Prelude,* sharing aspects of both. *The Cantos* is about Pound as the *Prelude* is about Wordsworth, with the significant difference that Wordsworth from the start intended to keep himself at the center of his poem, whereas Pound initially was determined to keep himself out of his as much as possible. Like the *Commedia, The Cantos* is the record of a moral quest, and Pound aspired—even confidently expected —to be able to write with as much moral certitude and authority as Dante, yet he did not intend to figure in his own poem as Dante the hero does in his. It is in this absence of a forward-moving narrative involving a hero who is kept in the reader's eye that Pound departs most radically from the conventions of the traditional epic. The poet in the first part of *The Cantos,* ordering and disposing the materials and events of his poem, and hidden from our eyes as he usually chooses to be, plays a role more like that of Beatrice than that of Dante—more like that of Athena and Hermes than that of Odysseus. Pound originally intended his "epic struggle" to be an intellectual one. He saw himself not like Odysseus, sailing to face physical dangers and trials, but "sail[ing] after knowledge"; not like "Dante the hero," traveling through Hell, but driven by a vision of his own times as a "hell" to give battle to the monster *Usura* through the power of the written word.

A thoroughly autobiographical poem such as the *Prelude* requires a kind of close self-scrutiny and uninhibited self-revelation that Pound found particularly uncongenial, yet he did not avail himself of the safe anonymity that would result from the choice of a hero like Odysseus. He had considered using a hero of this kind, but, as we see from the first of the *Poetry* cantos, he was not able to choose one hero who would serve his purposes as Sordello served Browning's. In *Sordello,* Pound says, Browning worked out a new form, "the meditative, / Semi-dramatic, semi-epic story" (Canto I/117), yet Pound asks, "What's left for me to do? / Whom shall I conjur up; who's my Sordello, / My pre-Daun Chaucer, pre-Boccacio, / As you have done pre-Dante?" Pound realizes that any one hero will be too limiting for the complex, fragmentary, and problematic nature of the wide range of material that he wishes to include in his poem—that his own sensibility can be the only "hero" of *The Cantos.* He chooses to keep "Pound the man" out of the reader's eye as much as possible, yet this deprives his poem of the highly visible and absorbing hero who gives the traditional epic its unity.

With the downfall of Mussolini, the ruin of Pound's hopes for a new and just economic order, and his arrest and imprisonment, the poet's social and economic struggle was inevitably eclipsed by a dramatic personal struggle. Now, instead of seeing only through the poet's eyes, we see Pound himself in the poem, standing forth in plain view. At this point the poem is given its "epic hero." Those autobiographical passages which focus on the personal struggle—carried on as it is until the end of *The Cantos* and beyond—give the poem a dramatic intensity and a unity that would otherwise have been lacking. *The Cantos* then is neither wholly epic, like the *Odyssey* and the *Commedia,* nor wholly autobiographical, like the *Prelude,* but has created for itself a genre of its own, which, in the absence of a better term, we could call "epic autobiography."

The element of personal struggle in the poem has hitherto received little critical attention, for several reasons. Because of the widespread anger at Pound's wartime activities, critics who wanted to insist on the value of his poetry could expect, with some reason, to be cast in the role of defenders of—or at least apologists for—the poet, even when they had no intention of making any overt defense of Pound's actions in their work. In addition, the feeling that the critic could not count on a sympathetic audience—that the reader might be hostile, not only because of the obscurity of the poetry but also because of the poet's notoriety—helps to account for the aloofness of some important Pound criticism and for the impression that it sometimes gives that this aloofness is a characteristic of the poet rather than of the critic alone. Because of the stigma attached to the poet's name, the first task for serious readers of Pound was to assert the respectability of the poetry, which, at first, was easiest to do by treating it in isolation from the poet. This understandable and initially effective separation has served its original function of enabling the critic to write about the poetry without being drawn into controversy about the actions of the poet; there is now a need to bring together the poet and his poem again. It is now important that we become aware of the urgency of the poet's voice and that we see the poem as a highly personal statement and not just as a literary *tour de force.* Pound is, above all, earnest in a way that makes sophisticated aloofness impossible, and it is from this earnestness that the impetus and dynamic unity of the poem spring.

In addition, the virtual proscription of biographical criticism under the dispensation of the New Criticism has had perhaps a more inhibiting influence on our understanding of *The Cantos* than is the case with any other modernist work. The habit of close and analytical reading which is the legacy of the New Criticism has of course been responsible for many sensitive and perceptive readings both of separate passages in the poem and of whole cantos. Yet there are larger questions of major form and of the poet's intentions which have hitherto been neglected or, at best, answered prematurely or incompletely. Until these questions are addressed directly and thoroughly, we will find ourselves hampered in a close reading of many crucial sections of the poem. Once we become sensitive to the earnestness of the moral struggle and the urgency of the increasingly anguished personal struggle, we begin to discover new depths of feeling in the poem and can arrive at new and more precise readings.

Pound himself is largely responsible for our slowness to grasp the centrality of the personal struggle in *The Cantos.* He had a strong aversion to direct self-revelation, and two of the reasons for this will particularly concern us in this study. In part he felt compelled to renounce subjectivity by his admiration for the aesthetic theories that he encountered when he arrived in London. As we see from his early poems, he initially had no compunction about being highly romantic and subjective, but he soon saw that this was out of tune with the commitment to "classicism" and objectivity that he found in Hulme and Wyndham Lewis. He was then quick to become an advocate of objectivity himself and to understand how this could revitalize poetry and save it from superfluities and unimaginative rhythms and diction.

Yet these external influences were very much second in importance to his habitual and deeply rooted reluctance to be open about his true feelings. We come to see that he was involved in an ongoing struggle between two sides of his own nature. He was torn between a romantic subjectivity and genuine humanitarian concern on the one hand, and, on the other, a fear of self-revelation and a strong desire to be objective and to approach problems dispassionately and theoretically. His efforts to maintain a kind of anonymity behind a pose of impersonality have hitherto succeeded only too well in deterring the critic from challenging the pose or investigating the relationships between the poet's dogmatic pronouncements and his feelings. His aversion to introspection seems to be not simply a matter of personal choice, but a fundamental part of his personality. This aversion is unquestionably a considerable liability and is responsible for the weaker parts of *The Cantos,* yet it is coupled with a genuine and deep humanitarian concern and we see that the personal and the social are curiously and closely related for him. His humanitarianism prompted his urgent desire for reform, but his reforming fervor allowed him to hide his emotional evasiveness from himself. The emotional evasiveness in turn made an unsteady foundation for his reforming endeavors and, by losing touch with the benevolent emotions which first motivated him, he fell into anger and hatred and lost his sense of proportion, relying increasingly on tirades, dogmatic pronouncements, and reiteration of "facts." Yet when he lost control of his emotions—at the time of his broadcasts for Rome Radio—he instinctively preserved the integrity of his poem by making a separation between his propagandizing self and his poetic self, and by choosing to concentrate in his poem on Confucianism in Chinese history and the virtues of John Adams, subjects which were fixed points for him and in which he never lost faith.

Pound's attempted flight from himself was abruptly halted by his arrest. In the stockade at Pisa, stripped of virtually all distractions from his own presence, he finally, belatedly, began to confront himself. There is a world of dignity in these confrontations, and his arrival at a remorseful self-awareness after so long and under conditions of such great physical and psychological stress, is testimony to the tenacity of his fundamental compassion and the strength of his suppressed emotions, but above all to the complete integrity of his whole career. He was never able to pretend to himself that any point he had reached was satisfactory. The sense of incompleteness, of something essential neglected, drove him on. After the *Pisan Cantos,* the personal struggle and the struggle against usury occupied him alternately. In *Rock-Drill* and *Thrones* we see how his faith in the reanimating power of love sustained him through his years in St. Elizabeths Mental Hospital and prevented him from falling into fatalism and despair. Even in *Drafts and Fragments,* however, he persisted in his self-accusation and was never free for long from his feelings of remorse at his past blindness and his sense of having failed.

If we are to do justice to Pound, we must never lose sight of the devastating impact that the events of his time had upon him.

He began with a strong faith in reform and belief in man's power to change his society, and this in a time when people seemed perhaps more than at any other to be at the mercy of events beyond their control. He felt that he was at the center of and in control of a vortex, and yet this gave way with the First World War to a series of vortices over which no one seemed to have control. It was his frustrating lot to be trying to hasten a renaissance just as Western civilization seemed to be collapsing; to be expansive in an age of introspection and retrenchment; to be preaching internationalism in the arts in a world torn apart by nationalism.

It is the intention of this work not just to offer new readings of important passages in *The Cantos,* but to invite the reader to see the poem from a new and broader perspective and to approach it in a new way. Since this requires some consideration both of the major form of the work and of the poet's moral vision, chapter 1 is devoted to these topics in an attempt to give as clear and accessible an account of them as possible. Chapter 2 addresses the question of Pound's evasiveness and looks to his personality and to the influence of Wyndham Lewis to discover the sources of that "habit of suppression" which is ultimately responsible for the tragedy in his life and so for the personal struggle which shapes the whole poem and gives it its dignity. Chapters 3–5 turn to the poem itself to trace the course of both kinds of struggle showing how the one determines the development of the first part of the poem and how an awareness of the other more personal struggle enables us to read many of the lyric passages in a new way. Critics have generally agreed in finding these passages the most impressive and successful; we find that in them Pound is most personal and self-revealing. This is obviously so in the *Pisan Cantos,* where the personal struggle clearly dominates everything else, but, more unexpectedly, it is equally true of many of the lyrical passages, even those in the first half of the poem. We discover that in many of the most moving and dramatic parts of the poem the poet is speaking not merely generally and mythically, but rather, specifically and very personally.

1 As Sextant

The poet's personal struggle is the most dramatic part of *The Cantos* and is finally responsible for its unity, yet the greater part of the poem is devoted to the struggle against the "forces of usury" both in the past and the present. The more personal cantos are embedded in this matrix and cannot properly be appreciated in separation from it. For this reason, the present chapter undertakes to provide an overview and elucidation of some of the more important and complex ideas and themes in the poem. Some consideration of the poem's form, of Pound's idea of the "divine or permanent world," and of *Usura,* and some familiarity with his pantheon of "heroes" are an indispensable preparation for any examination of his personal struggle.

The form of The Cantos

Pound's "epic autobiography" is a poem about good and evil as they manifest themselves in human society; it shares the high moral seriousness of *The Divine Comedy,* and Pound wants to be able to speak with as much authority about good and evil in his own time as Dante does for his. This presents no problem when Pound is writing on the subject of good, since he is as convinced as Dante of the existence of "eternal verities"–of "the reality of the *nous,* of mind, apart from any man's individual mind" (*GK,* 44);

7

of the absolute value of great works of literature, art, sculpture, and architecture, and of the spiritually and intellectually animating power of human love. On these matters he feels that he can speak with an authority more profound than that of his own intellect. In "The Serious Artist," for example, he talks of poetic passages which "have in them that passionate simplicity which is beyond the precisions of the intellect." Comparing these to some prose lines he writes, "In the verse something has come upon the intelligence. In the prose the intelligence has found a subject for its observations. The poetic fact pre-exists" (*LE,* 53–54). Because his most deeply held convictions about the "eternal verities" spring from intuitions and strong feelings, and are invulnerable to the fallibilities of the intellect, they provide a firm foundation for the poem. He formulates them early, never questions them, and continues to reassert them throughout the work.

When he comes to write on evil, however, serious problems arise, because he wishes to be absolute on this subject but to maintain at the same time a personal detachment. He presents the "eternal verities" as intense personal revelations but writes of evil as a phenomenon observed from a distance. Dante realizes, as Pound does not, that to study evil is to study human nature, and that this necessarily involves one to some extent in self-exploration. Pound has no intention of being introspective in his investigation of evil; he chooses not to consider its causes nor even its nature, but to describe the actions of evil men. He settles on *Usura* as the only deadly sin, elevating it from a social crime to the ultimate evil, making it the necessarily inadequate object of his intense moral outrage. He intends to write an "Inferno" and a "Paradiso"; he does not at first think about writing a personal "Purgatorio."

Pound does have a plan for his poem. In a letter to his father in April 1927 he writes:

> Have I ever given you outline of main scheme:::or whatever it is?
> 1. Rather like, or unlike subject response and counter subject in fugue.
> A.A. Live man goes down into world of Dead
> C.B. The "repeat in history"

B.C. The "magic moment" or moment of metamorphosis, bust thru from quotidien into "divine or permanent world." Gods, etc. [*L*, 210]

The "Rather like, or unlike" is a little disconcerting and the analogy with fugue is too vague to be of much help, but, as it happens, this brief schema proves to be the key to the literary form of the poem. When it is applied, as it usually has been, to "Pound the writer" as he appears in his poem, it is not particularly helpful. If it is taken to refer to "Pound the man" in the poem, it becomes a reliable guide to the poem's form and scope.

If the "live man" is Pound the writer, then the "Dead" are those great writers of the past whose works he has translated or "made new" in his own poem. The "repeat in history" would then have to refer to past instances of writers engaged in this kind of transmission of great literature. The first few cantos are highly "literary" in their subject matter, and it is likely that anyone studying Pound's schema will go first to the beginning of the poem to test it out. Here, although the process of translation and instances of metamorphosis are given such prominence, any definite or systematic plan is so hard to find that one is tempted to abandon the idea that the schema will prove very helpful. Pound's own comments about his first eleven cantos, made in 1922, are similarly discouraging. Of these cantos he says only that they are the "preparation of the palette"—an attempt to "get down all the colours or elements I want for the poem. Some perhaps too enigmatically and abbreviatedly." He adds—in exactly what tone of voice it is hard to say—"I hope, heaven help me, to bring them into some sort of design and architecture later" (*L*, 180). After Canto 11, however, and before 1927 when he formulates his schema, we find him writing for the first time in the poem whole cantos which deal directly and anecdotally with the events of his own time. We also find his "Hell Cantos" in which the "live man" among the dead is Pound himself.

When we reconsider the schema as it applies to "Pound the man" in the poem, we find that it offers a much more helpful and comprehensive account of the work. If the "live man" is Pound among his "dead" or atrophying or evil contemporaries, then all

those passages in which he describes the moral and cultural dead-
ness of his own times and those in which he makes the case against
the "usurers" will fit in the first of his three categories. The "re-
peat in history" would now refer to those instances in the poem in
which other energetic men of vision have similarly challenged the
sterility and corruption around them. These are Pound's heroes—
often rulers and lawgivers—and his account of their individual
heroic struggles will, as he foresees in this early comment, form
a very large part of his poem. He considers those passages which
deal with his heroes to be purgatorial, and, in the same letter in
which he gives his schema, he calls the "Hell Mouth" canto—in
which he writes both of heroes of the past and of the wartime
experiences of his own friends and acquaintances—a "purgatorio."
Yet the passages devoted to Pound's heroes are only purgatorial in
a very limited sense; the truly purgatorial cantos are those which
tell of his ordeal at Pisa and show the poet himself in purgatory.
Although Pound has no way of foreseeing this ordeal, because the
poem is fundamentally autobiographical, the *Pisan Cantos* can
take their place in it without threatening its unity.

With the *Pisan Cantos,* not only the purgatorial but also the
paradisal becomes more personal and more moving. In the previ-
ous cantos there are various kinds of paradisal moments. Some are
sudden states of exhilaration and euphoria which come unbidden
and which the poet dramatizes as the apparition of gods and god-
desses. Some are inspired by his contemplation of aesthetic per-
fection in great poetry, sculpture, architecture, and art, and are
doubly paradisal in being records of the visionary experiences of
their creators. Some are moments of transcendent awareness that
can sometimes accompany sexual passion. In the first part of the
poem, moments of this last kind are often generalized, but in the
process of self-examination the poet comes to look more closely
than before at his feelings for the women he has loved and to
acknowledge their individuality and their importance to him. As
a result, his paradisal moments become more intimately and spe-
cifically personal even though they remain fleeting. In the *Pisan
Cantos,* Cantos 90–93 (the heart of *Rock-Drill*) and *Drafts and
Fragments,* paradise is "jagged, / For a flash, / for an hour. / Then

agony, / then an hour, / then agony" (92/620). Until the end of the poem the poet persists in his self-accusation—his glimpses of paradise come to him while he is still in purgatory.

The Good: The "Divine or Permanent World"

Pound believes in an ordered cosmos, and the paradisal moments in *The Cantos* are revelations of this order. He feels that such revelations are only accessible to a person of strong emotions and incisive intellect, both of which must work together. Intimations of divine order are first apprehended by the senses, which are by their nature transitory, and then seized by the inspired intellect so that they can be held "in the mind indestructible." The artist goes one step further and attempts to capture the essence of this moment of inspiration in words, paint, or stone, engaging in what Pound calls "an approach to the infinite *by form*" (*LE,* 444).

Pound also finds that he can give some provisional form to his intimations of "eternal verities" through myth. His cosmology is essentially Neoplatonic and he refers specifically to the Plotinian *nous,* or Intelligence—the highest level of being which is the primal emanation of The One and the abode of Platonic "Ideas." The aim of the true Neoplatonist is to escape from the limitations of Matter (material existence) through a quest for moral perfection and intellectual enlightenment which allows the individual soul to rise to apprehension of the Intelligence, and hence The One. The individual intellect is moved by an instinctive love for its source in the *nous* and aspires to return. Pound, who has great faith in the intellect, seems early to have found Neoplatonism a congenial philosophy. He does not see it as a religion to which he could subscribe, but uses its concepts as he does those of myth as correlatives for his own intimations of the spiritual.

Pound remains very much at the center of his own cosmology. For him the momentary feeling of personal transcendence is the fixed point from which one's speculations go out and to which they return. These moments are not the prerogative of the mystic but occur "in the 'normal course of things' " as "certain times . . . when a man feels his immortality upon him" (*SR,* 94). These "magic moments" are the primary reality and the stories of the gods grow up around individual experiences of this kind. Pound expresses his opinion in "Religio, or the Child's Guide to Knowledge," when he says that "a god is an eternal state of mind" and becomes manifest "when the states of mind take form" (*SP,* 47). Finding that his own states of mind can correspond to those which the myths dramatize, he is prepared to accept the possibility of eternal states of mind like the Platonic Ideas or Forms, yet he treats their existence more as a workable hypothesis than as a matter of deep conviction. The emotions of the individual are the touchstone, as we see from his observation: "No apter metaphor having been found for certain emotional colours. I assert that the Gods exist" (*GK,* 299). He feels that one can only fully appreciate a myth by knowing intimately the state of mind which it dramatizes. He maintains that "myths are only intelligible in a vivid and glittering sense to those people to whom they occur. I know, I mean, one man who understands Persephone and Demeter, and one who understands the Laurel, and another who has, I should say, met Artemis. These things are for them *real*" (*SR,* 92).

From his poem "Plotinus," written in 1905 and published in *A Lume Spento,* we see how far back his interest in Neoplatonism dates and also how free he feels to adapt it to his personal predelictions. In it, the cosmology may be Plotinus's, but the speaker is the poet himself, who, in the final stanza, seems rather grandiosely to be drawing an analogy between the act of poetic creation and the operation of The One:

> As one that would draw thru the node of things,
> Back sweeping to the vortex of the cone,
> Cloistered about with memories, alone
> In chaos, while the waiting silence sings:
>
> Obliviate of cycles' wanderings
> I was an atom on creation's throne
> And knew all nothing my unconquered own.
> God! Should I be the hand upon the strings?!
>
> But I was lonely as a lonely child.
> I cried amid the void and heard no cry,

And then for utter loneliness, made I
New thoughts as crescent images of *me.*
And with them was my essence reconciled
While fear went forth from mine eternity.　　　[*CEP,* 36]

Pound's single-minded attention to his own states of mind seems, at least until he comes to write the *Pisan Cantos,* to blur the specifics of his emotional experiences and to leave out of consideration almost completely those people with whom he shared them. Where D. H. Lawrence, for example, emphasizes the physical particularity of sexual experience, Pound mythologizes, aetherializes, and depersonalizes it. Those passages in *The Cantos* which deal with sexuality are frequently more lyrical and less fragmented than other parts of the poem and give the appearance of beautiful set pieces. For all their beauty, such passages have a kind of insubstantiality—they lack the focus and resonance of the passages on love which we find in the *Pisan Cantos* and after. This reminds us that the poet's use of myth not only has an exploratory function, but also makes possible a kind of painless subjectivity in offering an effective alternative to direct expression of intimate emotions.

It is illuminating to consider the very different ways in which Pound, Eliot, and Yeats use myth. Myth in Eliot's poetry acts as a veil between the intensity and specificity of the personal and the eye of the reader. He uses myth to depersonalize intensely and painfully personal emotions for the purpose of his poetry. Mythic elements do not "stand for" the emotions themselves and are really not even an adequate way of articulating them; they are intended to divert the reader's close scrutiny from the powerful emotions whose presence is assumed but presented only obliquely. The poetic use of myth enables Eliot to write that kind of poetry which "is not a turning loose of emotion, but an escape from emotion; . . . not the expression of personality, but an escape from personality."[1] We see that the intensity of personal feeling prompts his desire for escape. For Eliot, myth cannot be "valid" in the way that Christianity and one's own emotions are, and is only of value to the extent that it can be aligned with and assimilated into the

1. T. S. Eliot, *Selected Essays 1917–1932* (New York, 1932), p. 10.

Christian tradition. He cannot begin to take myth "seriously" on its own terms, as Yeats does, and he disapproves of Yeats's "paganism." Pound is like neither of these poets. He is not committed to occult study as Yeats is, nor does he observe Eliot's clear demarcation between the artificiality of myth and the reality of the personal and the Christian. Myth serves both an evasive and an exploratory function in Pound's poetry. When the latter takes precedence over the former, his mythic vision fuses the multiplicity of the *Cantos* into a unity and generates some of his finest poetry. Myth can be used for purposes of evasion, to the extent that it allows one to communicate objectively feelings which are too dangerous to express literally and subjectively. Pound shows that he fully appreciates the safety in myth when he states his belief that "the first myths arose . . . when some very vivid and undeniable adventure befell [a man], and he told someone else who called him a liar. Thereupon, after bitter experience, perceiving that no one could understand what he meant when he said that he 'turned into a tree' he made a myth—a work of art that is—an impersonal or objective story woven out of his own emotion, as the nearest equation that he was capable of putting into words" (*LE,* 431). In *The Spirit of Romance* he expresses his concern that to reveal intimate feelings may expose one to something more dangerous than misunderstanding. Here he speculates that "Greek myth arose when someone having passed through delightful psychic experience tried to communicate it to others and found it necessary to screen himself from persecution" (*SR,* 92).

From the beginning Pound stresses the importance of love, but at first he seems to consider human passion primarily as the means to some "intellectual" end. A passionate experience is important because it arouses intimations of its perfect counterpart in the realm of the Intelligence, and the mind rises above the limited personal experience to attempt to grasp the elusive Idea of love—to trace the lineaments of Aphrodite. For the purposes of his poem, the story of Aphrodite and Anchises is particularly apposite, since in it the goddess herself is simultaneously the embodiment of the Idea of perfect beauty and passion, and also a lover of flesh and blood. He concludes Canto 23 with a reference to this story in which his crystalline imagery reminds us that the domain of the goddess is the *nous* which he has described elsewhere as a "sea crystalline and enduring, of the bright as it were molten glass that envelops us, full of light" (*GK,* 44). The canto concludes:

> "King Otreus of Phrygia,
> "That king is my father."
>   and saw then, as of waves taking form,
> As the sea, hard, a glitter of crystal,
> And the waves rising but formed, holding their form.
> No light reaching through them.   [23/109]

Aphrodite manages her metamorphosis into opaque flesh and, by lying about her parentage, deceives Anchises into believing her a mortal woman.

Pound is particularly fascinated by the fleeting glimpses of the world of the Intelligence to which the mind can sometimes aspire. To register these glimpses seems to him one of the highest achievements of the poet. Dante seems at home in this place of the mind, and his imagination moves freely through its mysteries. He seems to ascend effortlessly from the experience of earthly love to the contemplation of Divine Love. Pound describes the *Vita Nuova* as "the tale of Love the revealer, of Love the door and the way into the intelligence, of Love infinite 'That moves the sun and all the other stars' " (*SR,* 120), a description which applies equally to the *Commedia.* Pound feels that the poet of his own time does not have free access to this place of the mind. In an often-quoted passage from "Cavalcanti" he writes:

> We appear to have lost the radiant world where one thought cuts through another with clean edge, a world of moving energies *'mezzo oscuro rade', 'risplende in sè perpetuale effecto',* magnetisms that take form, that are seen, or that border the visible, the matter of Dante's *paradiso,* the glass under water, the form that seems a form seen in a mirror, these realities perceptible to the sense. . . . [*LE,* 154]

Here the glass and water imagery recurs and the extreme elusiveness of the "moving energies" is emphasized. Myth offers a simple solution to the problem of capturing these energies even if particularity must necessarily be sacrificed in the process of personification. It is for this reason that Pound contends that the *Metamorphoses* contains a "great treasure of verity . . . for mankind" which could not be "registered" in any other form (*GK*, 299). He is mainly interested in the process by which the gods assume a form within these stories. His rendering in Canto 2 of the story of Bacchus told by Acoetes to Pentheus in book 3 of the *Metamorphoses* illustrates this perfectly. When the god enchants the ship, the sailor feels:

> . . . out of nothing, a breathing,
>   hot breath on my ankles,
> Beasts like shadows in glass,
>   a furred tail upon nothingness.
>
> . . . .
> Rustle of airy sheaths,
>   dry forms in the *aether*.
>
> . . . .
>   void air taking pelt.
> Lifeless air become sinewed,
>   feline leisure of panthers.   [2/8]

The world of moving energies is only accessible to those of highly developed intellect and sensibility, and it is helpful to our understanding of Pound to recognize how, for the first part of his career, he is committed to the idea of an "elite of sensibility." He maintains that "more writers fail from lack of character than from lack of intelligence" (*ABC*, 193) and, in the same vein, that "a man's character is apparent in every one of his brush strokes" (*GK*, 91). He suggests that some people have an innate and infallible aesthetic sense which cannot be acquired, only refined upon. Those who possess this kind of sensibility belong automatically to an elite, and Pound is very assiduous in locating and cultivating other members of this elite.

His writings show how far he thinks of culture in terms of personalities, as emanating from and throwing into relief the most dynamic men of the age. In the interest of making his own case, it becomes important for him to assert the reliability of the taste not only of himself but also of whomever else he has judged to be of this elite. This accounts for his readiness to give his unqualified and sometimes unreflective support to the complete body of ideas of men whose intellect he admires or to causes whose proponents impress him. Unfortunately, the personalities and ideas to which he attaches himself can be harmful influences on him when they encourage him, by their example, in his impatience with the emotions. This is the case with his admiration for Wyndham Lewis, whose pathological disgust at any show of emotion must surely have been dangerous to Pound. Above all, Pound takes refuge in the idea that irresistible forces will determine one's artistic greatness; that the great artist will intuitively aim straight for the truth. Reflection, second thoughts, weighing all the evidence, tentative formulations—all these are rarely mentioned: "By genius I mean an inevitable swiftness and rightness in a given field. The trouvaille. The direct simplicity in seizing the effective means. . . . 'Human Greatness' is an unusual energy coupled with straightness, the direct shooting mind" (*GK,* 105–06).

We can best understand Pound's ideal of an elite of sensibility by examining *The Spirit of Romance* and his essay "Cavalcanti." In these works he studies the poets of Provence and Tuscany to establish his thesis that they themselves are members of an "elite of sensibility" whose roots can be traced back to the "ecstatic religions" of paganism, of which the Eleusinian mysteries are the most highly developed example. He stresses the connection between Provençal song and the pagan rites of May Day, and says that the initial impulse of these religions is not to establish "the one truth" but "to stimulate a sort of confidence in the life-force" (*SR,* 95). He believes that initially Christianity was a religion of this kind, but became adulterated by the "Mosaic or Roman or British Empire type" component which makes God into "a disagreeable bogie" (*SR,* 95). Pound's "ecstatic religion" is far removed from Eliot's Christianity. It caters to individuals rather than imposing limitations upon them; it seems not to require humility or self-abnegation. It is designed specifically for a sensitive elite and offers "a sort of working hypothesis acceptable to people of a certain range of temperament—a 'regola' which suits a particular constitution of nerves and intellect" (*SR*, 95). In *Guide to Kulchur* Pound claims that "Eleusis did not distort truth by exaggerating the individual, neither could it have violated the individual spirit," and he offers "for Mr. Eliot's reflection the thesis that our time has overshadowed the mysteries by an over-emphasis on the individual" (*GK*, 299). The rites of an "ecstatic religion" are communal in a way which offers the initiate some degree of protective anonymity, at the same time preserving the sanctity of the mystery by the individual's respect for the ineffable —by his acceptance of the fact that "the arcanum is the arcanum" (*GK*, 292).

Pound does not share Eliot's conviction of the need for sub-mission. Where Christianity has often called for the suppression of the senses as the only reliable way to spiritual enlightenment, Pound sees in Eleusis the idea that one comes to the divine *through* the senses, by refining the emotions. He feels that the Provençal troubadours with their code of chivalric love have inherited the legacy of Eleusis and kept alive the best of paganism and makes very ambitious claims for the troubadour love-cult, suggesting that its goal may have been "the purgation of the soul by the refine-ment of, and lordship over, the senses," and that it made stricter or more subtle demands on its adherents than did Christian asceticism. He imagines it inducing a state of ecstasy which would be "not a whirl or madness of the senses, but a glow arising from the exact nature of the perception," and believes that, in such a state, one could receive revelations of divine truth. He even con-siders it possible that some followers of the love-cult "developed their own unofficial mysticism . . . [that] the servants of Amor saw visions quite as well as the servants of the Roman ecclesiasti-cal hierarchy" (*SR*, 90–91, 94).

Once we come to the Tuscan poets, Pound feels that these matters are no longer only hypothetical. He chooses Cavalcanti's *"Donna mi prega"* as his prime exhibit in making his case for a Tuscan "unofficial mysticism" too eclectic to observe Christian orthodoxies. His own translation of Guido's poem forms the main part of Canto 36, and another somewhat different translation is the core and subject of his long essay "Cavalcanti." The transla-tion is preceded in the essay by a section called "Medievalism," in which Pound describes that part of the tradition of "intellectual light" which he calls "the Mediterranean sanity." This is followed by a "Partial Explanation," in which he speculates on Cavalcanti's philosophical views, suggesting that the poem is possibly "a sort of metaphor on the generation of light." After an Italian text of the poem, there are thirty-four pages of commentary on meter, vocabulary, and variant manuscript readings and translations. The last part of this, called "Guido's Relations," is largely concerned with Pound's own ideas about and experience with translating Italian poetry.

In the "Medievalism" section (*LE*, 149–55), he defines the "Mediterranean sanity" as "this 'harmony in the sentience' or harmony *of* the sentient, where the thought has its demarcation, the substance its *virtu*, where stupid men have not reduced all 'energy' to unbounded undistinguished abstraction." This lies between the objectionable extremes of "erotic sentimentality" and "idiotic asceticism." He gives, as an example of the former, the "Greek aesthetic," which, he says, seems "to consist wholly in plastic, or in plastic moving toward coitus, and limited by incest, which is the sole Greek taboo." The Provençal aesthetic avoids "erotic sentimentality" through its insistence that "there is some proportion between the fine thing held in the mind, and the inferior thing ready for instant consumption." The "Tuscan aesthetic" moves even beyond this to the "conception of the body as perfect instrument of the increasing intelligence." Writers like Cavalcanti and Dante have access to the "radiant world where one thought cuts through another with clean edge," and this world, now lost, is the one which Pound himself is intent on rediscovering. He values *"Donna mi prega"* so highly because he feels that it both defines and embodies the delicate balance between emotion and intellect which alone makes possible the apprehension of the "radiant world." Dante in the *Paradiso* portrays the radiance incomparably, but while he asserts the continuum of human and divine love, Cavalcanti anatomizes the operation of love and, Pound feels, speculates metaphysically with much more intellectual complexity and sophistication than Dante. He finds an "intellectual hunger" in Cavalcanti which is completely lacking in Dante and feels that as a result there is a "gulf" between their states of mind which "one can . . . scarcely exaggerate." Dante's orthodoxy leaves too little to the intellect. His truth is easily accessible; Cavalcanti's is "a truth for elect recipients, not a truth universally spreadable or acceptable."

Pound is not interested in the passivity of the Christian mystic who through surrender of the will and suppression of the reason prepares himself for the influx of divine revelation. His ideal is that of strenuous intellectual progress toward "The Truth," and he feels that Cavalcanti shared his faith in the intellect—that he "shows leanings toward not only the proof by reason, but toward the proof by experiment" (*LE,* 149). He claims that *"Donna mi prega"* is "a scholastic definition in form, . . . as clear and definite as the prose treatises of the period, it shows an equal acuteness of thought" (*LE,* 161). He suggests that Cavalcanti, like himself, finds Neoplatonism congenial in its avoidance of dogma and emphasis on the power of the human intellect. He traces the ideas behind *"Donna mi prega"* back to Averroes, Avicenna, and Avempace (Ibn Baja), who, as he has been reading in Etienne Gilson's *La Philosophie au Moyen Age,*[2] followed as the philosophy of Aristotle a mixture of Aristotelianism and Neoplatonism. Pound also speculates that Cavalcanti had read Robert Grosseteste (1175–1253), in particular his treatise on light, *De Luce seu de Incohatione Formarum.* Although Cavalcanti is eclectic and "swallows none of his authors whole," Pound insists that he is no "mere dilettante poetaster dragging in philosophic terms" (*LE,* 161). He believes that the Italian poem is a serious metaphysical speculation and raises the possibility that "the whole of it is a sort of metaphor on the generation of light" (*LE,* 161).

Gilson writes that "it is under the influence of neoplatonism and the Arabic *Perspectives* (or treatises on Optics), that Grosseteste came to attribute to light a central role in the creation and the constitution of the universe."[3] Pound quotes from Gilson's "most able, and most lucid" summary of Grosseteste's ideas on light in his essay:

2. Etienne Gilson, *La Philosophie Au Moyen Age* (Paris, 1947), p. 345, translation mine.
3. Ibid., p. 470.

Light is a very subtle corporeal substance, which approaches the incorporeal. Its characteristic property is to perpetually generate itself and to instantaneously diffuse itself spherically around a point. . . . This extremely attenuated substance is also the material from which all things are made; it is the primary corporeal form which some call corporeity. [*LE,* 160; translation mine.]

Gilson then goes on to explain Grosseteste's distinction between *lux,* the outward radiation of creating light which reaches its limits in matter (*hyle*), and *lumen,* the reflection of this light backwards toward the center of the world.[4] This simultaneous double movement of light parallels the operations of the Neoplatonic cosmos. Here, the light from the ineffable One permeates the *nous* and shines down into the realm of Soul and Matter. This movement is reversed when the individual soul mystically returns via the Intellect to The One. Pound's interest in Neoplatonic cosmology has led him to study the terminology of Arabic philosophers, not only in Gilson, but also in Ernest Renan's *Averroes et l'Averroisme.* In "Cavalcanti" he transcribes a passage from Albertus Magnus, cited by Renan, which shows the Christian theologian's debt to Arabic philosophy in his adoption of the concepts of the *intellectus agens, intellectus possibilis,* and *intellectus adeptus.* This passage from Albertus remains in Pound's mind and he refers to it again in Canto 51, where we find "Deo similis quodam modo / hic intellectus adeptus" (51/251). (See appendix 1.) The same canto begins with the Plotinian comparison of the radiation of *nous* from The One to the shining of the sun:

> Shines
> in the mind of heaven God
> who made it
> more than the sun
> in our eye.   [51/250]

When we turn to Pound's translation of *"Donna mi prega"* in 'Cavalcanti" we see how the poem has led Pound to an investiga-

4. Ibid., pp. 471–72.

tion of Neoplatonism and to the works of scholastic writers who have studied the Arabic philosophers. The poem speculates on the nature of love, its place of origin, the source from which it is created, its *virtù* and power, its essence and form, and the way in which it gives pleasure. Pound's translation of stanza 2 reads:

> In memory's locus taketh he his state
> [*In quella parte dove sta memoria . . .*]
> Formed there in manner as a mist of light
> Upon a dusk that is come from Mars and stays.
> Love is created, hath a sensate name,
> His modus takes from soul, from heart his will;
> From form seen doth he start, that, understood
> Taketh in latent intellect—
> [*. . . nel possibile intelletto*]
> As in a subject ready—
> place and abode,
> Yet in that place it ever is unstill,
> Spreading its rays, it tendeth never down
> [*Risplende . . .*]
> By quality, but is its own effect unendingly
> [*. . . in sé, perpetuale effecto*]
> Not to delight, but in an ardour of thought
> That the base likeness of it kindleth not.   [*LE,* 155–56]

"Nel possibile intelletto" has led Pound to consult Renan on Averroes and to discover there Albertus Magnus's statement about the *"intellectus adeptus."* Using this statement "solely as lexicography," he is guided by it to interpret *"Risplende / in sé perpetuale effecto / . . . / Perche non pote laire simiglglianza"* as "Radiates splendour in itself, itself's perpetual effect, as it cannot confer its likeness (on anything else)," and then as "glows through the possible intellect, which it has completely transfused, but does not penetrate into lower strata" (*LE,* 186). The *"dove sta memoria,"* he tells us, "is Platonism" (159), and he holds the phrase in his mind until he writes Canto 76, where, almost like an incantation, it revives his own memories of love. The canto begins:

And the sun high over horizon hidden in cloud bank
    lit saffron the cloud ridge
                dove sta memor[i]a   [76/452]

Later in the canto, the place of memories is no longer the cloud bank *nous,* but his own mind:

                nothing matters but the quality
    of the affection—
    in the end—that has carved the trace in the mind
    dove sta memoria   [76/457]

In an awkward line which Pound himself calls a forced translation (*LE,* 189), he says of the Love which issues from the beloved's eyes like a dart that it "falleth / plumb on to the spike of the targe [the bull's-eye]" (*LE,* 157). He decides that "bull's-eye" is probably too particularized a meaning for *"bianco,"* and leaves the reader to choose between "medieval doctrines of colour, of diaphana, of all colours united in the white" (*LE,* 190). In his Canto 36 translation he substitutes the last of these for the bull's-eye and makes other changes in the lines which follow to emphasize even more strongly the imagery of "radiant energies":

        Nor is he known from his face
        But taken in the white light that is allness
        Toucheth his aim
        Who heareth, seeth not form
        But is led by its emanation.
        Being divided, set out from colour,
        Disjunct in mid darkness
        Grazeth the light, one moving by other,
        Being divided, divided from all falsity
        Worth of trust
        From him alone mercy proceedeth.   [36/179]

In Canto 114, after which only two more complete cantos were written, Cavalcanti's phrase again shines out:

>   Falls white *bianco c(h)ade*
>   yet sentient
>   sees not.   [114/791]

After the translation in Canto 36, Pound gives a one-line reference
to the *Paradiso* and follows this with a passage on John Scotus
Erigena:

> Eriugina was not understood in his time
> "which explains, perhaps, the delay in condemning him"
> And they went looking for Manicheans
> And found, so far as I can make out, no Manicheans
> So they dug for, and damned Scotus Eriugina
> "Authority comes from right reason,
>   never the other way on"
> Hence the delay in condemning him.   [36/179]

Erigena falls into place before Avicenna and Averroes in Pound's
tradition of enlightened thinkers. Gilson describes him as "the first
heir of the Greek patristic writings in the West."[5] He translated
the works of Dionysius the Areopagite from Greek into Latin, and
Gilson says of his doctrine that "it offered to the Latins the possi-
bility, one might almost say the temptation, of entering once and
for all the way initiated by the Greek theologians, Denis [Dio-
nysius] and Maximus the Confessor. Had this invitation been
accepted, a neoplatonist philosophy would no doubt have pre-
vailed in Western Europe up to the end of the middle ages."[6] For
Pound, Erigena upheld the tradition of the inspired intellect and
conceded to human reason the same importance that he himself
did. Gilson expounds Erigena's position that, although faith must
precede reason, it does not preempt it: "God wills that faith
should engender in us a two-fold impulse—to put it into action
through the active life, and to explore it rationally through the con-
templative life."[7] Pound believes that Erigena was condemned by

5. Ibid., p. 205.
6. Etienne Gilson, *History of Christian Philosophy in the Middle Ages*
(New York, 1955), p. 113.
7. Gilson, *La Philosophie Au Moyen Age*, p. 202, translation mine.

the church three centuries after his death for the same reason that the Albigensians were exterminated. The Church accused them falsely of being Manicheans, but their only "crime" was to have kept alive the spirit of the Eleusinian mysteries and the light of Neoplatonism.

Pound believes that Cavalcanti in his poem has written on the subject of love with an intellectual complexity usually reserved for religious and philosophical speculation and says that it is "possible that Guido is claiming rank for *Amor*" beside those "divine things" already considered subjects worthy of contemplation (*LE,* 186). Already in *The Spirit of Romance* he has mentioned "the final evolution of Amor by Guido and Dante, a new and paganish god, neither Erôs nor an angel of the Talmud" (*SR,* 92). As we shall see, Amor assumes full divinity in Canto 90, but before this can happen, Pound's thinking about love will be significantly changed by his experience at Pisa.

At Pisa, Pound also rediscovers and "neoplatonizes" Confucius. As he turns again to the metaphysical, he finds the *Chung Yung* to be an ideal focus for his contemplation. In *Guide to Kulchur* there are many references to Confucius's writings, but the *Chung Yung* is mentioned only by its title as *The Standing Fast in the Middle.* Pound makes no mention of its contents and emphasizes instead the importance of the *Analects,* the *Ta Hio,* and *Odes.* The appeal of the *Analects* at this stage of Pound's career is clear from his comment that they show Confucius "filled with a sense of responsibility. He and his interlocutors live in a responsible world, they think for the whole social order" (*GK,* 29).

Pound had published an Italian translation of the *Chung Yung* (*L'Asse che non vacilla*) in February 1945, but most of the copies were burned after the Liberation, probably because of the suspicious "axis" in the title (*Life,* 406). He then made a translation into English which was published in 1947, the wording of which clearly reflects his Pisan metaphysical meditations.

The two most important concepts in the *Chung Yung* are that of the "process" and that of "sincerity." The "process," which is not even mentioned in *Guide to Kulchur,* is the "perfect way"; on the individual level it is the ideal of conduct which is determined for each man by his "inborn nature." In nature, "the process of

earth . . . causes straight plants to rise up" (*C,* 145), and finally
there is the all-inclusive "celestial and earthly process" which "per-
vades and is substantial; it is on high and gives light, it compre-
hends the light and is lucent, it extends without bound, and
endures" (*C,* 183). The person who allows himself to be ruled by
"the process" practices "sincerity" and through the exercise of
"sincerity" one remains in tune with "the process."

Hugh Kenner, reminding us that the character which Pound
translates as "the process" is *tao,* the "Way" of the Taoists, draws
attention to Pound's condemnation of "taozers" in the Chinese
History Cantos and suggests that the poet is not aware that the
Chung Yung is "dense with Taoism" (*Era,* 456), or that the
character for "the Process" is this same *tao.* Kenner wonders how
long it took for Pound to discover this (*Era,* 458n) but, in the text
of Pound's "Unwobbling Pivot" itself, when he writes that the wise
man "goes along naturally in the midst of the process," he follows
this with the names of the characters of this phrase: "[*Ts'ung
yung chung tao*]" (*C,* 169). Only on one other occasion in this
work does he consider the sound of the characters sufficiently
important to include in the translation. Even as late as Canto 99
he is still attacking "Taozers [who] turn out to chase devils,"
which makes it clear that it is not the Tao that he objects to but
a certain kind of purveyor of occultism, precisely those kinds of
people from whom Confucius distinguishes himself in the *Chung
Yung,* who "seek mysteries in the obscure, poking into magic and
committing eccentricities in order to be talked about later" (*C,*
113). Kenner emphasizes how much the Confucian *Four Books*
have been colored by Taoism, with its emphasis on harmony with
the universe, its lack of concern with forms of government, its
quietism, and its attraction to the hermitic life rather than to
leadership (*Era,* 456). By implying that all these are out of keeping
with Pound's ideals, Kenner seems to be considering only Pound's
conception of Confucius in *Guide to Kulchur,* and to be over-
looking the fundamental change which has taken place with the
Pisan Cantos, in which Pound has turned his attention once more
to the "radiant world." The Neoplatonic terminology of his
"Cavalcanti" shines out again both in his poem and in *The Un-
wobbling Pivot.* He "neoplatonizes" Confucius just as he has

"neoplatonized" *"Donna mi prega."* For example, Confucius's comment, which James Legge renders as "How abundantly do spiritual beings display the powers that belong to them!"[8] is translated by Pound: "The spirits of the energies and of the rays have their operative *virtu.* The spirits of the energies and the rays are efficient in their *virtu,* expert, perfect as the grain of the sacrifice" (*C,* 131).

The Neoplatonism reaches a climax in chapter 26, with which Pound concludes his translation of the *Chung Yung.* In Legge's translation this chapter first describes the wise man who possesses complete "sincerity," and then the operation of "the way of Heaven and Earth," and concludes with a reference to one of the odes. Legge complains that the extravagant claims made for the powers of the man of perfect "sincerity" are uncharacteristic of the thinking of Confucius and are the elaborations of Tsze-sze, his grandson (*Analects,* 52). Pound avoids this difficulty by attributing these powers not to an individual but to "the highest grade of this clarifying activity [*i.e.,* 'sincerity']" in a way that sounds highly Neoplatonic. This "perfect sincerity" moves slowly from "the seeds whence movement springs" but "goes far and with slow but continuing motion it penetrates the solid, penetrating the solid it comes to shine forth on high." There "it stands in the emptiness above with the sun, seeing and judging, interminable in space and in time, searching, enduring . . . standing on high with the light of the intellect it is companion of heaven persisting in the vast, and in the vast of time, without limit set to it" (*C,* 179–81). Pound ends his translation with:

> *As silky light, King Wen's virtue*
> *Coming down with the sunlight,*
> > *what purity!*
> *He looks in his heart*
> *And does.*
>
> > —*Shi King,* IV, 1,2,1.

8. James Legge, ed. and trans., *The Chinese Classics,* vol. 1, *Confucian Analects, The Great Learning and The Doctrine of the Mean* (Oxford, 1895), p. 397. Subsequent references to these three works in the text will be to this edition unless Pound's translations in *Confucius* are specified.

> Here the sense is: In this way was Wen
> perfect.
>   The *unmixed* functions [in time and
> in space] without bourne.
> This unmixed is the tensile light, the
>   Immaculata. There is no end
>   to its action.   [*C,* 187]

Pound has added all the light imagery himself—there is none at all in Legge's translation. Pound uses 顯 , *hsien* ("to be manifest," "illustrious"), as a kind of mystical equivalent for this composite idea of "radiant energies," and creates his own gloss for it—"the tensile light." The four small strokes in the bottom left-hand corner of the character represent silkworms, and Pound preserves this in the idea of "silky light." The "unmixed" is 純 , *ch'un,* which Legge translates as "Singleness" in the text, but which literally means "fine and pure" "unmixed" (*Doctrine of the Mean,* 422n.) and "silken" (*Doctrine,* 486). Here, as in the first of the *Pisan Cantos* (74/429), Pound brings together under the sign of *hsien* the Confucian ideal of perfect sincerity and harmony with "the process," the "light" of the Neoplatonic One, the sunlight, and even, in "Immaculata," a suggestion of the aura of the Christian Holy Spirit.

In Canto 83, the Pisan "canto of affirmation," Pound contemplates the brilliance of the early morning mist suffused with sunlight and, as we shall see in chapter 4, remembers Mencius's words on the power of the "passion nature." Pound's restatement of Mencius could well have been written of "sincerity":

> this breath wholly covers the mountains
>   it shines and divides
> it nourishes by its rectitude
> does no injury
> overstanding the earth it fills the nine fields
>   to heaven

> Boon companion to equity
>> it joins with the process
>>> lacking it, there is inanition   [83/531]

We can now understand the important hierarchy which we find in Canto 94: "Above prana, the light, past light, / the crystal. / Above crystal, the jade!" (94/634). In Pound's 1921 essay on Brancusi we read:

> But the contemplation of form or of formal-beauty leading into the infinite must be dissociated from the dazzle of crystal; there is a sort of relation, but there is the more important divergence; with the crystal it is a hypnosis, or a contemplative fixation of thought, or an excitement of the 'sub-conscious' or unconscious (whatever the devil they may be), and with the ideal form in marble it is an approach to the infinite *by form,* by precisely the highest possible degree of consciousness of formal perfection; as free of accident as any of the philosophical demands of a 'Paradiso' can make it. [*LE,* 444]

"Prana" is the Hindu "form-force" and Pound probably uses the Sanskrit word to make a connection with Apollonius of Tyana who learned a great deal from Indian mystics and whose story is about to be told in Canto 94. Prana is similar to Pound's concept of *forma,* as he describes it in *Guide to Kulchur:* "The *forma,* the immortal *concetto,* the concept, the dynamic form which is like the rose pattern driven into the dead iron-filings by the magnet, not by material contact with the magnet itself, but separate from the magnet. Cut off by the layer of glass, the dust and filings rise and spring into order. Thus the *forma,* the concept rises from death" (*GK,* 152). This is something existing apart from the human.

The "light" is involved in the coming together of human and divine. It can be the manner in which the divine manifests itself, as in the *Paradiso,* or it can represent a state of mystic enlightenment or intellectual inspiration in the person, or, as in Cavalcanti, the operation of love. Light is equivalent to the working of the process, and those who understand and further this working through the precision of their perceptions and their compassion manifest the light.

Pound sees in Scotus Erigena's "Omnia quae sunt, lumina sunt" [All things that are, are lights] a feeling for the "tensile light" which parallels his own. The great Chinese rulers, through their actions, enabled "the process" to take its course to the benefit of their people. These points come together in Canto 74:

> in the light of light is the *virtù*
>   "sunt lumina" said Erigena Scotus
>   as of Shun on Mt. Taishan
> and in the hall of the forebears
>   as from the beginning of wonders
> the paraclete that was present in Yao, the precision
> in Shun the compassionate
> in Yu the guider of waters
> . . . .
> Light tensile immaculata
>   the sun's cord unspotted
> "sunt lumina" said the Oirishman to King Carolus,
>   "OMNIA,
> all things that are are lights"   [74/429]

The crystal is the most complex of the four terms, since Pound uses it in a variety of ways. Its essential meaning is explained by the passage in which Pound says that he values the Neoplatonists because they "have caused man after man to be suddenly conscious of the reality of *nous,* of mind, apart from any man's individual mind, of the sea crystalline and enduring, of the bright as it were molten glass that envelops us, full of light" (*GK,* 44). Man has created his ideas of the gods from his consciousness of the *nous,* so the crystal is a fitting element for them. In Canto 91 we find "Gods moving in crystal," and the Princess Ra-Set "enter[ing] the protection of crystal," her sun barge moving "on river of crystal" (91/611, 613). The state of mind associated with crystal is visionary experience, the value of which varies from person to person. Apollonius of Tyana, in his quest for wisdom and spiritual enlightenment, has made the pursuit of this experience a way of life; for Joan of Arc, the experience is the saint's vision; for the poet, it is the inspirational state which generates the poem. The quality of crystal can even be transferred to the poem itself, as we see in Pound's comment on one of Hardy's poems: "There is a flood of life caught in this crystal" (*GK,* 287).

Extending the courtly lover's idea of the light of love issuing from the lady's eyes to enter her beloved's, Pound makes the eyes of women into miniature versions of the "crystal," containing the force which, through the agency of love, inspires their lovers to achievement. In Canto 91, the eyes of Elizabeth I impel Sir Francis Drake to defeat the Spanish Armada:

> Miss Tudor moved them with galleons
> from deep eye, versus armada
> from the green deep
> > he saw it,
> in the green deep of an eye:
> . . . .
> That Drake saw the splendour and wreckage
> > in that clarity   [91/611]

In the same way, as we shall see, the eyes of the women he loves are Pound's own inspiration.

Pound's main concern in *Rock-Drill* and *Thrones* is how to move from the "crystal" to the "jade," and we will examine this in more detail later. The sphere of activity which constitutes the "jade" goes beyond artistic creation alone and is the real object of Pound's quest. The "jade" represents the idea coming over into action, excellence of intellect and accuracy of perception manifesting themselves in a way which benefits the whole society and establishes a higher level of civilization. Fine sculpture and architecture become, for Pound, more than beautiful objects in their own right; they are a sign of the health of the culture which produced them. Because Pound becomes committed to the improvement of the whole society, and not of the arts alone, it is necessary for him to see beyond architectural beauty and to conclude that the economics of the culture which produced it must have been sound. Hence his conclusion that "A tolerance of gombeen men and stealers of harvest by money, by distortion and dirtiness, runs concurrent with a fattening in all art forms" (*GK*, 109). The "jade" can only be achieved through the agency of just rulers who choose wise counsellors and maintain a sound economic system. After the collapse of Pound's hopes that Mussolini would create the ideal state in Italy, he is forced to look to the past for examples of the "jade." For this reason *Rock-Drill* begins with an examination of the wisdom of the great rulers of ancient China, as it is recorded in the *Shoo King*. Pound says of two of these rulers: "Yao and Shun ruled by jade" (106/753). In the past, Pound can find examples of just rulers and great architecture, but in modern Europe the corrupting influence of usury blights everything.

Evil: Usura and the Hell of the Present

Where the "Good" in *The Cantos* is essentially a part of the poet's intimate, personal experience, "Evil" is something from which the poet himself stands removed—something observed from a distance. Pound approaches the problem of evil not psychologically or theologically but sociologically, concerning himself not with its origin or its nature, but with its manifestations in society around him. He insists that the artist should "settle the ethical problem without confusing it with the metaphysical" and blames Eliot for not observing this separation in *After Strange Gods* (*SP*, 320). He is concerned with justice, not with virtue.

His earliest formulations of "evil" are mainly secondhand. His friendship with Wyndham Lewis and his involvement in the *Blast* enterprise led him to pay lip service to Lewis's notions of "evil" and to imitate Lewis's "Enemy" pose, but his commitment to some of Lewis's more extreme ideas is not very convincing and he seems mainly to be caught up in protest for protest's sake. (These matters are discussed further in chapter 2.) Both Pound and Lewis denounce Protestantism but for different reasons. Lewis attacks it as antiauthoritarian, saying that it encourages emotion and individualism and paves the way for democracy, liberalism, socialism, and pacifism. Pound objects to Protestantism mainly because it reduces morality to sexual morality and because, he contends, it encourages usury. Where Pound finds too much repression, Lewis finds a dangerous incentive to self-expression.

The Hell Cantos give us a fairly comprehensive notion of Pound's idea of evil at that time, but before we examine them, we should determine what he means by *"Usura."* On one level, *Usura* is the machinations of the usurers and bankers which can be opposed by enlightened rulers or politicians, but its full meaning is considerably deeper and broader than this. In fact, Pound's conception of *Usura* is virtually identical to Dante's definition of it in canto 11 of the *Inferno.* Here Vergil explains how the last of the three rings of the Seventh Circle is reserved for the violent against God, Nature, and Art, and how "Violence may be done against the Deity, by denying and blaspheming Him in the heart, and despising Nature and her goodness; and therefore the smallest ring seals with its mark both Sodom and Cahors [notorious for its usury], and all who speak contemning God in their heart."[9] Vergil explains further how usury offends the Divine Goodness, saying that "Nature takes her course from divine Intellect and from Its art; and . . . your art, as far as it can, follows her, as the pupil does his master; so that your art is as it were grandchild of God. By these two, if you remember Genesis at the beginning, it behooves man to gain his bread and to prosper. But because the usurer takes another way, he contemns Nature in herself and in her follower, for he puts his hope elsewhere" (1. 11. 98–111). The virtuous man allows his acts—his "art"—to be governed by the rhythms of the natural world and in this way he is concurring with the "divine Intellect" which directs the course of nature. Pound expresses exactly this idea when he talks of the necessity of observing and acting in harmony with "the process." Dante is of course taking as the norm the agricultural society of his own day, and Pound in his condemnation of usury follows Dante so closely as often to seem

9. Dante Alighieri, *The Divine Comedy,* 3 vols., ed. and trans. Charles S. Singleton (Princeton, 1970, 1973, 1976), Bollingen Series 80, vol. 1, canto 11, lines 46–51. Subsequent references to *The Divine Comedy* in the text will be to volume, canto, and line in this edition.

anachronistic. His economic ideas sound unrealistic mainly because they frequently presume a very simple rural society which bears little relation to the reality of the technological society of twentieth-century cities. By choosing to live in Rapallo, he has, of course, maintained some contact with the simple life. At times he seems to be assuming that physical labor or the arts are the only legitimate and worthwhile human activities.

The three types of violence against God are "Sodomy," "Usury," and "blaspheming Him in the heart." The alternatives to these are fertile sexuality, husbandry, and religious observance and ritual. In pagan religions, the interrelation of these three life-affirming activities is the basis of the essential fertility and vegetation rites, and Cantos 39 and 47 are Pound's equivalent to these rites. Here, both sexuality and husbandry are sacramental and affirm man's "kinship with the vital universe," which gives him strength to continue to fight *Usura.* "The process" itself, the rhythm of the seasons, the inevitable recurrence of spring, all proclaim usury as a perversion and offer the reassurance that no matter how firmly entrenched it seems to be, it is always an aberration and can never be assimilated into the natural order.

The Hell Cantos are mainly concerned to attack "obstructors of knowledge, / obstructors of distribution" (14/63). The obstruction of natural increase is given much less attention and Pound only mentions in passing "sadic mothers driving their daughters to bed with decrepitude, / sows eating their litters," and "the vice-crusaders, fahrting through silk, / waving the Christian symbols" (14/62–63). The "obstructors of distribution" are, as we expect, the "usurers," "financiers," "war-profiteers," and "slum owners" and their "respecters," most notably "politicians," but also "fabians," "imperialists," and "agents provocateurs" guilty of the murder of Irish patriots. The "obstructors of knowledge" are the "betrayers of language" who have "lied for hire," "news owners," "orators," "preachers," "bigots," scholars "obscuring the texts with philology," and several specific individuals, one of whom "disliked colloquial language."

The "obstructors of distribution" are aided and abetted by the "obstructors of knowledge." Since the latter deal in language rather than in coin, they are more nearly in Pound's own province and he is particularly emphatic about the need for precision of language and clear definition of terms as the only effective weapons against the "perverters of language." He insists that "the mal-administration of an educational system, stupidity in the teaching of history, idiotic laws due to ignorance of legislature, both attain and are due to the mental realm and the indolence or cowardice of the literati."[10] All of these protect the usurers from scrutiny and allow them to continue to operate clandestinely: "there is one enemy, ever-busy obscuring our terms; ever muddling and muddy-ing terminologies, ever trotting out minor issues to obscure the main and the basic, ever prattling of short range causation for the sake of, or with the result of, obscuring the vital truth . . . (that is to say hogging the harvest, aiding the hoggers and so forth)" (*GK*, 31). Finding *"le mot juste"* has become an ethical imperative, and Pound insists on the need for this throughout *The Cantos*. In 99/711 we read "Precise terminology is the first implement, / dish and container," and are reminded in 97/680 that the poet is motivated by "an interest in equity / not in mere terminology." Pound uses 正名, ching[4] ming[2], several times in *The Cantos* to stand for his ideal of precise definition of terms.

The two scatological and almost hysterically shrill Hell Cantos ultimately tell us much more about Pound's anger and frustration than about the villains he is attacking, and the victims themselves are almost wholly left out of consideration. His approach in his *Usura* Canto is entirely different. Instead of rage spilling over into a proliferation of loathsome detail, we find an almost elegiac regret which calls up images of beauty. In the very act of asserting the power of *Usura* to stifle the arts, Pound names the very works of art and architecture that he values most highly and these go far toward determining the mood of the canto:

> with usura
> hath no man a painted paradise on his church wall
> *harpes et luz*
> or where virgin receiveth message
> and halo projects from incision,

10. Ezra Pound, "Newspapers, History, etc.," *Hound and Horn* 3, no. 4 (July/Sept 1930): 574–79.

with usura
seeth no man Gonzaga his heirs and his concubines   [45/229]

This canto also differs from the Hell Cantos in its concern for the victims of *Usura*. We can see this from the opening lines of the canto:

With *Usura*
With usura hath no man a house of good stone
each block cut smooth and well fitting
that design might cover their face,   [45/229]

It is significant that Pound begins with the *house* of stone which can afterwards be ornamented. He is not concerned with the arts in isolation but with the arts as cornerstone of a sound civilization. Shelter and nourishment for the body and nourishment for the mind and spirit belong together and usury jeopardizes them all. Not only are the people deprived of beautiful art in their churches but "with usura . . . / is thy bread ever more of stale rags / is thy bread dry as paper" (45/229). Pound makes this same protest in *Guide to Kulchur* when he says that, because of the usurers, "Millions starve or are kept on health-destroying short rations, diluted foods, Ersatz and offal" (*GK*, 131). His genuine distress at human suffering comes out clearly in Canto 46 also. Here he blames the usurers for the American Civil War which he says was fought as much over the debt of "two hundred million" owed by the South to the New York banks as over slavery. He holds the international bankers, profiteers, and armament manufacturers responsible for the "5 millions bein' killed off / to 1919" in Europe and holds the usurers responsible for the fact that in 1935 in America there are:

FIVE million youths without jobs
FOUR million adult illiterates
15 million 'vocational misfits', that is with small chance for jobs
NINE million persons annual, injured in preventable industrial
                                                                accidents
One hundred thousand violent crimes. . . .   [46/235]

The Struggle against Usura: The Heroes

A large part of *The Cantos* is a celebration of Pound's heroes. Many of them, particularly in the first part of the poem, are artists, sculptors, enlightened patrons such as Sigismundo Malatesta, or poets, and in *The Spirit of Romance,* Pound claims that "the study of literature is hero-worship" (*SR,* 5). As the poem progresses, we find an increasing number of heroes who are working more directly to counteract the power of the usurers. Some of these are historians who can help to make the case against the usurers by bringing to light hidden facts which detail their corruption—men like Thomas Hart Benton, Alexander Del Mar, and Brooks Adams. Some of the heroes are rulers who can take some positive action against the usurers, such as the Tuscan Grand-Dukes Ferdinand and Leopold, Thomas Jefferson, John Adams, Andrew Jackson, and Mussolini. Another group of heroes who particularly come into prominence in *Thrones* are "lawgivers" who, if their laws are just and are formulated clearly, can ensure that societies have some measure of protection from the usurers for generations.

As Pound increasingly turns his attention from the aesthetic to the ethical, he comes to require a highly developed sense of social responsibility from his heroes. A good indication of this new emphasis is found in the postscript to *Guide to Kulchur,* "As Sextant," which he calls "not a full list of books a sane man will want to enjoy [but] . . . books without which he cannot measure the force of the others." The list reads:

    I. The FOUR BOOKS (Confucius and Mencius)
   II. HOMER: Odyssey: intelligence set above brute force.
  III. The Greek TRAGEDIANS: rise of sense of civic responsibility.
  IV. DIVINA COMMEDIA: life of the spirit.
   V. FROBENIUS: Erlebte Erdteile . . .
  VI. BROOKS ADAMS: Law of Civilization and Decay: . . .
 VII. The English Charters, the essential parts of BLACKSTONE, that is those dealing with history and philosophy of law. The American Constitution. [*GK,* 352]

As we can see from the first item on this list, Pound considers Confucius to be the wisest of his heroes. In *Guide to Kulchur* he frequently commends the wisdom of the *Analects* and says that it shows that Confucius and his "interlocutors live in a responsible world, they think for the whole social order" (*GK*, 29).

To Pound, writing just before the outbreak of the Second World War, Mussolini alone of all the world rulers seems to have the sense of social responsibility that Pound considered necessary: "The heritage of Jefferson, Quincy Adams, old John Adams, Jackson, Van Buren is HERE, NOW *in the Italian peninsula* at the beginning of fascist second decennio" (*JM*, 12). Even after Pound's dream of the new Italy as the harbinger of a revitalized Western civilization was shattered, his attitude toward his heroes remained unchanged. He could no longer hope for any dramatic improvement in the conditions of his own time, but the efforts and example of his heroes became if anything more highly prized. He saw himself as the wise counsellor whose economic advice was not heeded, but he reaffirmed his faith in the efficacy of wise counsel and turned to the wise counsellors of the past to examine their achievements and the way in which their wisdom shaped the laws and institutions of their time. These seminal minds form a tradition of enlightened thought and action which Pound traces back to ancient China—he calls this tradition *Sagetrieb*. *"Sage"* means "legend," "saga," "myth," or "tradition," and *"Trieb"* has a variety of meanings from "sprout," "young shoot," to "driving force," "motive power," or "instinct." The "tradition" is of course all the written remains or artifacts or even hearsay which preserve the wisdom of the past. *"Trieb"* suggests both the "driving force" which makes possible the individual accomplishments which together constitute the tradition, and also the cumulative, forward-moving power of the tradition itself. Each new affirmation of the immemorial wisdom is like a young shoot—not so much a new growth on the parent tree, but perhaps something closer to a stalk of grain which springs up on its own yet duplicates the essential "idea" of "corn" or "wheat" because of that particular *virtù* of the seed which fascinates Pound, "the kind of intelligence that enables grass seed to grow grass; the cherry-stone to make cherries" (*C*, 193). He singles out as members of this tradition those who both show their faith in the power of human reason and have worked actively to implement their ideas and uphold their beliefs, often under difficult or dangerous circumstances requiring personal courage. Pound honors such men by awarding them "thrones"—hence the title of Cantos 96–109. In *Drafts and Fragments* we find "But these had thrones, / and in my mind were still, uncontending—" (114/793).

At the beginning of *Rock-Drill,* Pound presents the Great Emperors and wise counsellors of the Shang and Chow dynasties whose words and deeds are recorded in the ancient *Shoo King,* or *Book of Historical Documents.* To help explain his concept of *Sagetrieb,* Pound refers to the *San Ku,* or *Three Ku,* who with the three *Kung,* are the chief officers of the state and assistants to the emperor. The *Ku* are actually lower in rank than the *Kung,* but Pound has probably chosen to mention the former because of the use of light imagery in the description of their function. Legge's English translation reads: "they with reverence display brightly the powers of heaven and earth,"[11] but the French translation of Séraphine Couvreur, from which Pound was working, emphasizes more strongly both light and the idea of "the process," saying that they *"font briller l'action produtrice du ciel et de la terre."*[12] Hence we find in Canto 90:

> And from the San Ku
>
> . . . .
>
>   to the room in Poitiers where one can stand
>   casting no shadow,
> That is Sagetrieb,
>   that is tradition.
> Builders had kept the proportion,
>   did Jacques de Molay
>   know these proportions?
> And was Erigena ours?   [90/605]

11. James Legge, ed. and trans., *The Chinese Classics,* vol. 3, *The Shoo King,* p. 528. Subsequent references to *Shoo King* will be to this edition unless Séraphine Couvreur's edition, *Chou King,* is specified.

12. Séraphine Couvreur, ed. and trans., *Chou King* (Sien Hsien, 1927), pp. 333–34.

The room in Poitiers is the Tour Maubergeon (*Era,* 326), "the tower wherein, at one point, is no shadow" (87/573). Its architect, through the precision of his calculation, created a design on the principle of the greatest possible receptivity to light. This room of stone suggests itself to Pound as a useful symbol of his ideal of the intellect which lets the light of the Intelligence shine freely into it. As we shall see in the following chapter, Pound gives particular importance to works of stone, and he particularly values Romanesque architecture for which Poitiers is famous. Jacques de Molay, the last Grand Master of the Templars, is mentioned because Pound wants to suggest that he and his order were practising an enlightened form of economics. They ran a highly efficient banking system and were known to be honest and trustworthy, but Pound goes a step beyond this when he asks, "Was De Molay making loans without interest?" (87/576). He seems to be entertaining the idea that they were a threat to the "usurers" of their own time and that this would be sufficient reason, perhaps the real reason, for their extermination. Or perhaps there was some truth to the charge that they were Gnostics, like the Albigensians; that they had kept alive some valuable paganistic rites and that their sound financial transactions reflected this. In 85/559 we find:

> King Owen had men about him:
>   Prince of Kouo,
>   Houng Ieo, San I Cheng

Sagetrieb

as the hand grips the wheat,

The character which follows the names of the three excellent ministers of King Owen (Wăn) is *chiao,* "to teach." Their instruction is an example of *Sagetrieb.* This refers us to part 5, book 16 of the *Shoo King,* where we read: "But for the ability of these men to go and come in his affairs, developing his constant lessons, there would have been no benefits descending from King Wăn on the people. And it also was from the determinate favour *of Heaven,* that there were these men of firm virtue, and acting according to their knowledge of the dread majesty of Heaven, to give themselves to enlighten King Wăn" (*Shoo King,* 13-14). *Ping,* the second character, shows "a hand grasping stalks of grain" (*Shoo King,* 300n.) and is used in the passage above with the meaning "to maintain virtue." As the hand grasps the stalks of grain, so those who study ancient wisdom hold firm to the tradition and thereby maintain virtue.

From ancient China, Pound turns, in *Rock-Drill,* to nineteenth-century America to honor, for their integrity, courage, and concern for justice, Andrew Jackson, Martin Van Buren, Thomas Hart Benton, and Randolph of Roanoke. Above all, Pound praises them for the part they played in the fight against the Bank of the United States:

> And in the time of Mr. Randolph, Mr. Benton, Mr. Van Buren
> he, Andy Jackson
> POPULUM AEDIFICAVIT   [89/596]

Although *Rock-Drill* begins with the transmitters of *Sagetrieb,* Pound changes his emphasis abruptly and returns, with Canto 90, to the metaphysical to affirm his conviction: "Beyond civic order: / l'AMOR" (94/634). Cantos 90-93 are like the *Pisan Cantos* in their personal meditations, their celebration of the power of love and their descriptions of the intellect rising to intimations of the *nous.* Pound follows them with a tribute to Apollonius of Tyana, in whom reverence for the divine and the love of wisdom is united with deep concern for the spiritual and political well-being of the people. The only full account of the life of Apollonius is the biography written by Philostratus from which Pound excerpts passages for Canto 94. It seems most likely that he first learned of Apollonius from G. R. S. Mead, the editor of *The Quest,* a publication devoted to studies of Gnosticism, theosophy, and pagan mystery religions. Pound had met him in London in 1911 and presented as a lecture to "The Quest Society" what is now chapter 5 of *The Spirit of Romance* (*Life,* 104, 113). In 1901 Mead had published a critical study of Philostratus's *Life of Apollonius* in a book called *Apollonius of Tyana.* The picture of the philosopher which emerges from these pages is one that could not help but appeal to Pound. Apollonius, as Mead presents him, comes as close as it is possible to get to Pound's ideal of conduct and wisdom. In his search for divine truth he observed the strict rules of purity of the Pythagoreans but combined piety and meditation with a highly active life. He was "one of the greatest travellers known to antiquity,"[13] visiting shrines and temples wherever he went to restore the rites to their ancient purity and to receive instruction from those like the Brahmans, whom he considered more enlightened than himself. Mead says that to him "the mere fashion of a man's faith was unessential; he was at home in all lands, among all cults."[14] He divided his time between developing his own wisdom and sharing the benefits of it with others, devoting the mornings "to the divine science" and the afternoons to "instruction in ethics and practical life."[15] On his travels, the philosopher "discoursed on the life of a wise man and the duties of a wise ruler, with kings, rulers, and magistrates [and] . . . endeavoured to advise for their good those of the emperors who would listen to him."[16] Vespasian, Titus, and Nerva followed his counsel, but Nero and Domitian ignored it and persisted in their evil. Apollonius had concentrated on the reforming of religious practices, but Mead says that Nero's tyranny "opened his eyes to a more immediate evil, which seemed no less than the abrogation of the liberty of conscience by an irresponsible tyranny," and from then on he concerned himself with the conduct of the rulers of his own time.[17] Apollonius was also courageous. Domitian was incensed at the philosopher's criticisms of his conduct, but Apollonius, instead of avoiding the Emperor, expressly travelled from Egypt to Rome to confront him, was arrested, tried for treason and for being a magician, and acquitted. From Philostratus we learn that before Apollonius came to trial he had an interview with Casperius Aelianus, a prefect of

13. G. R. S. Mead, *Apollonius of Tyana* (London & Benares, 1901), p. 75.
14. Ibid., p. 63.
15. Ibid., p. 71.
16. Ibid., p. 106.
17. Ibid., p. 107.

the praetorian guard. Unknown to Domitian, the prefect was an admirer of Apollonius and advised the philosopher how best to prepare his defense. Apollonius's companion Damis was afraid at the prospect of their trial, but when his master told him that they had the friendship of Aelianus, he replied: "Now I am ready to believe that Leucothea did really once give her veil to Odysseus, after he had fallen out of his ship and was paddling himself over the sea with his hands. For we are reduced to just as awful and impossible a plight, when some god, as it seems to me, stretches out his hand over us, that we fall not away from all hope of salvation." Apollonius upbraids him for not yet realizing that "wisdom amazes [terrifies] all that is sensible of her, but is herself not amazed by anything."[18] Pound, having experienced Damis's precise fear himself, takes heart from Leucothea's rescue of Odysseus and chooses it for the conclusion to *Rock-Drill* (91/615–16). Pound, confined to an asylum for the criminally insane, cannot avoid some anxiety about his powers of endurance:

> Without guides, having nothing but courage
> Shall audacity last into fortitude?"   [93/632]

Apollonius's example heartens him, and it is certain that he decides to give the philosopher a prominent place in *Rock-Drill* for highly personal reasons.

Where *Rock-Drill* begins with the deeds of the rulers of ancient China, as recorded in the *Shoo King, Thrones* introduces the Lombards through Paul the Deacon's *History of the Langobards.* Paul himself, as the writer of histories, furthers *Sagetrieb,* but Pound clearly intends us to think of him as an individual as well as a historian by making him talk confidentially and informally: "and my grand-dad got out of what is now Jugoslavia / with a bow, arrows and a wolf acting as guide / till it thought gramp looked too hungry" (96/652). Pound probably has several reasons in addition to his interest in Paul for choosing to begin this sequence with the

18. Philostratus, *The Life of Apollonius of Tyana,* ed. and trans. F. C. Conybeare, 2 vols. (Cambridge, Mass., 1960), The Loeb Classical Library, 2: 211.

Lombards. He has turned from the Italian present to its early history and is perhaps somewhat reassured to be reminded that the European chaos of his own times is nothing new; that Italy, for example, has managed to survive centuries of political upheaval. He is also particularly interested in the fact that "Rothar got some laws written down" (96/652), since bodies of law will be his main theme in *Thrones*. In Canto 96, he moves from the Lombards to the Byzantines and the flourishing of the Eastern Empire under Leo VI. In counterpoint to the consolidation of the Byzantine Empire, we inevitably find the collapse of the Western Empire— "Barbarians enjoying Roman calamities"—and Pound surely intends to draw a parallel between the latter and the fate of Italy (he would say of all Europe) with Mussolini's overthrow and the end of the Second World War.

Beginning with Diocletian, Pound mentions several Emperors whose financial and legal policies helped to strengthen the Eastern Empire, but Leo VI receives special emphasis because Pound chooses to examine and present in some detail the *Eparch's Book*, a collection of statutes regulating the activities of merchants and craftsmen and compiled by Leo. This is only one small example of this Emperor's extensive legal writings, but Pound probably values it because of its specificity and practicality in carrying sound legal principles down into the details of the lives of tradesmen and artisans and in safeguarding the ordinary citizen. The *Eparch's Book* gives us a close-up on the functioning of Byzantine society at its peak. One sign of Byzantine supremacy is the fact that no other rulers of the West presume to usurp the Basileus's prerogative of coining gold. The coining of gold is a sign of sovereignty and it is not until the fall of Constantinople that the rulers of Europe begin to mint their own gold coins. Pound had been studying this matter in the works of Alexander Del Mar, and the first half of his next canto is a compilation of information taken mainly from *History of Monetary Systems*. Del Mar fully supports Pound's contention that rulers are renouncing an important part of their sovereignty when they hand over the prerogative of creating money to banks— "When kings quit, the bankers began again" (97/672)—and that this is "wholly inconsistent with the safety of the State, and that it demands revision."[19] Del Mar is yet another exponent of *Sage-trieb:* trained as a civil and mining engineer, he became interested in the history of money and made an intensive study of the subject, at the same time holding various government positions including Director of the Bureau of Statistics and Mining Commissioner to the United States Monetary Commission. Pound is clearly attracted to his contention that there is a direct connection between monetary systems and social justice, that money is "perhaps the mightiest engine to which man can lend an intelligent guidance," having power to "so distribute the burdens, gratifications, and opportunities of life that each individual shall enjoy that share of them to which his merits or good fortune may fairly entitle him, or, contrariwise, to dispense them with so partial a hand as to violate every principle of justice, and perpetuate a succession of social slaveries to the end of time."[20]

Cantos 98 and 99 celebrate the wisdom of the Chinese *Sacred Edict* and thereby pay tribute to the three men responsible for it—the Emperor K'ang-hsi, his son Yong-cheng, and Wang-iu-p'uh, "Commissioner of the Salt-Works," who rendered the existing text into colloquial Chinese and expounded on it to make its meaning accessible to the common people. Where the *Eparch's Book* is expressly directed to the conduct of business, the Chinese *Edict* makes pronouncements on almost all aspects of the lives of the people, from the education of children to agricultural methods, from "Heretical Sects" to "Payments of Taxes." Above all, it extols harmony within society and within the family, and the virtues of compassion, filiality, mutuality, and deference. It emphasizes that the essence of law is reciprocity and that conscientious work is the root of honesty, good manners, and good custom—that "there is worship in plowing / and equity in the weeding hoe" (99/711). The impression of the *Edict* which we form from these cantos is wholly favorable, but when we turn to the Chinese text itself, what we find is somewhat unsettling and we realize that

19. Alexander Del Mar, *History of Monetary Systems* (Chicago, 1895), p. 7.
20. Ibid., p. 5.

Pound has excerpted from it only what suits his purposes. The culture which emerges from the pages of the *Edict* is alien and disturbing and raises obstacles to a sympathetic reading which are not raised by the Confucian classics. The problem particularly centers on those passages concerned with punishments. For example, the first three chapters on "Duteousness and Subordination," "Clan Relationships and Harmony," and "Keeping the Peace" all conclude with lists of punishments such as: "Sons or grandsons who use abusive language to their parents or grandparents, or wives or concubines who abuse the husband's parents or grandparents, are alike strangled; those who strike (the afore mentioned) are beheaded: those who kill them, are put to death by slow degrees."[21] The logic behind the severity of the laws is of course that, knowing these penalties, "none will dare to follow the impulses of their savage dispositions."[22] The reiteration of these punishments severely compromises the value of the *Sacred Edict* as a guide to the ideal of a humane society. Nor is the writer's attitude toward the common people very attractive either: "Granting that you soldiers and civilians are naturally stupid and perverse, and cannot fully understand reason and equity, is it possible that none of you have any concern for yourselves and families? Give it a moment's thought. To break the law of the land is to suffer endless misery; in some cases it involves beating, in others torture: —call on the gods as you may, you certainly won't be let off. Your best course is thoroughly to reform without delay."[23] Altogether, the book is an odd choice for a pivotal source, and makes us feel that in these cantos, Pound's comments about human virtues and emotions must be seen as generalizations made ultimately without reference to his deepest feelings and intimate experience. We begin to realize that in *Thrones* he is still hoping that "the truth" about the human condition will manifest itself in some objective way and specifically in the wording of just laws. His conviction of the importance of legal justice is sincere and not just an intellectual

21. F. W. Baller, ed. and trans., *The Sacred Edict* (Shanghai, 1924), p. 17.

22. Ibid., p. 94.

23. Ibid., p. 95.

but an emotional conviction, yet in itself it is not enough. We feel that he is using his absorption in this subject as a distraction from or alternative to personal meditations of the kind that we find in *Rock-Drill* and in *Drafts and Fragments.*

Canto 105 on Saint Anselm and the Anglo-Saxon kings of Britain partly serves as a transition to Pound's tribute to Sir Edward Coke and to the British common law in the last three cantos of *Thrones.* The kings are mentioned only briefly and as members of a tradition of enlightened British rulers under whom the law of the people evolved and became established. Anselm's intellectual brilliance and faith in the power of human reason to prove the existence of God makes him an obvious choice for a Poundian hero. He also conveniently ties together the beginning and end of *Thrones,* being a Lombard by birth and finally becoming an English Archbishop. He was, in addition, a man of courage, upholding the power of the Church against the King, William Rufus, although deserted by the English bishops and finally driven to exile until William renounced the right of investiture of clergy.

Cantos 107–09, with which *Thrones* concludes, are a celebration of the Magna Carta, the foundation of British law and justice, and of Sir Edward Coke, the great English jurist and champion of common law. *The Second Part of the Institutes of the Laws of England,* which is Pound's major source for these cantos, is Coke's commentary on the Magna Carta. In 1648 Coke's defense of common law against the power of the throne culminated in his drawing up of the Petition of Right establishing the liberties guaranteed by the Magna Carta and by ancient legal precedence. Charles was forced to concede to the unanimous request of the Lords and Commons and to give his royal approval to this instrument for the curtailing of royal prerogative. Coke himself had an encyclopedic knowledge of the law and an unwavering commitment to the defense of the liberties of the common people. He also showed courage in defying both James and Charles, and was imprisoned in the Tower of London for nearly seven months on a charge of treason which had finally to be dropped in the absence of any evidence.

Pound is clearly celebrating the enduring value of British common law as the instrument of justice. Growing organically from the consciences and customs of generations, it symbolizes the human aspiration toward justice itself. He reminds the reader in his reference to "Woolcott" (109/773) that this same common law is the basis of American law also. Henry Woolcott, who emigrated to New England in 1628, was the grandfather of Roger Woolcott, lawyer, Colonial Governor of Connecticut, and the author of the first volume of verse published in Connecticut. Roger's son was also Governor of that state, member of the Continental Congress, and one of the signers of the Declaration of Independence. In a lecture delivered at the Hall of Lincoln's Inn to commemorate the four hundredth anniversary of Coke's birth, Samuel E. Thorne, Professor of Legal History at Harvard, speaks of Coke's contribution to American law, saying that "some of his doctrines and ideas . . . have taken firmer root abroad than they have at home, and more American than English law can be traced back to his books and no further. . . . If he was born and died a British subject, he has since achieved dual nationality."[24] Pound, who has already made his personal peace with England in Canto 80, is now ready to turn from the laws of Byzantium and China to his more immediate heritage.

Although most of his references in the Coke Cantos are taken from part 2 of the *Institutes,* some refer us to his second main source, Catherine Drinker Bowen's life of Coke, *The Lion and the Throne.* In this work, Coke is no longer just the author of the *Institutes,* but the whole man in all his moods and roles and relationships. Written against this background, the cantos on Coke represent a definite movement away from the objectivity of the *Eparch's Book* and the *Sacred Edict.* The details of Coke's life make it clear that what Pound says of himself can, with equal justice be said of Coke—that he "had been a hard man in some ways" (74/431). Samuel Thorne, after paying tribute to him as "an extraordinarily able lawyer, a great judge, and a remarkable parliamentary leader" goes on to observe that "he was, as well, an unpleasant, hard, grasping, arrogant, and thoroughly difficult man, of whom his widow, after thirty-six years of married life, could write,

24. Samuel E. Thorne, *Sir Edward Coke 1552–1952,* Selden Society Lecture (London, 1957), pp. 3–4.

not without more than sufficient cause, 'We shall never see his like again, praises be to God.' "[25]

His brutal prosecution of Sir Walter Raleigh was one of his harshest public acts, but his own family was not spared his "unpleasantness" either. He forced his fourteen-year-old daughter into a marriage which would be to his political advantage, and to do so kidnapped her from the house where her mother was hiding her. Pound refers obliquely to this incident when he reminds us that this same daughter was later tried for adultery, convicted, and sentenced to walk publicly "in a white sheet in the Savoy" in penance (107/761). Coke's contribution to British and American justice was without doubt of the utmost significance, but it was only one part of his life.

Pound's Struggle with Himself

Pound became so involved in the struggle against usury that he came to neglect not only the aesthetic and the metaphysical, but also the personal. His opinions became increasingly dogmatic and formulaic, and by the time of the Rome Radio broadcasts he seemed to have lost touch with his deepest, positive emotions. In *After Strange Gods,* Eliot observed that Pound did away with "the idea of intense moral struggle" and replaced it with a belief that the world would become "as good as anyone could require" through "benevolence . . . and a redistribution or increase of purchasing power, combined with a devotion, on the part of an élite, to Art."[26] During the time that he spent in the Disciplinary Training Center (D.T.C.) at Pisa, however, he became involved in an "intense moral struggle" which took precedence over the struggle against usury and which was to be the most important subject of the second half of the poem.

Although before 1945 Pound had come to feel that the pursuit of metaphysical and aesthetic harmony must temporarily take second place to the cause of monetary reform, he never ceased to

25. Ibid., p. 4.
26. T. S. Eliot, *After Strange Gods* (London, 1934), p. 42.

hold the former as his highest ideal. The political and economic chaos of his own times seemed an insuperable obstacle to the attaining of such a harmony, but he continued to hope that, with time, this obstacle would be removed. In the meantime he hypothesized, from a distance, an ideal of "totalitarian art" which would be characterized by inevitability and perfect equilibrium and would show no trace of struggle. In *Guide to Kulchur* he describes the performance of a Boccherini piece as "utterly beautiful" because "no trace of effort remained," and contrasts this to Bartok's Fifth Quartet, to much of Beethoven, and to his own *Cantos,* which all contain defects precisely because they are "record[s] of a personal struggle" (*GK,* 135). He prizes most highly moments of perfect repose and equilibrium at the center of the vortex of activity or the whirl of "facts." He has faith that if all the facts are correct they will irresistibly spring into a symmetry and a synthesis, that the *"immortal concetto"* will manifest itself, as the random iron filings spring into a rose in the presence of the magnet (*GK,* 152).

A later chapter in *Guide to Kulchur* called "The Promised Land" shows Pound taking stock of the progress he had made toward his ideal of "totalitarian" art. It shows how even in 1938 he was trying to examine and understand the causes of his uneasiness about his own work and ideas. It shows him arguing out his own positions with himself, realizing the weaknesses of his course but persisting anyway, modifying earlier views which he had held to so dogmatically, but also reasserting some of his most rigid and limiting ideas.

He begins by looking back at the "serious Victorians, from Hardy to Swinburne," and decides that although with the exception of Browning they "wrote as non-interveners," they still did not accept the social irresponsibility of the current Victorian "code of morality"—the irrelevance and platitudinousness of the Church, which was careful not to interfere with "a man's politics or his religion." Browning is unique among these writers in that he has "a revivalist spirit," but Pound suggests that the others saw the problems which he himself saw as a young writer but, unlike him and his generation, made no attempt to do anything concrete about them. He wonders why they were "non-interveners" in their writing; whether this was "an artistic device to rouse pity and terror" or "the hopelessness of staving off a great and unguessed war" (*GK,* 290–91). Their failure to act on their misgivings left Pound's contemporaries without clear guidelines, forced to be "a generation of experimenters . . . unable to work out a code for action." He says of them: "We believed in the individual case. The best of us accepted every conceivable 'dogma' as a truth for *a* situation, as the truth for a particular crux, crisis or temperament" (*GK,* 291). One had to learn to adjust to this total relativity.

Pound's purpose in this chapter is to praise Hardy's poetry, but, at the same time, to consider his own poetry in light of it and to decide why it lacks the emotional immediacy of Hardy's. By choosing this particular poet he has forced himself to examine the painful matter of the impersonality of his own writing and we see that the self-analysis which is undertaken so openly in the *Pisan Cantos* is not a completely new departure. When he singles out Hardy's ultimate conviction that "the greatest of things is charity," he anticipates his own realization in the first of the *Pisan Cantos* that "the greatest is charity" (74/434). Yet it is still difficult for Pound to talk openly about emotions and he postpones this briefly by veering off into economics:

> a few saw a dissociation of personal crises and cruces, that exist above or outside of economic pressure, and those which arise directly from it, or are so encumbered by, and entangled in, the root problems of money, that any pretended ethical or philosophical dealing with them is sheer bunk UNTIL they be disentangled. [*GK,* 291]

He realizes that he is avoiding the issue and reassures the reader and himself that he does not intend "to deny the permanent susceptibility to tragedy, the enduring tangles, situations etc. that depend wholly on free emotion, emotion conditioned only by hungers, appetites, affinities, and durabilities of attachment." But he then returns to his original assertion and maintains that a general inability to distinguish personal crises which *are* caused by economics from those which are not places all current professional writing below the level of Crime Club stories which he disconcertingly suggests are popular because "the whole people [have] an intuition of a crime somewhere, down under the Bank of England and the greasy-mugged regents, but [accept] an escape mechanism of murder, burglars and jewel-thefts" (*GK,* 291–92).

Pound's self-confidence was at a low ebb. He felt that it was almost in bad taste to quote from Hardy's final poems in "a book of yatter such as the present" (*GK,* 292). He felt that he was in a "No-Man's land," between "the hell of money" and "the undiscussable Paradiso." He quotes from canto 5 of the *Paradiso* to give an example of a literary triumph which is beyond his reach as poet, critic, and translator. "The arcanum is the arcanum," and in his present mood he feels very much excluded from it. Then follows his tribute to Hardy's poetry, resumed from the previous chapter where he had praised the poems without reservation: "No man can read Hardy's poems collected but that his own life, and forgotten moments of it, will come back to him, a flash here and an hour there. Have you a better test of true poetry?" (*GK,* 286). Pound registers "a vain regret that one couldn't have written novels for thirty years or whatever before courting the muses." In "The Promised Land" he really comes to grips, as far as he can, with the issue of Hardy's romanticism. His high praise stands, he insists, "despite all the rocks anyone can throw at Hardy for romance and sentiment," but Pound cannot bring himself to confront directly the possibility that he may have limited himself by avoiding a personal treatment of emotion in his work. Instead, he suggests that the time has now already passed when one could "concede such emphasis to the individual elegy and the personal sadness"; that we may have moved by now from a "literary" to a merely "rhetorical" age. He sees his personal dilemma not as the result of his own deliberate choices, but as a problem of the whole society; yet every aesthetic decision which he has made has shown his determination to *resist* the individual elegy.

Although Pound does not take up the question of his impersonality explicitly, he does so indirectly when he hints, for a moment, that he might have overemphasized the technical dimension of poetry: "a craft that occupies itself solely with imitating Gerard Hopkins or in any other metrical experiment is a craft mis-

directed. We engage in technical exercise faute de mieux, a neces-
sary defensive activity." But he reasserts himself by underlining
"solely" and also "necessary," which mitigates "defensive" some-
what. And then as one would change the subject abruptly from
awkwardness at some unaccustomed self-revelation, he interjects:
"Is one however permitted to detect a damned lack of sociability
in late Victorian writers?"

Returning to the problems of the modern poet, he feels that
even if literature has gained in "narrative sense" between 1600 and
1900, English verse has lost the tones that accompany the experi-
ence of "Eleusis"; he suggests that "a modern Eleusis [is] possible
in the wilds of a man's mind only" (*GK*, 294).

One by one, Pound calls his most cherished beliefs into ques-
tion, the next being his ideal of a literary elite:

> The requirements [for Eleusis are] far beyond those of merely
> an intelligent literary circle (which doesn't in any case exist).
> We lack not only the means but the candidates. Think of any
> modern waiting five years to know anything! Or wanting to
> know! . . . Was it ever possible save with conviction and sim-
> plicity beyond modern reach? now that knowledge is a drug
> on the market, said knowledge being a job lot of odds and
> ends having no order, but being abundant, superhumanly
> abundant. [*GK*, 294]

The real desperation here reveals his disillusionment as the
accumulations of "facts" in *The Cantos* fails to assert its own
order. What is the answer? "A divine parsimony of ideas? Or an
ultimate sophistication? Sophistication is not, emphatically is not,
enough." He ends the chapter with an admission that "the fore-
going pp. are as obscure as anything in my poetry." Yet these
pages are not obscure to the reader and we suspect that Pound is
not really thinking about the reader's reaction to them as much as
he is registering his own. The implications of these remarks are not
as surprising and unforeseen to the reader as they are to Pound
himself. We have seen the inevitability of the confrontation with
himself which is already beginning in these pages, yet no one could

have foreseen how dramatic, how thoroughgoing, and how painful the full confrontation would be during the long months in the D.T.C. at Pisa.

He closes this chapter by reaffirming his belief that

> certain truth exists. Certain colours exist in nature though great painters have striven vainly, and though the colour film is not yet perfected. Truth is not untrue'd by reason of our failing to fix it on paper. Certain objects are communicable to a man or woman only 'with proper lighting', they are perceptible in our own minds only with proper 'lighting', fitfully and by instants. [*GK*, 295]

In Cantos 52–71 he has concentrated on what is clear-cut and definite—on "good" and "evil" as responsible or irresponsible political action. In the *Pisan Cantos* he has to pursue a more elusive "truth" and to meditate on "good" and "evil" as states of mind and as the result of personal choices. In many significant respects the attitudes and concerns of the Chinese and Adams cantos are opposite to those of the *Pisan Cantos* and these two sharply contrasted emphases divide the rest of the poem between them. The spirit of Cantos 52–71 is summed up by the quotation from Cleanthes' hymn to Zeus which concludes the section and which is translated for us by Pound at the beginning of the section: "Glorious, deathless of many names, Zeus aye ruling all things; founder of the inborn qualities of nature, by laws piloting all things" (256). Pound's main subject in these cantos is civic justice as it is maintained by just laws and administered by intelligent, courageous, and public-spirited leaders. Objectivity and precision of terminology are the main requirements of efficient laws, and the poet's activities as he writes these cantos (studying his sources and capturing the spirit of the original as succinctly as possible) involve him in a similar objectivity and precision. In the *Pisan Cantos,* as we will see in chapter 4, all this has changed—instead of Zeus and Law we find Aphrodite and Love; political activity gives way to meditation on "the quality of the affection." The codified and the programmatic are eclipsed by the revelation that "What thou lovest well remains, / the rest is dross." Although in the first five cantos of *Rock-Drill* Pound has turned again to objectivity and to sustained examination of texts, he returns to his personal struggle in Cantos 90–93. The revelations in the *Pisan Cantos* are of the strength of past affections now newly rediscovered and retrospectively appreciated; in Cantos 90–93 the poet's celebration of the power of love is prompted by his experiences in the present when his love for a woman quickens his poetic creativity—raising him from "under the rubble heap" and bringing him back from "the dulled edge beyond pain" to "Castalia." Here he celebrates not only love but also compassion and "good nature" and affirms that "energy is near to benevolence." Although here he writes "Beyond civic order: / l'AMOR" (94/634), he chooses to make "civic order" his main concern in *Thrones,* where only Canto 106 is predominantly personal.

With *Drafts and Fragments,* Pound returns to himself and his own emotions. He meditates on his shortcomings and tries to assess his achievements, striving "to confess wrong without losing rightness" (116/797). The tension and the struggle are still there. He realizes that he has failed in his highly idealistic but ultimately impossible attempt to "make a paradiso / terrestre" (117/802), but he hesitates to take the impossibility as a justification for the failure. He is still inclined to blame himself. He has counted so much on discovering a definite and clear "truth" that he is hardly able to recognize that the wisdom which he has finally arrived at in these concluding cantos is, in fact, wisdom. It is still a mystery to him that men "go wrong, / thinking of rightness" (116/797), but he can take some comfort from his faith that "it coheres all right / even if my notes do not cohere" (116/797). In the first canto of this sequence he writes: "pray / There is power" (110/781), and Canto 120 is a prayer for forgiveness.

2 Pound the Man of Letters versus Pound the Man: The Influence of Wyndham Lewis and Henri Gaudier-Brzeska

The two kinds of struggle in *The Cantos* correspond to the two sides of Pound—Pound the man and Pound "the man of letters"—and, to a surprising degree, the latter was not just a role, but a complete personality. From the time of his close association with Wyndham Lewis until his imprisonment at Pisa, the "man of letters" came to dominate so entirely that eventually the man himself virtually disappeared from the poem and, it seems, from the life also. In Pound, to an unusual degree, his sense of personal identity was bound up with his sense of literary mission, and, as with any other "true believer," there was always the possibility that he would be guided by his sense of mission rather than by his feelings—that he would make choices on a theoretical rather than on an emotional basis. If we can begin to understand the usurpation of Pound the man by Pound the man of letters, we can better understand the course of his struggle against usury and the dangerous extremes to which it finally led him. Our purpose here is not to try to decide why Pound was this way, but to notice that he was. His writings provide the most complete evidence of this, but the comments of those who knew him also offer interesting insights.

Pound's sense of literary mission was very clear to himself. In "How I Began" he writes: "I knew at fifteen pretty much what I wanted to do. I believed that the 'Impulse' is with the gods; that technique is a man's own responsibility. A man either is or is not a great poet, that is not within his control, it is the lightning from heaven, the 'fire of the gods,' or whatever you choose to call it."[1] His faith in a kind of "poetic predestination" shows how he omits from consideration the place in the writing of great poetry of the development and maturing of the poet's views and sensibilities. He seems to imagine that personal character is a given quantity—static and inviolable rather than dynamic and fallible—and that it can set the seal of genius upon creative work in a fairly automatic way as long as artists work hard enough to perfect the tools of their craft.

William Carlos Williams provides us with an interesting description of Pound as he was at eighteen when he and Williams were students together at the University of Pennsylvania. After spending a weekend with Pound's family, Williams writes to his mother:

> If he ever does get blue nobody knows it, so he is just the man for me. But not one person in a thousand likes him, and a great many people detest him and why? Because he is so darned full of conceits and affectation. He is really a brilliant talker and thinker but delights in making himself just exactly what he is not: a laughing boor. His friends must be all patience in order to find him out and even then you must not let him know it, for he will immediately put on some artificial mood and be really unbearable. It is too bad, for he loves to be liked, but there is some quality in him which makes him too proud to try to please people. [Quoted in Stock's *Life,* 17–18]

Even at this age, "making himself just exactly what he is not" was an ingrained habit. Williams's comments do not guess at Pound's motives, but, if he was right in believing that Pound loved to be liked, then this affected manner was not only self-punishing but also somewhat beyond Pound's control.

After Pound's arrest and trial, Williams said of him that "he always felt himself superior to anyone about him and could never brook a rival."[2] Yet this impression, although understandable, is

1. Ezra Pound, "How I Began," *T. P.'s Weekly* 21, no. 552 (June 6, 1913): p. 707.
2. Quoted in Charles Norman, *The Case of Ezra Pound* (New York, 1968), p. 85.

misleading because it does not take into account the separation
between Pound the man of letters and Pound the man. Eliot and
Lewis, who knew him as he was in Europe, could see both sides of
him, although they were puzzled by the discontinuity. Williams,
naturally enough, assumes that because Pound is arrogant he must
also be vain, but Eliot and Lewis show us why, in Pound's case,
this is not so. Eliot explains that for Pound, "to discover a new
writer of genius is as satisfying an experience, as it is for a lesser
man to believe that he has written a great work of genius himself.
He has cared deeply that his contemporaries and juniors should
write well; he has cared less for his personal achievement than for
the life of letters and art" (*LE,* xii). Lewis's observations corre-
spond to Eliot's exactly: "In his attitude towards other people's
work Pound has been superlatively generous. . . . He does not in
the least mind of [*sic*] being in service to somebody (as do other
people it is usually found) if they have great talent. No envy of the
individual is attached to the work. *I have never known a person
less troubled with personal feelings*"³ (italics mine). Lewis sees
very clearly the surprising extent to which the man of letters dis-
places the man, and he elaborates on this later in *Blasting and
Bombardiering.* He speaks of Pound "*transacting* his social life"
because, he says, "there was nothing social for him that did not
have a bearing upon the business of writing. If it had not it would
have been dull. He was a man of Letters, in the marrow of his
bones and down to the red follicles of his hair. . . . He breathed
Letters, ate Letters, dreamt Letters. A very rare kind of man."⁴

What Eliot and Lewis do not mention is the reciprocity of
Pound's literary "transactions"—the extent to which the writers
and artists and thinkers whom he admired influenced his own
opinions. We find that Pound was capable of almost slavish attach-
ment to the ideas and views of such people, so that someone like
Lewis had an extreme effect upon his attitudes and his rhetoric.
Before we examine the influence on him of Lewis and Gaudier-
Brzeska, however, we should first make some brief inquiry into

3. Wyndham Lewis, *Blasting and Bombardiering* (Berkeley & Los
Angeles, 1967), p. 280.
    4. Ibid., pp. 288–89.

the nature of Pound the man, overshadowed as this side of him so often was. Pound was certainly given to adopting poses, and, at the time of his close association with Lewis in 1914, he affected a manner that was much more abrasive than his former behavior and was clearly an adaptation of Lewis's "Enemy" pose. Richard Aldington called attention to the discrepancy between this version of Pound and the "real Pound" which he felt lay behind it. In a review of *Blast* which appeared in *The Egoist* for July 15, 1914, he writes: "Mr Pound is one of the gentlest, most modest, bashful, kind creatures who ever walked the earth; so I cannot help thinking that all this enormous arrogance and petulance and fierceness are a pose." There is no question that Pound could be kind and affectionate, and yet he seems to have developed the habit of suppressing this side of himself, or at least of allowing it to be suppressed by the demands of his professional life. His daughter even says of him that, until his imprisonment at Pisa and the soul-searching that accompanied this, his "attitude toward personal feelings had been somewhat Henry Jamesian: feelings are things other people have" (*Disc.,* 258). She recalls one incident which particularly illustrates Pound's clumsiness in managing emotional situations, or perhaps rather his insistence on treating an emotional as a practical matter. At the *Quiete,* her convent school, she had asked for a Latin-German rather than the customary Latin-Italian missal. It had to be specially ordered and turned out to cost almost three times more than expected and the bill was forwarded to Pound. Overlooking all the most obvious reasons why a twelve-year-old girl, homesick for her adoptive family (and whose first language was after all German) would naturally prefer a German translation, Pound overreacted most unreasonably. He accused the Mother Superior of encouraging Mary to choose the expensive missal; he thought it "silly to study Latin via German"; he assumed that Mary wanted the book because it was "a handsome object." Then he was drawn into a diatribe which would have been more appropriate in *Guide to Kulchur:* "the lack of precise statement will do more to destroy any morality than mixing it up with piety, which is of all places the field where honesty is or should be most emphasized. There is no beauty in inexactitude, and the church was most holy when its theologians attained the greatest clarity of expression." He was ready, though, to accept the Mother Superior's further explanation and reassurances: "So long as Maria did not say she was given permission to spend more than had been discussed I am quite content." He decided to let her pay ten lire of her own money "not as punishment, but simply to get it into her head that one cannot be careless about 57 lire UNLESS one is much richer than she is . . . I am not quite sure that Latin should be learned from German . . . so far as association of words is concerned. BUT, I don't wish to make this as more than an interrogation, in M's case she may learn better from German, though I doubt it. She might be asked about this. Her own view is worth quite as much as mine on the subject" (*Disc.*, 108–10). Everything is strictly in accordance with Pound's principles: his eagerness to be fair and to forgive, his respect for philology, his anxiousness not to be dogmatic, his concern for her education, his readiness to concede the value of her opinions. Yet his daughter had chosen the German missal for purely emotional reasons and he was unable to accept this as justification for her choice. Later, after his time of soul-searching at Pisa, he was able to state openly the warmth and consideration that he felt for her. When Olga Rudge disapproved of her daughter's proposed marriage, Pound was "the only one who hadn't inveighed against the folly of our marriage, who had understood and sent his message under the letterhead 'J'Ayme Donc Je Suis,' from St. Liz" (*Disc.*, 274).

As we would expect, his personal aversion to introspection and demonstrativeness shows also in his reactions to other writers. In an early judgment on Whitman, which he later changed, he demotes Whitman's poetry from art to only "a human document" because of the author's failure to show himself "in some degree master of the forces which beat upon him" (*SP*, 114). The self-revelations of the Romantics bother Pound also and he omits these poets from "How to Read," which is intended as a "minimum basis for a sound and liberal education in letters" (*LE*, 38). Their self-involvement provokes his criticism that "Romantic poetry . . . almost requires the concept of reincarnation as part of its mechanism" (*GK*, 299). As one would expect, Pound is particularly irritated by D. H. Lawrence. Noel Stock notices in Pound "a sort of irrational dislike which he never . . . defined, but [which] was

very strong and almost always came to the front when he dis-
cussed Lawrence's work."[5] In Pound's review of *Love Poems and
Others* in the July 1913 issue of *Poetry,* he states his objection to
Lawrence clearly. He wonders if the "Love Poems" of the title are
"the middling-sensual erotic verses in this collection," which he
finds to be "a sort of pre-raphaelitist slush, disgusting or very
nearly so." He concedes though that "when Mr Lawrence ceases
to discuss his own disagreeable sensations . . . there is no English
poet under forty who can get within shot of him."[6]

His criticisms of subjectivity and self-analysis often have a ring
of defensiveness, and this becomes increasingly evident as time
goes on. He finds the introspection of Russian writers repulsive
and has no time for "the slightly alcoholic or epileptic and de-
formed profundity of Dostoievsky, his disciples and his inferiors"
(*PE,* 86). He shows nothing but disgust for the whole field of
psychiatry, which he calls a "quagmire" because of its tendency to
"give disproportionate importance to the subjective, and to lose
all, or too much, of one's sense of relative importance of the total
external world" (*I,* 232). He thinks that Freud's ideas encourage
morbid introspection, and that his writings "are the flower of
a deliquescent society going to pot" (*JM,* 100), claiming that
external discipline or distraction from personal problems is more
effective than obsessive self-analysis. Freud's ideas, in his opinion,
aggravate the problem and encourage people to become "Dos-
toievskian duds, worrying about their own unimportant innards"
(*JM,* 100). Yet it seems likely that he senses very early that his
avoidance of self-analysis is in itself more extreme than it need be.
One telling paragraph in *The Spirit of Romance* suggests that he is
to some degree aware of how much of the personal he is leaving
out of his poetry, and is possibly even uneasy about this:

> The *accurate* artist seems to leave not only his greater self,
> but beside it, upon the films of his art, some living print of
> the circumvolving man, his taste, his temper and his foible—

5. Noel Stock, *Poet in Exile: Ezra Pound* (Manchester, 1964), p. 73.
6. Ezra Pound, Review of *Love Poems and Others,* by D. H. Lawrence,
Poetry 2, no. 4 (July 1913): pp. 149–51.

of the things about which he felt it never worth his while to
bother other people by speaking, the things he forgot for
some major interest . . . things that his audience would have
taken for granted; or . . . things about which he had, for some
reason or other, a reticence. We find these not so much in the
words—which anyone may read—but in the subtle joints of
the craft, in the crannies perceptible only to the craftsman.
[*SR*, 88]

He seems here to be expressing the hope that this unspoken part
of himself will somehow shine out from his work.

Wyndham Lewis: The Mystique of Loathing

When he went to England in 1909, Pound as a man of letters was
very sure of his own poetic talent and critical judgment and of his
mission to help bring about a literary and cultural renaissance.
Wyndham Lewis, remembering the occasion of his first meeting
with Pound, recalled the poet's obvious desire to impress on him
and his friends "that he was superior to all other intellectuals in
intellect, and all poets in prosodic prowess, [that they] were the
spectators merely—they were of very little account." The rest of
Lewis's account, however, makes Pound's egotistical demeanor
seem not only understandable but necessary:

> It was announced one day that a certain Ezra Pound was to
> come in to lunch. . . . I remember he was not a particularly
> welcome guest. Several of our party had already seen him.
> And it was reported that S. had pronounced him a Jew. . . .
> I was mildly surprised to see an unmistakable 'nordic blond.'
> . . . But this moment of disillusion past, I took no further
> interest in this cowboy songster. . . . I turned my back: I
> heard the staccato of the States: I 'sensed' that there was
> little enthusiasm.[7]

7. Lewis, *Blasting and Bombardiering,* pp. 273–75.

Pound the man of letters might easily take refuge in his conviction of his "superiority to all present," but Pound the man could hardly have remained entirely unaffected by such condescension. His writings from 1914 on show that he decided not to hold out against these attitudes and chose instead deliberately to imitate Lewis's supercilious manner and to echo both his rhetoric and his opinions. It turned out to be a very dangerous decision. Many years later, Charles Olson saw this only too clearly: "There is an assumption on Pound's part that he can traffic with snobs and bastards, and get away with it. I don't believe he or any man can, and I figure on this path he went to fascism."[8] At the time, "trafficking with snobs" seemed to Pound to be the most efficient way of getting a renaissance under way.

Initially, Pound was mainly concerned with the possibility of an *American* renaissance. In a letter to Harriet Monroe in August 1912 he writes: "Any agonizing that tends to hurry what I believe in the end to be inevitable, our American Risorgimento, is dear to me. That awakening will make the Italian Renaissance look like a tempest in a teapot!" (*L*, 10). *Patria Mia,* which appeared serially in *The New Age* of 1913, is specifically devoted to convincing Americans of the possibility of a renaissance of their own and to pleading for state support and encouragement of the artist, so that great American art can be produced without delay. This renaissance, he promises, will be "an intellectual awakening" which will "have its effect not only in the arts, but in life, in politics, and in economics" (*SP*, 111). He is sure that "there is more artistic impulse in America than in any country in Europe" and encourages his reader to see in the architecture of New York "our first sign of the 'alba.' " In his essay "The Renaissance," published in *Poetry* in 1914, he continues his campaign to enlighten America. He gives a brief course in great authors, warning the reader, for example, about the dangers of Milton and the limitations of the Elizabethans (excepting Shakespeare). He urges the need for "taking stock of what we have, and devising practical measures" and warns that

8. Catherine Seelye, ed., *Charles Olson and Ezra Pound* (New York, 1975), p. 88.

"we have not defined the hostility or inertia that is against us . . . and we have not realized to what extent a renaissance is a thing made—a thing made by conscious propaganda" (*LE,* 219-20).

In *Blast* we see Lewis making the same claims of cultural potential for England, and as Pound became more involved in Vorticism he turned his attention to the *individuals* who were bringing about this renaissance, and exchanged his nationalistic bias for a strong enthusiasm for internationalism in the arts. Pound transferred his allegiance, and with it his expectations of renaissance, to London. In "Affirmations VI: Analysis of this Decade," he continues his propaganda, but this time in support of a movement which is already underway. "The Renaissance sought for a lost reality, a lost freedom. We seek for a lost reality and a lost intensity. We believe that the Renaissance was in part the result of a programme. We believe in the value of a programme in contradistinction to, but not in contradiction of, the individual impulse" (*GB,* 117).

Pound had high hopes for Vorticism and was enormously impressed by Lewis:

> Lewis had just sent in the first dozen drawings. They are all over the room, and the thing is stupendous. The vitality, the fullness of the man! Nobody knows it. My God . . . Nobody has *any* conception of the volume and energy and the variety . . . Lewis has got Blake scotched to a finish. He's got so much more *in him* than Gaudier. I know he is seven years older. Ma chè Cristo! . . . It seems to me that Picasso alone, certainly alone among the living artists whom I know of, is in anything like the same class. It is not merely knowledge of technique, or skill, it is intelligence and knowledge of life, of the whole of it, beauty, heaven, hell, sarcasm, every kind of whirlwind of force and emotion. Vortex. That is the right word, if I did find it myself. [*L,* 73-74]

Lewis was bound to attract Pound; not only was he a fine painter but he also had an impressive intellect and was at least as forceful and flamboyant in presenting his conclusions as Pound himself. Where Pound had many doubts about the direction he should take in his writing, Lewis had, or seemed to have, no doubts about anything. Pound was ashamed of his own romanticism and felt that it was a hindrance in his writing, tying him too firmly to the past, so that the present seemed intractable as material for poetry. Lewis's whole philosophy was premised on the evils of romanticism. Pound was inhibited in confronting or directly expressing his own emotions; Lewis preached that the emotions should be stifled and always dominated by the intellect, particularly in the artist. Yet Pound's uneasiness about self-revelation paled in comparison with Lewis's unrelenting and complete revulsion at both emotion and human physicality. "Merely by living," he wrote in *The Hitler Cult,* "we contaminate ourselves."[9]

As we would expect, fear of the emotions goes hand-in-hand with authoritarianism, and Lewis was, of course, only one of a great many who were attracted to the authoritarian views of his time. The writers of the *Action Française* group in France were particularly influential in propounding such views and Lewis's philosophy was virtually identical to theirs. Like them he was anti-democratic, anti-Semitic, anti-woman and anti-pacifist. Like them, and like T. E. Hulme, he believed in Original Sin, as he explained in *Men Without Art:* "If . . . you regard man as a perfectly fixed and 'static'—corrupt, evil, untidy, incomplete—animal, as I do, as Mr. Hulme did, it is pretty evident that a kindly, tolerant and humanitarian attitude is the last thing to expect of us."[10] Hulme was the first to introduce the ideas of contemporary French neo-classicism into England, but Lewis, who could not bear to be thought of as anyone's follower, was anxious to play down Hulme's influence and his own debt to him. Lewis, like Hulme, began as an admirer of Bergson, but, unlike Hulme, did not commit himself to Bergsonism in writing. When Benda and the *Action Française* group turned against Bergson, Lewis could easily renounce his old allegiance and, by denouncing Bergson, insist on the difference between his views and Hulme's: "Hulme was not a 'master-mind', or anything of that sort . . . and he was highly influenceable. Bergson dominated him, of course, with great facility: and anything

9. Wyndham Lewis, *The Hitler Cult* (London, 1939), p. 173.
10. Wyndham Lewis, *Men Without Art* (London, 1934), p. 211.

tainted with Bergsonism could not help being suspect to me."[11] "Although he has been called 'a philosopher', he was not that, but a man specializing in aesthetic problems"; "he was a journalist with a flair for philosophy and art, not a philosopher." In this way Lewis gave himself the ascendancy because he then appeared as the gifted exponent of what, with Hulme, were merely theories: "All the best things Hulme said about the theory of art were said about my art . . . We happened, that is all, to be made for each other, as critic and 'creator'. What he said should be done, I *did*. Or it would be more exact to say that I did it, and he said it."[12] In *Gaudier-Brzeska* we find Pound taking exactly the same position: "So far as I am concerned, Jacob Epstein was the first person who came talking about 'form, not the *form of anything.*' It may have been Mr. T. E. Hulme, quoting Epstein. I don't know that it matters much who said it first; he may have been a theorist with no more than a sort of scientific gift for discovery. He may have been a great sculptor capable of acting out his belief" (*GB*, 98–99). In fact, Pound was as intent as Lewis on discounting Hulme's influence and he was mainly concerned to deny that Hulme's aesthetic ideas lay behind Imagism (see appendix 2).

Both Lewis and Hulme claim that the whole liberal position is wrongheaded because it is posited upon people's essential goodness and potential for progress. Hulme calls humanism "a heresy, a mistaken adoption of fake conceptions." Romanticism, he says, acts on the assumption of man's "unlimited" existence and this "creates the bastard conception of *Personality*" and "distorts the real nature of ethical values by deriving them out of essentially subjective things, like human desires and feelings."[13] This is reminiscent of Pound's comment, much later, that Romantic poetry "almost requires the concept of reincarnation as part of its mechanism." Despite the similarity of their views, there is a strong contrast between Hulme's presentation and Lewis's; Hulme seems dispassionate, general, and logically methodical in comparison to

11. Lewis, *Blasting and Bombardiering*, p. 107.
12. Ibid., p. 99–100.
13. T. E. Hulme, "A Notebook by T. E. H.," *The New Age* 18, no. 13 (Jan. 27, 1916): pp. 305–07.

Lewis, who is often passionate to the point of obsession. It is clear that, for Lewis, this philosophy answered an urgent personal need and gave him the opportunity to castigate and mock the largest possible number of people. It seems, at times, as though anyone other than Lewis is liable to be indicted for "romanticism," but the more prominent the artists or intellectuals are, the more likely Lewis is to set upon them. His antiromanticism then is not original, but it is surely unique in its inclusiveness.

To Lewis, the vast majority of people are mindless and selfish. The mass are enslaved to "Group Rhythms": the "Age War," between the young and the old (discussed in *The Doom of Youth*); the "Sex War," between men and women; and the "Color-War," between white and black (in *Pale-face*). Youth, the Negro, and women are all a threat to "masculine" rationality and to discipline because of their emotionality. He sees everywhere around him the emasculation of men and the strengthening of the forces of infantile emotion, encouraged by capitalists and socialists whose aim is to undermine the rationality which could curtail their power over other people. Feminism is, needless to say, a great perversion: "The 'homo' is the legitimate child of the 'suffragette.' "[14] Lewis denounces pacifism as a manifestation of effete liberalism and also, like the French neoclassicists, attacks Protestantism for emphasizing and encouraging individualism and emotion—"the evangelical heresy." Compared to the Catholic philosophy, Protestant moralism is strongly antiauthoritarian and, under Jewish leadership, responsible for democratic liberalism.[15]

Given this set of opinions, Lewis's philosophy could not help but be nihilistic, yet Pound was prepared to overlook this, as was Eliot, who called him "the most fascinating personality of our time."[16] Both of them were particularly impressed by Lewis's "Inferior Religions," which presents a drastically nihilistic view of human existence. This piece was published in *The Little Review*

14. Wyndham Lewis, *Rude Assignment: A narrative of my career up-to-date* (London, 1950), p. 177.

15. Wyndham Lewis, *Count Your Dead: They Are Alive! or A New War in the Making* (London, 1937), p. 268.

16. T. S. Eliot, "Tarr," *Egoist* 5 (1918): 106.

of September 1917, and Pound at that time considered it "the most important single document that Lewis has written," saying that it "makes Bergson look like a gnat."[17] In it Lewis shows how physicality, in all its forms, seems to him a kind of delayed putrefaction, and people as they are known to each other and as they interact socially are almost completely unreal. This unreality deprives all relationships of significance, and this reminds us of the hero's comment in *Tarr* that "there are no 'friends' in this life any more than there are 'fiancées'. So it doesn't matter. You drift on side by side with this live stock—friends, fiancées, colleagues and what not."[18] Given this depressing and absurd condition of life, Lewis says, one has two possible responses. The majority of men, either because they cannot or do not wish to see that this *is* the nature of reality, allow themselves to be distracted by the "Inferior Religions" of the title. A few individuals, like Lewis, see the absurdity and their response is "Laughter." The "inferior religions" are the tasks or interests on which most men focus all their attention and to which they devote all their effort—the innkeeper's restaurant or the fisherman's boat—in the service of which they become "creaking men machines," "puppets" who are "only shadows of energy, not living beings."[19] "Laughter," as Lewis uses the word, is a kind of stoicism and a badge of superiority; it is a sign that one knows the full extent of man's degraded and embarrassing condition, and this knowledge makes one superior to those who are ignorant of it. "Laughter" is the only possible stance before a world of men as futile and as repulsive as they are to Lewis, a world that is completely intractable and incapable of any change or improvement.

Pound's admiration for Lewis confronted him with a dilemma. He did not himself believe that people are fundamentally and irretrievably absurd and depraved, and he was very far from being nihilistic, yet it seemed to him at first that Lewis's denunciations of human weaknesses were made in the service of the arts. Lewis's rantings in *Blast* could be taken as a histrionic eruption of high

17. Ezra Pound, unpublished letter to Margaret Anderson, June 22, 1917, cited by Kenner, *The Pound Era*, p. 242.
18. Wyndham Lewis, *Tarr* (New York, 1918), p. 29.
19. Wyndham Lewis, *The Wild Body* (London, 1927), pp. 232-34.

spirits and his description of the embattled artistic intellect making a stand against the mediocrity and mindlessness around him seemed mainly an act of bravado, appropriate to the air of optimism in the arts before the war. As long as he felt that Lewis's real object was a revitalization of the arts, Pound had no compunction about adopting Lewis's "Enemy" pose and echoing his rhetoric and many of his opinions, as we see from his contributions to *Blast*. After the Vorticist group was disbanded because of the war, it became clearer to Pound that many of his friend's more extreme ideas were not just weapons in the war against the enemies of the arts but matters of personal conviction, and this made him more guarded in his response to them.

In Pound's contributions to *Blast*, however, we see no such guardedness and they suffer greatly as a result. Most of his poems are weak and some are embarrassingly bad. In *Blast No. 1* we find, in "Salutation the Third," "Come, let us on with the new deal, / Let us be done with Jews and Jobbery, / Let us SPIT upon those who fawn on the JEWS for their money."[20] *Blast No. 2* contains "Et Faim Sallir Le Loup des Boys":

Cowardly editors threaten: "If I dare"
Say this or that, or speak my open mind,
Say that I hate may [*sic*] hates,
    Say that I love my friends,
Say I believe in Lewis, spit out the later Rodin,
Say that Epstein can carve in stone,
That Brzeska can use the chisel,
Or Wadsworth paint;
                Then they will have my guts;
Then they will cut down my wage, force me to sing their cant,
  . . . .
Cowardly editors threaten,
Friends fall off at the pinch, the loveliest die.
That is the path of life, this is my forest.[21]

20. Wyndham Lewis, ed., *Blast: Review of the Great English Vortex*, No. 1 (June 20, 1914): 45.

21. Wyndham Lewis, ed., *Blast: Review of the Great English Vortex*, No. 2 (July 1915): 22.

The very awfulness of this tells us two interesting things. First we realize that Pound cannot readily fall into the callousness which is essential to an exponent of Lewis's philosophy, and instead remains painfully self-conscious. Second, we can begin to understand why Pound keeps to the impersonal and to the persona when at all possible—to be explicitly personal can make him very awkward. This poem is a highly personal response to Gaudier-Brzeska's death and to being boycotted by G. W. Prothero of the *Quarterly Review* for his part in *Blast No. 1*.

Pound's prose in *Blast* shows Lewis's influence even more strongly than the poetry. The ideas in his "satiric" pieces are virtually all Lewis's: " 'BLAST' alone dared to present the actual discords of modern 'civilization,' DISCORDS now only too apparent in the open conflict between teutonic atavism and unsatisfactory Democracy." "The melancholy young man, the aesthetic young man, the romantic young man, past types; fabians, past; simple lifers past. The present: a generation which ceases to flatter. Thank god for our atrabilious companions."[22] *Blast No. 2* also contains a series of repetitious fulminations against "homo canis," for example: "BLAST does not attempt to reconcile the homo canis with himself. Of course the homo canis will follow us. It is the nature of the homo canis to follow. They growl but they follow. They have even followed thing [*sic*] in black surtouts with their collars buttoned behind."[23] Pound attacks Protestantism, not, as Lewis does, for encouraging liberalism, but rather for collaborating with the usurers and perverting the concept of morality by making it mean sexual morality. In "Imaginary Letters," he merely contends that Christianity "has reduced itself to one principle: 'Thou shall attend to thy neighbour's business in preference to thine own,' " but in *Guide to Kulchur* he is more specific and very Lewisian:

> The puritan is a pervert, the whole of his sense of mental corruption is squirted down a single groove of sex. The scale and proportion of evil, as delimited in Dante's hell (or the catholic hell) was obliterated by the Calvinist and Lutheran churches

22. Ibid., pp. 85–86.
23. Ibid., p. 85.

... I mean that the effect of Protestantism has been semiticly to obliterate values, to efface grades and graduations. [*GK,* 185]

But, above all, usury is the real villain: "Putting usury on a pedestal, in order to set avarice on high, the protestant centuries twisted all morality out of shape. 'Moral' was narrowed down to application to carnal relations. Thus acting as usurer's red herring" (*GK,* 256). In *Impact* he even theorizes that "Protestantism as factive and organized, may have sprung from nothing but pro-usury politics" (*I,* 241).

After *Blast,* although Pound's admiration for Lewis seems undiminished, we sense that he is beginning to have some reservations about some of his friend's more extreme views. We see this, for example, in his review of Lewis's *Tarr* which he calls "the most vigorous and volcanic English novel of our time" (*LE,* 424). Tarr's feelings of revulsion toward women and his ideas on the relationship between sexuality and artistic creation are diametrically opposite to Pound's. Lewis, through his hero, suggests that the greater an artist one is, the more necessary it is to neglect sexuality. Tarr deliberately seeks out women who are as uncongenial as possible to him and believes that his coarse, foolish, slovenly taste in women frees him to be the more an artist: "All the delicate psychology another man naturally seeks in a woman . . . I seek in my work and not elsewhere."[24] He also suggests that the "art instincts" of most men are so inadequate that they "should be kept firmly embedded in *sex,* in *fighting,* and in *affairs.*"[25] In his review Pound chooses to write of the novel as though it were primarily a piece of social criticism, saying that it shows "a highly-energized mind performing a huge act of scavenging; cleaning up a great lot of rubbish, cultural, Bohemian, romantico-Tennysonish, arty, societish, gutterish" (*LE,* 429). In fact Lewis is less concerned to attack any particular social milieu or set of values than to dramatize his loathing of the "female chaos" of which the social behavior of his characters is merely an excrescence. Throughout the work we are aware of the author's violent aversion to women:

24. Lewis, *Tarr,* p. 26.
25. Ibid., p. 357.

How foul and wrong this haunting of women is!=they are everywhere!=Confusing, blurring, libelling with their half-baked gushing, tawdry presences! It is like a slop of children and the bawling machinery of the inside of life, always and all over our palaces.[26]

Toward the end of *Tarr* he writes: "There was only one God, and he was a man.=A woman was a lower form of life. Everything was female to begin with. A jellyish diffuseness spread itself and gaped on the beds and in the bas-fonds of everything."[27]

Pound avoids commenting on Tarr's view of sex and women in his review but it is clear that the two preceding passages have stuck in his mind. We hear echoes of them in his comment that "Kriesler . . . [is] a 'powerful' study in sheer obsessed emotionality . . . who has, over and above his sombre emotional spawn-bed, a smouldering sort of intelligence, combustible into brilliant talk" (*LE,* 428). Even more significant are the echoes in Canto 29:

> Chiefest of these the second, the female
> Is an element, the female
> Is a chaos
> An octopus
> A biological process
> > and we seek to fulfill . . .
> TAN AOIDAN, [the song] our desire, drift . . .
> . . . .
> Our mulberry leaf, woman, TAN AOIDAN,
> 'Nel ventre tuo, o nella mente mia,
> 'Yes, Milady, precisely, if you wd.
> have anything properly made.'   [29/144]

The pompousness and silliness of this are a pose which misrepresents Pound's real feelings about women as we quickly see when we compare this passage to those parts of Cantos 39 and 47 on

26. Ibid., p. 28.
27. Ibid., p. 371.

this same subject. The dignity and poignancy which he achieves through his "mythicizing" of sexuality in Canto 47 could not be farther from Lewis:

> The light has entered the cave. Io! Io!
> The light has gone down into the cave,
> Splendour on splendour!
> By prong have I entered these hills:
> That the grass grow from my body,
> That I hear the roots speaking together.   [47/238]

Pound's review of *Tarr* is actually quite evasive and we notice how, by concentrating on Lewis's style—with which he finds considerable fault—he is able to withhold his consent to *what* is said in the novel: "When Tarr talks little essays and makes aphorisms they are often of intrinsic interest, are even unforgettable. Likewise, when the author comments upon Tarr, he has the gift of phrase, vivid, biting, pregnant, full of suggestion" (*LE,* 426). It seems likely that he can accept Lewis's ideas when they are presented in a general and theoretical manner, as in "Inferior Religions," but is made more aware of their unpleasant implications when they are dramatically presented through characters.

We see Pound again torn between his fascination with and reservations about Lewis's nihilism in his contributions to *The Little Review* in 1917 and 1918. In his first editorial, he explains why he has accepted the post of Foreign Editor and ends with what amounts to a paraphrase of Lewis: "There is no misanthropy in a thorough contempt for the mob. There is no respect for mankind save in respect for detached individuals." This May 1917 number contains Lewis's first "Imaginary Letter," but the series is interrupted when he leaves for the war. In September 1917 Pound picks up the series, writing the fourth and fifth letters while Lewis sends in the short stories "Cantleman's Spring Mate" and "A Soldier of Humor." (Lewis resumes the letters in March and April.) Lewis, as William Bland Burn, writes to his wife, Lydia, and Pound, taking the name of Walter Villerant, decides to address his first four letters to Mrs. Bland Burn too.

A passage from Lewis's "The Code of a Herdsman" from *The Little Review* will give a good idea of the tone which Lewis sets and Pound feels to some extent compelled to imitate:

> Mock the herd perpetually with the grimace of its own garrulity or deadness. If it gets out of hand and stampedes towards you, leap on to the sea of mangy backs until the sea is still. That is: cast your mask aside, and spring above them. They cannot see or touch anything *above* them. . . . *Never* fall into the vulgarity of being or assuming yourself to be one ego. . . . Each single self—that you manage to be at any given time—must have five at least indifferent to it. You must have a power of indifference of *five* to *one*. . . . Spend some of your spare time every day in hunting your weaknesses, caught from commerce with the herd, as methodically, solemnly and vindictively as a monkey his fleas. You will find yourself swarming with them while you are surrounded by humanity. But you must not bring them up on the mountain. . . . *There are very stringent regulations* about the herd keeping off the sides of the mountain. In fact your chief function is to prevent their encroaching. . . . Those traps and numerous devices you have seen on the edge of the plain are for use, of course, in the last resort. . . . Contradict yourself. In order to live, you must remain broken up. . . . Always come down with masks and thick clothing to the valley where we work. Stagnant gasses from these Yahooesque and rotten herds are more dangerous often than the wandering cylinders that emit them. . . . The terrible processions beneath are not of our making, and are without our pity.[28]

Pound's "Imaginary Letters" are unsuccessful because he is trying to do two different things which get in the way of each other. His main concern is clearly to comment on the state of literature in the present, but he feels that he must, at the same time, affect a species of world-weary and urbane hauteur and there

28. Wyndham Lewis, "The Code of a Herdsman," *The Little Review* 4, no. 3 (July 1917): 3–7.

is no smooth continuity between the two. The tension between the basic earnestness of his real intent and the languor of the pose produces an awkwardness which prevents the letters from being witty in the way that they would have to be to succeed. His pieces lack the shock value of Lewis's because he cannot bring himself to be as extreme as his friend and it is impossible to be truly out-rageous if one is holding back. He decides to create a character for himself who shares Lewis's condescending sense of superiority to all around him, but is free of Lewis's loathing: "I live as a man among herds . . . for which I have a considerate, or at least con-siderable, if misplaced, affection. 'Herds' is possibly a misnomer. A litter of pups that amuses me. I am not prey to William's hostili-ties" (*PD,* 59–60). Instead of being revolted by the physicality of women, Villerant is merely annoyed by their sentimentality, domesticity, and poor taste in furnishings, and, although he "can not talk to the English 'lower-classes' " when he is sober, he can manage to be very friendly with them when drunk.

Perhaps he feels that he has been too temperate and is reassert-ing his solidarity with Lewis when he includes in his final letter his inexcusable version of Baudelaire's *"Une Nuit que j'étais près d'une affreuse Juive":*

> One night stretched out along a hebrew bitch—
> Like two corpses at the undertakers—
> This carcass, sold alike to jews and quakers,
> Reminded me of beauty noble and rich.
> Although she stank like bacon in the flitch,
> I thought of her as though the ancient makers
> Had shown her mistress of a thousand acres,
> Casqued and perfumed, so that my nerves 'gan twitch.
>
> [*PD,* 72]

This provides us with a depressing and somewhat prophetic illus-tration of what happens when Pound experimentally adopts a cal-lous and offensive manner for the sake of the shock value and without consulting his real feelings. At least Lewis's loathing is a gut reaction, but to dabble experimentally in such states of mind is perverse and, as Pound's case shows, dangerous.

Pound may have believed that he shared Lewis's views on important points, but Lewis knew perfectly well that this was not so and that Pound was radically different from himself. Above all, he thoroughly understood the genuine naiveté at the center of Pound's character. In *Time and Western Man,* in the chapters called "Ezra Pound, Etc." and "A Man In Love With The Past,"[29] Lewis shows how anxious he is to dissociate himself from Pound's ideas and theories and describes Pound in a way that is both derogatory and illuminating. Beyond the insults, which one comes to expect in Lewis, there is an interesting core of truth. He has chosen to be scathing about Pound's ideas—he calls him "a kind of intellectual eunuch"—but is highly complimentary about his character. He puts his finger on the essential naiveté of Pound and uses this to excuse him. Lewis is so anxious to ridicule Pound's ideas because he is determined to bring an end to the idea that there is any longer a connection between the two of them. He particularly stresses Pound's borrowing of his ideas and describes him as "the most gentlemanly, discriminating parasite I have ever had" (*Time,* 69), and we can see how much truth there is in this. Lewis admires the way in which Pound writes of the past, or rather becomes one with the past himself, but he has nothing but scorn for his attempts to understand or write about the present: "He cannot at all manage the unruly shape of things that are in-the-making, and which demand of him also some effort of a creative sort—ask him to set them limits, or direct them even. Ezra, in such a situation, is at his wit's end." "Life is not his true concern. . . . Ezra for preference consorts with the dead, whose life is preserved for us in books and pictures. He has never loved anything living as he has loved the dead." But always, Lewis concedes Pound's complete sincerity: "So I like, respect, and, in a sense reverence Ezra Pound; I have found him a true, disinterested and unspoilt individual. He has not effected this intimate entrance into everything that is noble and enchanting for nothing. He has really walked with Sophocles beside the Aegean; he has *seen* the Florence of Cavalcanti . . . And he

29. Wyndham Lewis, *Time and Western Man* (London, 1927), pp. 38–48, 69–74. Subsequent page references to *Time* are to this edition.

is not unworthy, in himself, of these many privileges" (*Time,* 70–71). "If Ezra Pound as a living individual were less worthy and admirable . . . were there any vulgarity or sham in the essential Ezra," Lewis feels that he would not be able to adopt these personae as effortlessly as he does (*Time,* 70). Yet Lewis sees a negative side to Pound's naiveté which comes to the fore when he deals with the present. In the rather obvious and heavy-handed depiction of comic characters in Pound's poetry, Lewis sees merely a caricature of the terse mannerisms which Pound uses himself in conversation: "If Pound had not a strain of absolutely authentic naïveté in him . . . he could not write in this clumsy and stupid way, when attempting to stage scenes from contemporary life. . . . And a simpleton is what we are left with. That natural and unvarnished, unassimilable, Pound, is the true child, which so many people in vain essay to be. But some inhibition has prevented him from getting that genuine naïf (which would have made him a poet) into his work. There, unfortunately, he always attitudinizes, frowns, struts, looks terribly knowing, 'breaks off,' shows off, puffs himself out, and so obscures the really simple, charming creature that he is" (*Time,* 74).

The painstaking way in which Lewis explains exactly what he means by Pound's "terseness" shows how seriously he is approaching this task of "explaining" his former colleague. The instances of terseness are widespread enough to warrant comment. Lewis reminds us that "such violent expressions as 'bunk, junk, spoof, mush, slush, tosh, bosh,' are favourites with him; and he remains convinced that such over-specifically *manly* epithets are universally effective, in spite of all proof to the contrary" (*Time,* 72). Lewis is right to single these out as a sign of weakness but doesn't suggest an explanation for Pound's frequent use of them except for observing that they are an attempt to be manly. In fact, they seem to be a way of masking his self-consciousness at speaking in his own person and a way of keeping the reader at arm's length. This suggestion is particularly borne out by the high incidence of such expressions in his personal letters. If these colloquialisms appeared only in the poetry, or in the prose works, one could perhaps make a case for some deliberate *literary* effect. As it is, the lapses into this strange, self-parodying style are always either annoying or distracting—in much the same way that Pound's behavior was to many people.

Although Lewis does not make the connection between some of Pound's "terseness" and his self-consciousness at speaking in his own voice, he has seen other evidence of Pound's problem: "When he writes in person, as Pound, his phrases are invariably stagey and false, as well as insignificant. There is the strangest air of insincerity about his least[,] purely personal utterance. . . . When he writes about living people of his acquaintance . . . he never seems to have *seen* the individual at all . . . there is no direct contact between Ezra and an individual person or thing. Ezra is a crowd; a little crowd. People are seen by him only as types" (*Time*, 69–70). Ultimately, Lewis cannot hope to see deeper than the symptoms of Pound's problem because he is fundamentally so different from Pound. Lewis can hold people at arm's length with no compunction whatever—he positively enjoys it. Pound, who is driven to holding them at arm's length all the time, would be much freer if he could get closer to them. Lewis is quite justified in deploring Pound's impersonal posing and in pointing out his indecision about his main artistic goals: "This certain discrepancy between what Pound said—what he supported and held up as an example—and what he did, was striking enough to impress itself on anybody" (*Time*, 39).

Lewis errs, though, in seeing only simple naiveté beneath this posing and inconsistency. His appraisal of Pound's artistic worth is unreliable because he is not aware of the complexity and dynamism of the "essential" Pound which may often be suppressed by, or at least in conflict with, the poet's public practice and professions, but which persists as a source of inspiration and potential stability and ultimately restrains Pound from abandoning himself to the excesses which, in Lewis, invalidate much in his later writings. Lewis's label "naïf" is most justified in describing Pound's perverse ability to hide from himself the true nature of his personality and to make himself believe in the public persona which he creates for himself.

Lewis's comment on Pound's relationship with "Vorticism" and later with Antheil are also full of provocative insights. He contends that Pound was somewhat out of place among the other Vorticists because, unlike them, he was not in the least extremist: "What struck them principally about Pound was that his fire-eating propagandist utterances were not accompanied by any very experimental efforts in his particular medium." He describes Pound's work at the time as "a series of pastiches of old french or old italian poetry" (*Time,* 39). Lewis sees Pound's association in 1928 with Antheil, and his experimental collaborations in music, as of the same kind as his association with the Vorticist painters and sculptors: "The Blast situation, on a meaner scale, repeats itself. Pound is there with a few gentle provençal airs, full of a delicate scholarship and 'sense of the Past,' the organizer of a musical disturbance. The real business is done by a young musician, Antheil, of a fiery accomplishment and infectious faith in the great future of jazz." Prophetically, Lewis writes: "With all his admirable flair for 'genius' (in which he has described himself as 'a specialist'), it leads him into the support of things that are at once absurd and confusing. He is not always so lucky as I believe him to be in his choice of Antheil" (*Time,* 40–41).

Pound must have been disturbed by Lewis's judgment of him, but his response, which appears very publicly as a footnote to *Guide to Kulchur,* is surprisingly conciliatory: "Mr. W. Lewis, calling me in one place a revolutionary simpleton, makes honorable amend, calling himself a chronological idiot in another. Music is the least of his troubles, or interests, yet I wdn't go so far in a censure. On the only occasion I can remember his being present during the execution of some English music in the prevalent manner, he said that he knew nowt about it, but thought such things should not happen. There is more hope for such an illiterate than for the graduates of what corresponds in music to the London School of 'Economics' " (*GK,* 234). Pound's unwillingness to dismiss or refute Lewis's harsh criticism shows, I think, not just Pound's deference toward his friend's opinions, but his uncertainty about his ability to handle the present artistically. He frankly acknowledges this uncertainty when, on December 12, 1918, he writes to Joyce about himself: "The Signore Sterlina has rash moments of believing the gift of immortality lies within his reach, but Giorgio and Lucia had much better trust to their connection con il loro illustrissimo padre. The Signore Sterlina is perhaps better at digging up corpses of let us say Li Po, or more lately Sextus Propertius, than in preserving this bitched mess of modernity" (*PJ*, 147–48).

As we look back on Pound's association with Lewis, we understand how crucial the fundamental differences in their attitudes are. Pound may borrow Lewis's rhetoric, but he does not accept his premises. He does not believe that people are depraved and that human physicality is a detestable absurdity and indignity. He does not find women and children repulsively emotional. He never convinces himself, as Lewis seems to do, that he is infallible, and never stops looking for new evidence to shape his conclusions; it is his willingness to examine new material that gives his work a complexity and fascination which survives the obscurity. Pound is at times wrongheaded, which we can bring ourselves to excuse; Lewis seems to be wronghearted, and that is a more serious matter.

Pound is saved from nihilism not only by his faith in human nature, but also by his belief in the possibility of change. The extreme pessimism of Lewis's view of human nature and human society is frighteningly claustrophobic because it is posited on the impossibility of any significant change or improvement. In *Blast No. 2* he says of artists that "They change less than other people. A good artist is more really 'of his time' and therefore makes less fuss about his accidental surroundings. Well, then, I should be perfectly content that the Present Time should always remain, and things never change, since they are new to me."[30] The implications of changelessness are somewhat less bright for "the herd." He continues: "Do not let us, like Christan [*sic*] missionaries, spoil the savages all around us."

Pound is also helped by his love of the past which provides him with a series of fixed points and also affirms a valuable and certain tradition which is of real use in establishing some sense of balance and proportion in the present. Lewis denounces both past and future and even physical existence in the present, and will only concede value to the workings of his own intellect. He claims that the past makes the artist "weakly relax and slip back." With

30. Lewis, *Blast No. 2*, p. 13.

a characteristic emphasis, he calls the past and the future "prostitutes" from whose "brothel" art must escape.[31]

Also, Pound and Lewis mean different things when they write about the need for order. When Pound is being antidemocratic, it is not for the same reasons as Lewis, and in the beginning this is evident. Where Lewis despises the common man and insists that he must be kept in line by an elite of intelligent men, Pound has a much vaguer notion of the need for order, which can only be explained by his feelings about himself and not by his feelings about the average man. He doesn't want anyone to "control" any one else; he only wants to be left alone and assumes, insofar as he thinks about it at all, that everyone (except those who are dangerous to society) should have that right. This is clear in *Patria Mia:* "I dare say I give disproportionate attention to the status of authors [in society] but I have always felt that it was the essence of democracy that each man should look after his own sort of affairs. . . . Whereas the essence of Fabianism, [and] Webbism . . . would seem to be that every man, . . . should look after everybody else's affairs" (*PM,* 41).

Pound relies heavily on order as an alternative to coming to terms with himself. His ideal is a "totalitarian" condition where order *establishes itself* because the individual has been entirely accurate in all his perceptions and sentiments. Subjectivity seems too complex and arbitrary to generate an order that one can believe in. Lewis has made subjectivity, emotion, and romanticism synonymous with democracy. But Pound is only interested in Mussolini's fascism, for example, because he convinces himself that it will take a stand against "usury" and make possible a higher level of civilization; in fact because he believes that it will give the individual, including "the last ploughman and the last girl in the olive-yards," the freedom which Lewis is so concerned to prevent them from having (*JM,* 34). Even though Pound frequently uses Lewis's rhetoric and at times gives Lewis's opinions as his own, he categorically does *not* believe with Lewis that "the human being . . . is a very helpless child, dependent on others (like a horse or dog) . . . [who] finds his greatest happiness in a state of depen-

31. Lewis, *Blast No. 1,* p. 148.

dence and subservience when (an important condition) it is named 'freedom.' "[32]

With the war, Pound's thinking and attitudes changed drastically. Before the war he had adopted Lewisian rhetoric and denunciation in the service of the arts, but with the collapse of the Vorticist experiment and the death of Gaudier, Pound felt great anger which gave substance to the vituperations which had, up to then, been largely a matter of rhetoric. He wanted to be able to assign blame for the overthrow of his hopes and the death of his friend and, because he did not wish to subscribe to Lewis's totally pessimistic view of humanity, he decided that the real villain was the "usurer." The Lewisian rhetoric was already there as a model, and in his anger Pound developed a dangerous habit of unreflective overstatement. From then on he sounds most like Lewis in attacking "usury" in all its manifestations. By 1920—in "Hudson: Poet Strayed into Science"—this style is full-fledged; by 1923 he is writing the "Hell Cantos." His outrage in the "Hudson" article against "a bloated usury, a cowardly and snivelling politics, a disgusting financial system, the sadistic curse of Christianity" (*SP*, 430), expresses itself through the kind of rhetoric that reminds us of that of some of his radio broadcasts.

In January 1948 Olga Rudge had a booklet of six of Pound's Rome Radio Broadcasts published. It was called *If This Be Treason . . .* and was to help in the effort to secure his release from St. Elizabeths. Here, Pound comments on Lewis's limitations (and on Joyce's) and chooses Cumming's *Eimi* as a greater book than *Ulysses* or *The Apes of God,* both of which he feels are limited by being merely records of the ills of the nineteenth century, "the age of usury." He quotes Lewis on *Ulysses:* "Don't seem (meaning Mr. Joyce doesn't seem) to have a very NEW pt. of view about anything," and Pound feels that this is true of both Lewis and Joyce. He says of *Apes:* "Lewis had survived the END of a period. Did a smashing big canvas of the boil on ole England's neck, heritage of Rowlandson, Smollet, Fielding, and Hogarth." Similarly, he considers Ulysses "the END, it was the completion (literarily speakin) of an era. It cooked up and served the unmitigated god damn stink of the decaying usury era." But he goes on to wonder

32. Wyndham Lewis, *The Art of Being Ruled* (New York, 1926), p. 95.

"why the hell waste all that work paintin the mould on the top of the omelet. Damn well, I am sometimes impatient, but the peeve remains as a LIMIT of that great performance." Of both Joyce and Lewis he claims: "I nacherly never agreed with either of 'em about much of anything." Pound realizes that Lewis's ideas are not congenial to him; that "Lewis has and has had what I think a fairly wrong headed philosophy. Anschauung."[33] But by now this recognition is almost too late. In the most dogmatic and obsessive of these broadcasts we can see the final outcome of Pound's failure to look critically at the rhetoric and stance for which Lewis had been a model.

In Canto 78, Pound writes: "Gaudier's word not blacked out / nor old Hulme's, nor Wyndham's" (78/479). Yet in *Thrones* he claims: "But the lot of 'em, Yeats, Possum, Old Wyndham / had no ground to stand on" (102/728), referring to their lack of interest in economic theory. He is contrasting them here to Orage. When we read in Canto 111, "Orage held the basic was pity / *compassione,*" we realize the extent to which Orage's humanitarianism must have stood, for Pound, as the antithesis to Lewis's scorn for "the herd." It seems likely that the intensity of Pound's commitment to Orage's economic ideas was partly an index of the strength of his reaction against Lewis's misanthropy. In his last reference to Lewis in *The Cantos,* Pound chooses to mention not his views, but his courage, commenting on his refusal to have his eyes operated on and his persistence in writing even when his sight failed (*Era,* 549). "Wyndham Lewis chose blindness / rather than have his mind stop" (115/794). A few lines later in this fragment of Canto 115 he writes, "Their asperities diverted me in my green time," thinking not only of how they entertained him, but also of how they turned him aside from his true course.

Gaudier-Brzeska: The Spirit Clear in the Stone

When Gaudier-Brzeska was alive, he had a very strong, positive influence on Pound. As a result of this friendship, the poet devel-

---

33. Ezra Pound, *If This Be Treason* (privately printed) (Siena, 1948), pp. 6–10.

oped a deep fascination with the art and the history of sculpture, and from watching his friend work he came to have great respect for the difficult skill of carving directly in stone and a strong conviction of the young sculptor's genius. Gaudier's work became a proof that the new renaissance was already under way. When his friend was killed in the trenches at the age of twenty-three, the shock to Pound was overwhelming and generated the intense anger which plunged him into his obsessive campaign against the usurers.

Charles Olson, visiting Pound in St. Elizabeths thirty-one years after Gaudier's death, found him repeatedly referring to the sculptor and insisting that his genius was still unmatched. This led Olson to a very perceptive and important conclusion:

> The curious thing in all this is that everything Pound has to say and feel *politically* is . . . 30 years old and dead as a duck . . . It is clear he only experienced war and politics once: in England, World War I . . . Maybe it was accidental, but the conjunction of Gaudier Brzeska's death to the whole conversation appears to me to be important. It is as though Pound has never got over it, that Gaudier's death is the source of his hate for contemporary England and America, that then, in 1915, his attack on democracy got mixed up with Gaudier's death, and all his turn since has been revenge for the boy's death.[34]

Olson is absolutely right about Pound's desire for revenge, although wrong about his attack on democracy—for Pound, the villain is not democracy but usury. It is important to understand that the poet's desire for revenge did not just spring from sorrow at a personal loss, but from anger at a loss to the arts. It was because he believed Gaudier's genius to be indispensable to the new renaissance that his need for revenge was so intense. Pound the man clearly grieved for his friend, but Pound the man of letters saw the sculptor's death as part of a deliberate and malicious campaign against the arts and felt that he must take the offensive

34. Seelye, *Charles Olson and Ezra Pound,* pp. 4–5.

against the "obstructors of knowledge" who were also "obstructors of distribution."

Pound's main objective was still the revitalizing of Western civilization, but it was now clear to him that artists would not be able to do this alone. Gaudier's death had shown how vulnerable they were to the usurers who had a vested interest in silencing them. The true artist's commitment to clarity of thought and precision of definition was a particular threat to the usurers who depended for their success on confusing and deceiving the public and who thrived in times of social upheaval and especially in times of war. In a 1934 "Postscript" to his memoir of Gaudier, Pound writes:

> For eighteen years the death of Henri Gaudier has been unremedied. The work of two or three years remains, but the uncreated went with him.
>
> There is no reason to pardon this either to the central powers or to the allies or to ourselves. . . .
>
> With a hundred fat rich men working overtime to start another war or another six wars for the sake of their personal profit, it is very hard for me to write of Gaudier with the lavender tones of dispassionate reminiscence. [*GB,* 140]

To Pound, Gaudier's sculpture is talismanic. He sees it as "a three dimensional assertion of a complete revaluation of life in general, of human life in particular, of man against . . . social and physical necessity." His extravagant claims for it show that he thinks of the sculpture as though it were itself the new renaissance: "There is still enough energy even in what I was able to get into my memoir of his (i.e. all his own writing and 40 half-tone reproductions) to modernize Russia, to bring communism to date, I mean into harmony with the best thought of the occident, and to make America fit to live in." Pound's "Postscript" makes it clear that his campaign against the usurers is more than just a matter of revenge and that he believes that a renaissance of some kind is still possible: "A few blocks of stone really carved are very nearly sufficient base for a new civilization. The garbage of three empires collapsed over Gaudier's marble. And as that swill is cleared off, as the map of a new Europe becomes visible Gaudier's work reemerges, perfectly solid" (*GB,* 144). Here, of course, Pound is referring to his hope that Mussolini will help to create a "new Europe" in which the power of the usurers will be curbed. We come to see that there is a strange but nevertheless definite continuity between Pound's enthusiasm for Gaudier and his enthusiasm for the Duce. Mussolini becomes important to him as someone who can help to remove the obstacles to a new renaissance and "make Europe safe" for the arts. Pound not only insists that the Duce is similar to Jefferson in his aims, but even makes him into a kind of "honorary artist": "I don't believe that any estimate of Mussolini will be valid unless it *starts* from his passion for construction. Treat him as *artifex* and all the details fall into place. Treat him as anything save the artist and you will get muddled with contradictions" (*JM,* 33–34). And again: "The more one examines the Milan Speech the more one is reminded of Brancusi, the stone blocks from which no error emerges, from whatever angle one look at them" (*JM,* viii).

Pound's motives for counting on Mussolini were certainly defensible, but they were highly unrealistic, and this, in conjunction with the habit, learned from Lewis, of relying on invective and sweeping denunciation, quickly led him into danger. Lewis's rhetoric, authoritarianism, and loathing of humanity joined with Pound's anger and outrage at Gaudier's death to produce the almost uncontrolled excesses of the Hell Cantos and of the Rome Radio broadcasts.

Fortunately, Gaudier had a strong, positive influence on Pound also and this, in the long run, proved to be the more enduring and was a means of healing. Pound felt a strong affection for Gaudier, and the fact that his friend was dead seemed to free him from his usual inhibitions about dwelling on his own emotions. His reminiscences of Gaudier and sorrow at the thought of his death helped him to maintain contact with his most intimate feelings. In those passages in the first half of the poem in which he remembers his friend, we find the elegiac note which is to become the dominant mood in the *Pisan Cantos.*

Gaudier-Brzeska: A Memoir is by far the most self-revealing of all Pound's prose works, and, writing on his friend, Pound is personal in an unprecedented way: "He was certainly the best company in the world, and some of my best days, the happiest and the most interesting, were spent in his uncomfortable mud-floored studio when he was doing my bust." He says that sitting for Gaudier was an escape from the present into the Italian Renaissance: "He was, of course, indescribably like some one whom one had met in the pages of Castiglione or Valla, or perhaps in a painting forgotten. . . . I knew that if I had lived in the Quattrocento I should have had no finer moment, and no better craftsman to fill it. And it is not a common thing to know that one is drinking the cream of the ages" (*GB*, 47–48). There are few other places where Pound is as explicitly personal as he is when he recounts his feelings on getting to know Gaudier:

> I was interested and I was determined that he should be. I knew that many things would bore or disgust him, particularly my rather middle-aged point of view, my intellectual tiredness and exhaustion, my general scepticism and quietness, and I therefore opened fire with 'Altaforte,' 'Pierre Vidal,' and such poems as I had written when about his own age. . . . He even tried to persuade me that I was not becoming middle-aged, but any man whose youth has been worth anything, any man who has lived his life at all in the sun, knows that he has seen the best of it when he finds thirty approaching; knows that he is entering a quieter realm, a place with a different psychology. [*GB*, 45–46]

In many ways, Gaudier was similar to Pound—his feverish energy and his often arrogant pose really hid a highly romantic and gentle disposition. In his public pronouncements he could appear callous and impersonal, as when from the trenches he writes: "THIS PALTRY MECHANISM, WHICH SERVES AS A PURGE TO OVER-NUMEROUS HUMANITY. THIS WAR IS A GREAT REMEDY. IN THE INDIVIDUAL IT KILLS ARROGANCE, SELF-ESTEEM, PRIDE. IT TAKES AWAY FROM THE MASSES NUMBERS UPON NUMBERS OF UNIMPORTANT UNITS, WHOSE ECONOMIC ACTIVITIES BECOME NOXIOUS AS THE RECENT TRADES CRISES HAVE SHOWN US" (*GB*, 27). Or when he writes: "My temperament does not allow of formless, vague assertions, *'all what is not like me is evil'*; so is Kandinsky" (*GB*,

33). Yet he was living under great physical strain in extreme poverty which forced him to work as a clerk during the day to get enough money to buy materials. He rarely had enough food and made do with very little sleep so that he could work on his sculpture at night. He was infinitely patient and gentle with Sophie Brzeska, the woman who lived with him (though not as his mistress) and whose name he added to his own. Gaudier's vitality and love of nature must have particularly appealed to Pound, who could never bring himself to despise the physical and vital as Lewis did. In "Vortex"—Gaudier's brief, impressionistic "history of sculpture"—which Pound considers the most important single document of Vorticism, Gaudier sees fecundity as the most outstanding characteristic of the sculpture of a civilization in its maturity. Pound admires Gaudier's "abnormal sympathy with, and intelligence for, all moving life, its swiftness and softness" (*GB,* 79). Describing his first sight of the sculptor, Pound says that Gaudier followed him "like a well-made young wolf or some soft-moving, bright-eyed wild thing." After talking to Pound briefly, "he disappeared like a Greek god in a vision" (*GB,* 44). Together with his love of nature, Gaudier had a ritualistic and pantheistic sense which must have fascinated Pound. In a letter written in 1910 to a former teacher of his, Gaudier says:

> I begin to understand the Greek and pagan antiquity, which I now prefer to the Gothic . . . now I have finished with . . . Christian philosophy, that hysterical egoism which contemplates the material sufferings of a material body and says: 'I have no wish to be crucified. I thank you, Christ, for having suffered in my stead, to save me from Hell where my body would have burned eternally.' This now seems to me only a repugnant sadism, and I much prefer the pantheistic idea.[35]

He chooses to worship the sun and says, in a letter to Sophie: "I should never be happy all day if I did not, each morning when I get up, kneel down before [the sun] . . . We can only follow the fine and natural religion of the ancients, and no one can laugh at

35. H. S. Ede, *Savage Messiah* (New York, 1931), p. 22.

us, for our prayers are addressed to a Being, true and real."[36] And we remember that in Canto 113 Pound begins and ends with "Pater Helios" and follows the sun toward consolation where "Out of dark, thou, Father Helios, leadest" (113/790). It seems appropriate that Pound, toward the end of his life—and by great indirection—should come again to a communion with the sun like that of the very young Gaudier, whose influence has remained with him throughout *The Cantos* and who had, all those years ago, tried to persuade him that he was not becoming "middle-aged."

Gaudier's presence is implicit in *The Cantos* whenever there are allusions to carved stone—to sculpture and to architecture, but there are other, more particularized references to him also. Gaudier was killed in action on June 5, 1915, and Pound began to write the first *Three Cantos* in September of this year, so it seems likely that his friend's death was partly responsible for his decision to make Odysseus's descent into Hades the main subject of his third canto and later to use this *nekuia* as Canto I. Pound's emphasis on Elpenor seems to support this idea. In Canto 1 only Odysseus's meeting with him is given in detail; Tiresias's long soothsaying is condensed to ". . . 'Odysseus / 'Shalt return through spiteful Neptune, over dark seas, / 'Lose all companions,' " and Anticlea is passed over with a few words (1/4–5). Elpenor's plea takes on a particular poignancy when we think of Gaudier, killed just as he is beginning a life's work:

> "But thou, O King, I bid remember me, unwept, unburied,
> "Heap up mine arms, be tomb by sea-bord, and inscribed:
> "*A man of no fortune, and with a name to come.*   [1/4]

The Hell-Mouth Canto takes on a new and moving dimension when we realize how much Pound must have Gaudier in mind as he writes it. As the poet struggles out of Hell Mouth, he finds:

>   Palux Laerna,
>   the lake of bodies, aqua morta,
>   of limbs fluid, and mingled, like fish heaped in a bin,
>   and here an arm upward, clutching a fragment of marble,

36. Ibid., pp. 53–54.

And the embryos, in flux,
      new inflow, submerging,
Here an arm upward, trout, submerged by the eels;
      and from the bank, the stiff herbage
the dry nobbled path, saw many known, and unknown,
for an instant;
      submerging,
The face gone, generation.   [16/69]

Donald Davie says that the hand clutching the marble here is "the first glimmer of convalescence after the passage through the infernal regions,"[37] but in the context this seems an image of loss rather than of hope. These bodies are not struggling upward but being sucked down—"the new inflow, submerging"—and Pound uses "submerging" or "submerged" three times in six lines. The connection between the bodies in the lake and the dead and dying on a battlefield becomes unavoidable when we find that the rest of the canto is largely devoted to war and those killed in war. In "submerging, / the face gone, generation," the last word surely refers to the generation of young men killed in 1914–18. Once he has passed the swamp the poet falls asleep and hears the voices which tell him of war—of the Franco-Prussian War, the Greek War of Independence, and finally of the First World War. An anecdote of one of Richard Aldington's experiences in the trenches is followed by the bald statement: "And Henri Gaudier went to it, and they killed him, / And killed a good deal of sculpture" (16/71). There seems little doubt that the arm "clutching a fragment of marble" as it submerges in the swamp is Gaudier's arm, and that this is really his canto, even though only these three lines are explicitly about him.

Pound has a particular reason for beginning this canto with a vision of Blake fleeing from the horrors that he has "seen" in Hell and, once we realize this, we are able to visualize the "lake of bodies" quite specifically.

37. Donald Davie, *Ezra Pound: Poet as Sculptor* (New York, 1964), p. 129.

Figure 1. William Blake, *Charon and the Condemned Souls.*

And before hell mouth; dry plain
      and two mountains;
   On the one mountain, a running form.

  . . . .
And the running form, naked, Blake,
Shouting, whirling his arms, the swift limbs,
Howling against the evil,
     his eyes rolling,
Whirling like flaming cart-wheels,
     and his head held backward to gaze on the evil
As he ran from it.   [16/68]

Blake is described here like a figure from one of his own paintings,
and if we turn to his *Illustrations to the Divine Comedy* we notice

Figure 2. William Blake, *The Angel Crossing Styx*.
  "the lake of bodies, aqua morta,
    of limbs fluid, and mingled, like fish heaped in a bin." [16/69]

a resemblance between Pound's description of Blake and Blake's drawing of Charon in "Charon and the Condemned Souls." Charon, bracing himself on the deck while he brandishes his oar, has been drawn by Blake in the stance of a runner and is, in addition, "shouting," "whirling his arms," and "howling against the evil," in this case raging at the souls of the damned on the shore who hesitate to get into his boat. In the *Inferno* Dante tells that "the ferryman of the livid marsh . . . had wheels of flame about his eyes" (1.3.98–99), and Blake has represented these only roughly with two concentric circles. Pound refers more explicitly to Dante's description when he presents his Blake with "eyes rolling, / whirling like flaming cart-wheels." As Charon ferries souls— and presumably Dante and Vergil also—across Acheron to Hell, so Blake himself, through his paintings, has led both Pound and all those who see the paintings into these regions.

Another of Blake's illustrations for the *Inferno* seems to lie behind Pound's description of Palux Laerna. "The Angel Crossing the Styx" shows the filthy swamp full of bodies and more bodies within a great spiral current above the marsh. Blake's spiral is a whirlwind, drawing some of the souls up "out of the pit of annihilation,"[38] but there is no precedent for this in Dante, and the drawing itself is only roughly sketched, so that Pound's assumption that the bodies are being sucked down into the lake is entirely reasonable. Although Blake leaves this drawing in an unfinished state, he picks up the motif of the spiral current again in the most detailed and carefully finished of all his illustrations for the *Commedia*–"The Circle of the Lustful: Francesca da Rimini"– and, as we shall see, Pound makes this engraving the central image in Canto 20.

Canto 51 focusses on the connection between usury and war in a way that makes us think particularly of Gaudier. In recapitulating the *Usura* Canto, the poet has made changes which emphasize stonecutting much more strongly than in Canto 45. Also, this section is preceded by an indirect reminder of the First World War: "Fifth element; mud; said Napoleon." Gaudier is clearly in Pound's mind and we are made particularly aware of this by the last episode in the canto. We are conveyed to the Seventh Circle of Hell where Geryon presides over the usurers and the fraudulent, where we find the bankers:

> sang Geryone; I am the help of the aged;
> I pay men to talk peace;
> Mistress of many tongues; merchant of chalcedony
> I am Geryon twin with usura,
> You who have lived in a stage set.
> A thousand were dead in his folds;
> in the eel-fisher's basket.   [51/251–52]

The thousand dead in the eel-fisher's basket recall the Hell-Mouth Canto where the limbs in Laerna are "mingled, like fish heaped in a bin" with "here an arm upward, trout, submerged by the eels." The "eel-fisher's basket" reappears most strategically in Pound's

---

38. Albert S. Roe, *Blake's Illustrations to the Divine Comedy* (Princeton, 1953), p. 74.

addendum for Canto 100. As it stands, Canto 100 must surely be one of the most feverish and fragmentary of the Cantos. It reiterates with disconcerting rapidity many points already made in detail in previous cantos. The synthesis, or at least the focus which we hope for in the hundredth canto is conspicuously absent. Pound's decision to write an addendum is a recognition of this and we find that, unlike the main body of the canto, the addendum is very clearly focussed. It hearkens back to Cantos 16, 45, and 51, since *"Usura,"* here called *"neschek,"* is both the Hydra and Geryon:

> Poisoner of the fount,
>   of all fountains, *neschek,*
> The serpent, evil against Nature's increase,
> Against beauty
>   Τὸ χαλόν [the beautiful]
>   formosus nec est nec decens
> A thousand are dead in his folds,
>   in the eel-fisher's basket
>   [100/798–99]

Here, in 1941, in the middle of another war, Pound is still seeking an exit from the hell of his own times as he was in the "Hell-Mouth Canto":

>   Χαῖρη! Ω Διώνη, Χαῖρη [Hail! O Dione]
>   pure Light, we beseech thee
>   Crystal, we beseech thee
>   Clarity, we beseech thee
>   from the labyrinth   [100/799]

Throughout *The Cantos,* works in stone are fixed points and focus some of the poet's deepest and most intense feelings. In one sense, works of architecture are presented as "affirmations"—both as affirmations of the craftsmanship of individuals and as affirmations of the cultural and spiritual values of the times in which they were built. Pound believes that great works of architecture can only be built in times of cultural health, and since most of his references are to churches, cathedrals, temples, and shrines, these works are the manifestation of spiritual as well as cultural energies. Yet the great age of these monuments gives them a timeless quality —the "dimension of stillness"—and the poet's response to them is meditative and elegiac. Whenever he writes of carved stone, his verse is particularly moving, not only because of his love for the past, but also because of his memories of Gaudier.

Sculpture, for Pound, is "the approach to the infinite by form." Paradisal energies are translated into forms in the sculptor's mind and he knows these forms before he transfers them to the stone. To Pound, the apprehension of the form by the sculptor is similar to the apparition of the gods and to the focussing of divine energies in the experience of love. In Canto 20 he interpolates in his description of the poet Sulpicia's passion for her lover the lines:

> "as the sculptor sees the form in the air
>   before he sets hand to mallet,
> "and as he sees the in, and the through,
>   the four sides
> "not the one face to the painter   [20/117]

He then compares the sculptor's visualizing of the form to Aphrodite's assumption of human form when she reveals herself to Anchises:

> "as the sculptor sees the form in the air . . .
> "as glass seen under water,
> "King Otreus, my father . . .
> and saw the waves taking form as crystal,   [20/119]

Pound insists on the need to reverence the divine energies that were celebrated in ancient times at pagan shrines and in sacred groves. In those places where all traces of former shrines have now disappeared, he imagines that the form of the shrine still remains in the air, as though waiting for a sculptor to see it and reestablish it in stone. One of his favorite walks from Rapallo takes him to Castellaro, the site of just such a shrine: "to Jupiter and to Hermes where now is the castellaro / no vestige save in the air / in stone is no imprint and the grey walls of no era" (74/438).

In the *Pisan Cantos,* Pound finds a symbol for his spiritual and emotional confusion in the sacred grove whose altar has been obliterated. The reappearance of the altar will coincide with the poet's own breakthrough into the paradisal and will represent a personal vision of coherence and unity. In Canto 74, he recalls Elpenor—and Gaudier—when he writes: " 'and with a name to come' " and follows this with "aram vult nemus" [the grove needs an altar] (74/446). He repeats this last phrase in 78/481 and also at the end of the "Lynx chorus" which concludes Canto 79, when Aphrodite makes a triumphal entry into the forest of the lynxes:

> a petal lighter than sea-foam
> Κύθηρα
>> aram
>> nemus
>> vult   [79/492]

At this point the altar is built only out of words, and the building of it in stone cannot be effected by Aphrodite alone. When the altar finally comes to the grove, in Canto 90, "Amor" rather than Aphrodite is the presiding genius. Where Aphrodite in Canto 79 was "deina" [fearful] and "terrible in resistance," "Amor" is personal and beneficent, showing how, because of his experience at Pisa—as we find it recorded in the *Pisan Cantos*—Pound has learned to confront his own emotions as they are rather than as they can be represented by the stories and goddesses of myth. In Canto 90 the healing power of love is revealed to the poet and he witnesses the apotheosis of Amor which is proclaimed by the substantiation of an altar of carved stone in the grove:

> water jets from the rock
> and in the flat pool as Arethusa's
>> a hush in papyri.
> Grove hath its altar
>> under elms, in that temple, in silence

. . . .
The architect from the painter,
　　　the stone under elm
Taking form now,
　　　the rilievi,
　　　the curled stone at the marge
Faunus, sirenes,
　　　the stone taking form in the air　　　[90/607]

The coming of the altar to the grove is not just symbolic, but is an intimately personal experience which takes place under the elms in the grounds of St. Elizabeths:

woodland ἐπὶ χθονί [upon the earth]
　　　the trees rise
　　and there is a wide sward between them
　　　　　myrrh and olibanum on the altar stone
giving perfume,
. . . .
　　　thick smoke, purple, rising
bright flame now on the altar
　　　the crystal funnel of air　　　[90/608]

Bill MacNaughton tells how, when he visited Pound at St. Elizabeths, the poet would sometimes burn olibanum on a small stone that he kept for this purpose.[39]
　　Wyndham Lewis would not have approved of the change of heart that has set up this altar to "Amor," but, as Charles Olson shows us, it is not Lewis but Gaudier whom Pound speaks of with deep feeling during his ordeal in "Erebus, the deep-lying."

39. Bill MacNaughton, "Pound: A Brief Memoir: 'Chi Lavora, Ora,' " *Paideuma* 3, no. 3 (Winter 1974): 323.

3 Cantos 1-71

We have seen in chapter 1 how, by 1927, Pound had realized that the material of greatest interest to him in his poem fell into three categories and how, by recognizing and naming these categories, he had provided a schema for the poem. In Cantos 31–71 these categories are very clearly defined, but Pound comes to this definition gradually; as we move from the *Poetry* Cantos I–III to Cantos 1–30, we find the poet struggling with different kinds of problems and becoming progressively more troubled, more disillusioned, and more grim.

In Cantos I–III Pound is mainly struggling with his uncertainty about what kind of poem to write and what kind of material to concentrate on. His uncertainty was probably aggravated also by his sense that what he had come up with was not very satisfactory. By the time that he had put Cantos 1–7 into their present form, he was in the process of making a major revision of his earlier idea of what his duty as a poet should be. The Pound of Cantos 1–7 was in a state of transition—turning from his original, more purely aesthetic concerns to a more socially conscious and reformist position. Essentially, this transition continues throughout the whole of Cantos 1–30, although, as we have seen, it is not until after Canto 11 that we find him devoting whole cantos to the problems of his own times.

Cantos 1–30 focus on complications and difficulties—both those which the poet must confront in the present and those which have faced his counterparts in the past. Even the "bust thru" into the "divine or permanent world" presents problems: the euphoric states of mind that result from it can tempt the poet to be escapist; the intellectual apprehension of paradisal perfection can make him painfully aware of the gulf between this and the sordid present; and sexual passion can be dangerous and destructive as well as the means to transcendant awareness. In Cantos 31–51, the three categories of the schema are even more rigidly distinct and Pound avoids much of the complexity of Cantos 1–30 by focusing more narrowly on economic problems and by writing on the paradisal more generally and at less length.

The Poetry Cantos

If we briefly consider Cantos I–III, we find that each canto has a different focus. In I, Pound is most concerned about the difficulty of finding a hero for his poem complex and dynamic enough to serve as an adequate vehicle for his strongest feelings. He considers Browning's solution to this problem, which was

> To set out so much thought, so much emotion;
> To paint, more real than any dead Sordello,
> The half or third of your intensest life
> And call that third *Sordello;*   [I/114]

but he realizes that what will work for a nineteenth-century poet is not likely to accommodate the complexities of the twentieth century:

> You had one whole man?
> And I have many fragments, less worth? Less worth?
> Ah, had you quite my age, quite such a beastly and
>   cantankerous age?
> You had some basis, had some set belief.   [I/115]

In fact, as he anticipates here, he will not use his "heroes" as a way of projecting part of his "intensest life." He has already considered, and rejected, Arnaut, Bertrand de Born, Uc St. Circ, and Cavalcanti, and it is clear from this canto that his strongest feelings, and those that fascinate him most, are those "paradisal" states of mind that are stirred by beautiful landscapes in which he has felt himself so close to the divine energies of a pagan past that he can readily imagine gods, nymphs, and satyrs revealing themselves. Foremost among these is Sirmione on Lake Garda:

> This is our home, the trees are full of laughter,
> And the storms laugh loud, breaking the riven waves
> On "north-most rocks"; and here the sunlight
> Glints on the shaken waters, and the rain
> Comes forth with delicate tread, walking from Isola Garda—
>   *Lo soleils plovil,*
> As Arnaut had it in th' inextricable song.
> The very sun rains and a spatter of fire
> Darts from the "Lydian" ripples . . .
> . . . .
>   Gods float in the azure air,
> Bright gods, and Tuscan, back before dew was shed,
> . . . .
> 'Tis the first light—not half light—Panisks
> And oak-girls and the Maenads
> Have all the wood. Our olive Sirmio
> Lies in its burnished mirror, and the mounts Balde and Riva
> Are alive with song, and all the leaves are full of voices.
>
>   [I/116–18]

Throughout the canto Pound talks openly about his difficulty in planning his poem and also voices two other concerns. He wonders how far it is justifiable to claim to know the past on the strength of his intimations alone, "Or say the filmy shell that circumscribes me / Contains the actual sun; / confuse the thing I see / With actual gods behind me?" (I/120). He also hints at a feeling that his verse should in some way acknowledge and reflect the new form-sense of contemporary artists: "the new world about us: / Barred lights, great flares, new form, Picasso or Lewis" (I/121).

He does not pursue this further, but in Canto II turns back to those characters and authors of the literature of the past who have seemed particularly alive to him. He has already written on most of these in *The Spirit of Romance* and in "Troubadours—Their Sorts and Conditions," and we sense that he feels some misgivings about the inconclusiveness of this compendium of literary enthusiasms. This shows in the rather mechanical and awkward way in which the various episodes are linked: "Leave Casella. / Send out your thought upon the Mantuan palace—"; "There's the one stave, and all the rest forgotten. / I've lost the copy I had of it in Paris,"; "Thus St. Circ has the story:"; "So ends that novel."; "Dig up Camoens, hear out his resonant bombast." Perhaps the anecdote which concludes the canto also makes an oblique comment on his uncertainty about his chances of making a success of his ambitious poem and, ultimately, of his projected career as a poet. In this anecdote, an Indiana farm boy, whose father had wanted to be an artist himself, spends ten years as an artist in Paris only to end up back in Indiana "Acting as usher in the theatre, / Painting the local drug-shop and soda bars, / . . . / dreaming his renaissance" (II/188).

In the opening section of Canto III, on John Heydon, Pound seems still to be holding his subject at arm's length and finally rejects the vague Neoplatonism of Heydon and Ficino for the more solid achievement of Lorenzo Valla whom he considers to have "more earth and sounder rhetoric" (III/249). His 1914 essay, "The Renaissance," (*LE,* 214–26) explains his enthusiasm for Valla. He singles him out as a hero, claiming that the Italian Renaissance began with his tribute, in the preface to his *Elegantiae linguae latinae,* to the Latin language as a great sacrament, the foundation of the liberal arts and of law, and the road to all knowledge. Valla understood, Pound says, "the value of a capital, the value of centralization, in matters of knowledge and art, and of the interaction and stimulus of genius foregathered." This led, not to "a single great vortex," but to "the numerous vortices of the Italian cities, striving against each other not only in commerce but in the arts as well." Pound reassures the reader that the lives of Erasmus and Valla show that "scholars of the quattrocento had just as stiff a stupidity and contentment and ignorance to contend with" as those who wish to bring about a renaissance in the twentieth century.

Valla is concerned to encourage not only the use of more elegant classical Latin, but also the translation into Latin of classical Greek texts, some of which, including books 1–16 of the *Iliad,* he translates himself. In Paris, in 1910 or before, Pound had bought Andreas Divus's Latin translation of the *Odyssey,* made about a hundred years later than Valla's *Iliad,* but undertaken in the same spirit. In Canto III, he follows his tribute to Valla with a reference to Divus's translation and with his own versions of Odysseus's descent into Hell.

When he decides to use this translation for his Canto 1, he omits the tribute to Valla and the Latin language. Valla's case, as we see from "The Renaissance," was intended to show how one can get on with a renaissance despite opposition, but, by the time that Pound comes to write Canto 1, Valla's case no longer seems applicable. In Canto 5, he writes of later Renaissance Latinists whose careers were much less successful and much more thwarted by circumstance than Valla's was. When Pound writes of the Renaissance in Cantos 1–30, as he does a good deal, the emphasis is always on difficulties and complications, and this represents a significant break with his earlier tendency to idealize the past. Before, he was always very ready to lose himself in the past, but now he has misgivings about this. To understand this change we must look briefly at *Hugh Selwyn Mauberley,* since it is in this poem that he squarely confronts his "escapism" and reorders his priorities.

Hugh Selwyn Mauberley

From December 1919 to the spring of 1922, Pound, having reached an impasse, suspended his work on *The Cantos.* During this period he wrote *Hugh Selwyn Mauberley,* which represented an important reorientation in his thinking about his role as a poet and made it possible for him to return to *The Cantos* with a much surer sense of direction. In 1922 he settled on Sigismundo Malatesta and devoted four cantos to him. As a result, "the design of the poem suddenly crystallize[d]" and he was "able to rethink the poem sufficiently to change drastically those parts of it left untouched since the appearance of the *Lustra* volumes [1917]."[1]

Pound had been strongly influenced by the political and economic ideas of A. R. Orage and Major Douglas and had read the latter's *Economic Democracy* just before writing *Mauberley,* the first of his poems to refer to usury. He felt more and more strongly that the poetic program which he had established for himself (which had largely been set forth in his statements on Imagism and Vorticism) was not capable, in itself, of bringing about the revitalizing of civilization which he was striving for. As his disgust at the deterioration of British civilization grew, the need for an understanding of the economic causes of the decay seemed increasingly urgent. His anger made his criticisms of society more violent and bitter, and the bitterness made him increasingly unpopular. Unless he could find some justification for modifying his disillusionment with British society, he had little choice but to try and find a more hospitable intellectual climate elsewhere. After considering the possibility either of returning to America or of studying medicine, he finally decided to go to Paris (*Life,* 234).

The complexities of these decisions are clearly reflected in *Hugh Selwyn Mauberley* and explain his need to dispense with E. P. and to create and then destroy Mauberley. His creation of the latter was Pound's way of justifying to himself his belief that his impulse toward a more socially conscious art was a reliable one, and that economic theory warranted a place in his program important enough to make some of his earlier, purely aesthetic goals less than all-sufficient.

Pound ingeniously made Mauberley the depressing and clearly exaggerated projection of the kind of writer whom E. P. might have become had he carried out his original program and not revised it to accommodate his new economic and political insights. Mauberley was offered as a warning of what might have happened to Pound himself if he had not adjusted some of his earlier ideas. If we are not convinced of Mauberley's resemblance to Pound, or

1. Myles Slatin, "A History of Pound's *Cantos I-XVI,* 1915-1925," *American Literature* 35 (May 1963): 192. I have followed Slatin's dating throughout.

of the likelihood of Pound turning into a Mauberley, this is simply evidence of how little convincing Pound really needed to pursue his new enthusiasms.

What have appeared to earlier critics to be ambiguities in the poem can be easily understood once we realize the nature of Pound's relationship to Mauberley. His impulse to place his character's isolation "under a more tolerant, perhaps, examination" (*P*, 201) becomes understandable once we see their close connection. His tendency to be unduly harsh toward Mauberley (which alternates, even in the same poem, with his tolerance) can now be seen as a testimony to the urgency of his need to discredit his former program in his own eyes and leave himself free to follow up the new interests to which he is by now strongly drawn.

Kenner's idea that "E. P. Ode Pour L'Election de Son Sepulchre" is not written by "Pound" so much as "seen through the eyes of uncomprehending but not unsympathetic conservers of the 'better tradition' "[2] is an unconvincing and puzzling attempt to remove any trace of Pound's self-criticism in the poem, particularly since Pound is so involved in self-examination at this time. It seems very likely that Pound himself would immediately counter the suggestion that he has been "wrong from the start" with: "No, hardly but seeing he had been born / In a half savage country, out of date . . ." (*P*, 187). It seems very unlikely that he would present a critic who could be this considerate. It is the younger, less socially conscious Pound for whom this "epitaph" is written and who, we are told, ceased to exist after 1916, "*l'an trentuniesme / De son eage.*" Nor is Pound wholly aloof from Mauberley. In "The Age Demanded," for example, his character's "sense of gradations" is certainly a virtue in Pound's estimation, but to maintain it exclusively now "amid . . . current exacerbations" is to be forced to eliminate too much of life from consideration. A purely aesthetic credo is inadequate, Pound is saying, as a guide to how to proceed in this postwar world. He is, of course, making a case for the importance to the serious writer of

2. Hugh Kenner, *The Poetry of Ezra Pound* (Norfolk, Conn., 1951), p. 170.

an economic philosophy. Without this, and armed only with his theories of art, the implication is that he, like Mauberley, would be a prey to "The discouraging doctrine of chances," his "desire for survival" reduced to "an Olympian *apathein* / In the presence of selected perceptions." By presenting Mauberley in this way, Pound is dramatizing his own fear that finally even his poetic creativity would be dammed up completely. This explains why he lightly mocks his own earlier poetic program when he presents Mauberley as:

> Incapable of the least utterance or composition,
> Emendation, conservation of the "better tradition,"
> Refinement of medium, elimination of superfluities,
> August attraction or concentration   [*P,* 202]

Pound turns most decisively against Mauberley in the stanza that follows, where he makes him guilty of "maudlin confession" and "irresponse to human aggression" and of "lifting the faint susurrus / of his subjective hosannah." But Pound immediately re-affirms his brotherhood with him by accusing him of "Non-esteem of self-styled 'his betters,' " which by now was giving Pound himself considerable trouble in "the world of letters." Early in 1920, while he was still composing *Mauberley,* Pound had been angered by criticisms of *Quia Pauper Amavi* in *The Observer* of January 11 and the *Spectator* of February 7. His review in the *Athenaeum* of a production of Gogol's *The Government Inspector* brought complaints which necessitated an apology by the magazine and in late July of 1920 he was fired from the magazine (*Life,* 228–29). In *The New Age* of January 13, 1921, Orage explained some of the reasons for Pound's decision to leave England: "Much of the Press has deliberately closed by cabal to him; his books have for some time been ignored or written down; and he himself has been compelled to live on much less than would support a navvy" (*Life,* 235).

With poem 4 which follows, all tension has disappeared and complete detachment and passivity takes its place. Mauberley fades into oblivion, but is no more dead than the "E. P." of the

"Ode." Mauberley cannot be taken seriously any more, having lost all contact with reality, just as "E. P." must be abandoned because his purely artistic goals are not in themselves sufficiently oriented toward action. All that is left of Mauberley, by the end of the poem, is his poem "Medallion" from which he himself is absent and which makes a work of art of the woman who is its subject by reducing her to a condition of inanimate beauty. An art whose highest achievment is to reduce its living subject to a condition of complete stasis can no longer serve the turn of a writer who is increasingly moving toward the conviction that "the truth of a given idea [is] measured by the degree and celerity wherewith it goes into action . . ." (*GK,* 182).

Pound found a man of action to suit his immediate purposes in Sigismundo Malatesta. In May 1922, when he started working on *The Cantos* again, he made rapid progress. He was busy with research for the Malatesta Canto and actually started writing it in August or September. By December it had turned into three cantos, by July 1923 a fourth had been added, and the group was published as "Cantos IX–XII of a Long Poem" in *Criterion.* With only a few minor changes, this group stands as the present Cantos 8–11. Then Pound was able to rearrange the rest of *The Cantos,* and they appeared in their new order in *A Draft of XVI Cantos* (May–December 1924).

Cantos 1–7

In Cantos I–III, Pound was dealing with the same dilemmas that are central to Cantos 1–7, but then, although he had been aware that there were problems, he had not fully understood them. As a result, in Cantos I–III, he was more concerned to present his confusion than to examine the nature of it and its causes. This accounts for the major difference between the two groups of cantos —the directness of address in I–III and the obliquity of 1–7. When we compare a passage from Canto II with a related passage from Canto 3 we can readily appreciate what a difference is made by the poet's shift from intrusiveness to obliquity. In Canto II, for example, he writes:

Send out your thought upon the Mantuan palace—
Drear waste, great halls,
Silk tatters still in the frame, Gonzaga's splendor
Alight with phantoms! What have we of them,
Or much or little?
Where do we come upon the ancient people?
"All that I know is that a certain star"—
All that I know of one, Joios, Tolosan,
Is that in middle May, going along
A scarce discerned path, turning aside,
In level poplar lands, he found a flower, and wept.
"*Ya la primera flor,*" he wrote
"*Qu'ieu trobei, tornei em plor*
There's the one stave, and all the rest forgotten.
I've lost the copy I had of it in Paris,
Out of the blue and gilded manuscript
Decked out with Couci's rabbits,
And the pictures, twined with the capitals,
Purporting to be Arnaut and the authors.
Joios we have.   [II/180]

Here the poet, worrying out loud about his exact relationship to
these monuments from the past, had compromised their imme-
diacy by interposing between them and the reader the picture of
himself at work on the literary texts in which he had encountered
them. In Canto 3 he also refers to the palace of the Este in Mantua,
but with quite different effect. He begins this canto with a per-
sonal reference, but to himself as "Pound the man" rather than as
"Pound the writer": "I sat on the Dogana's steps / For the gon-
dolas cost too much, that year, / And there were not 'those girls',
there was one face." He then cuts to a landscape in which "Gods
float in the azure air," and follows this with a direct presentation,
without any personal interjection, of one of the incidents from *El
Cid*. The canto concludes:

Ignez da Castro murdered, and a wall
Here stripped, here made to stand.
Drear waste, the pigment flakes from the stone,

> Or plaster flakes, Mantegna painted the wall.
> Silk tatters, 'Nec Spe Nec Metu.'   [3/12]

The elimination of all distractions from the physical details of the scene leaves the reader with no choice but to enter into the poet's mood, and the effect is moving and disturbing. The reader passes with the poet through the rooms of the palace, very much aware of the gulf between the present and the past of "Gonzaga's splendor" and uncertain about the relationship between the two. In Canto II, the poet had presented the reader with the problem; now he confronts it himself as he stands contemplating a past which insists on its distance from him, into which he cannot escape and which seems to advise only resignation—that he proceed "Nec Spe Nec Metu," "Neither With Hope Nor Fear."

In Canto 1 the poet writes with complete assurance on matters that are straightforward, but in Canto 7 everything in the present seems problematic. By distinguishing the straightforward from the problematic in these cantos and by noticing how the problematic comes to dominate the poet's concern, we can understand the progression of this sequence and its unity. In Canto 1 he celebrates the genius of Homer, pays tribute to the writer of "The Seafarer," and—by referring us to Andreas Divus's translation of *The Odyssey* and to a Latin version of the *Homeric Hymns* by the Cretan, Georgius Dartonis—insists on the importance of those who transmit the great literature of the past from generation to generation. Here we see Pound at his most assured. His hero, Odysseus, succeeds in his quest, and Pound himself, in his version of Odysseus's descent into Hades, has succeeded in a task which he knows he can execute with the greatest possible skill and assurance. Even in the Cantos I–III, when nothing else seemed entirely satisfactory, this one section satisfied him and is the only passage of any length that he transfers intact to his new version of the poem. In Canto 1, Aphrodite also, shown as she has been presented in the Second Homeric Hymn to her, is beneficent and "mirthful."

In Canto 2, the central episode of Dionysus's enchantment of the sailors is similarly straightforward, but in the rest of the canto, which serves as a frame to the tale, there are hints of the problematic. This story of Dionysus is told in the first Homeric Hymn to the god, but Pound bases his version not on this directly, but on Ovid's rendering of it in *Metamorphoses* 3. By doing so, he places more emphasis on danger. In the Hymn to Dionysus, the singer simply tells how Hecator (Acoetes) escaped the fate of his companions and was rewarded by the god. In Ovid, Acoetes tells his own tale but his narrative is only one part of the main story which tells of Pentheus's denial of Bacchus's divinity and how the king's sacrilege is punished when his mother, in a Bacchic frenzy, mistakes him for a wild boar and tears his body to pieces. Pound intends us to think of this when he has Acoetes say: "And you, Pentheus, / Had as well listen to Tiresias, and to Cadmus, / or your luck will go out of you" (2/9). The speaker, then, in this canto is saved and honored by the god, but he is more passive than Odysseus. Like the *Odyssey* passage in Canto 1, this section of Canto 2 shows Pound at his most assured and the challenge of presenting the imminence of divine energies on the point of taking visible form, calls forth some of his greatest poetic strengths:

> And, out of nothing, a breathing,
> > hot breath on my ankles,
> Beasts like shadows in glass,
> > a furred tail upon nothingness.
> Lynx-purr, and heathery smell of beasts,
> > where tar smell had been,
> Sniff and pad-foot of beasts,
> > eye-glitter out of black air.
> . . . .
> > fur brushing my knee-skin,
> Rustle of airy sheaths,
> > dry forms in the *aether.*   [2/9]

For Acoetes, these energies manifest themselves so completely that the natural gives way to the supernatural, but for the poet in this canto, the natural world remains the primary reality. It offers ambiguous glimpses of the divine world, but these are willed by the poet more than granted by the gods. One can imagine Tyro in Neptune's embrace, but only the water, the beach, and the sea-birds are clearly seen:

> Lithe turning of water,
>> sinews of Poseidon,
> Black azure and hyaline,
>> glass wave over Tyro,
> Close cover, unstillness,
>> bright welter of wave-cords,
> Then quiet water,
>> quiet in the buff sands,
> Sea-fowl stretching wing-joints,
>> splashing in rock-hollows and sand-hollows   [2/10]

The natural scene still offers hints—a "Naviform rock" and a coral formation which suggests the face and arms of a girl—around which one can construct stories of metamorphosis. The poet is ready to respond to this with his own myth of a maritime Daphne:

> If you will lean over the rock,
>> the coral face under wave-tinge,
> Rose-paleness under water-shift,
>> Ileuthyeria, fair Dafne of sea-bords,
> The swimmer's arms turned to branches,
> Who will say in what year,
>> fleeing what band of tritons,
> The smooth brows, seen, and half seen,
>> now ivory stillness.   [2/9]

Yet this reality is very much secondary to the details of the sea-scape itself and pales into insignificance next to the spectacular enchantments of Dionysus. The poet's readiness to grant the immanence of divine energies in the natural world is strong enough to make other earlier writers' accounts of metamorphoses come alive for him, but not sufficient to provide him with a fully satisfactory subject for his own poetry. The natural world remains in all its particularity, but the canto ends retrospectively and fades out—"And we have heard the fauns chiding Proteus / . . . . / And . . ." (2/10).

Pound chooses to begin the canto with a reference to the problem of finding an appropriate form or model for his poem by acknowledging, as he had in Canto I, the impossibility of using Browning's *Sordello* as a model. Shortly after raising this problem, he considers a problem of another kind by alluding to the fatal consequences of the beauty of Helen, "ἐλέναυς and ἐλέπτολις," destroyer of ships and destroyer of cities, for fear of whom the old men of Troy say:

> "Let her go back to the ships,
> Back among Grecian faces, lest evil come on our own,
> Evil and further evil, and a curse cursed on our children,
> Moves, yes she moves like a goddess
> And has the face of a god
>   and the voice of Schoeney's daughters,
> And doom goes with her in walking.   [2/6]

Through Helen, Aphrodite's only protegée, we are reminded that the goddess has a sinister as well as a "mirthful" face.

   ·   In Canto 3 the poet writes of himself more directly, but of how he was in the past:

> I sat on the Dogana's steps
> For the gondolas cost too much, that year,
> And there were not "those girls," there was one face,
> And the Buccentoro twenty yards off, howling "Stretti",
> And the lit cross-beams, that year, in the Morosini,
> And peacocks in Koré's house, or there may have been.
>   [3/11]

The situation is less than ideal. He is short of money, and the fascination of one particular girl is intruded upon by the music of a popular song blaring from the rowing club, "twenty yards off." We learn from Canto I that the girl in question was anyway "young, too young" (I/117). "Or there may have been" has the same deflating effect as the blaring music, and he turns from the imperfections of Venice in 1908 to the more idyllic setting of Lake Garda and Sirmione, whose landscape is hospitable to "Bright gods," "panisks," dryads, and maelids, and where the past supplants the present. The literary hero of this canto, El Cid, is as involved in strenuous activity as Odysseus, but is much closer to us in time and concerned with more mundane problems than Odysseus and Acoetes:

> And he came down from Bivar, Myo Cid,
> With no hawks left there on their perches,
> And no clothes left there in the presses,
> And left his trunk with Raquel and Vidas,
> That big box of sand, with the pawn-brokers,
> To get pay for his menie;   [3/11-12]

We have already seen how the flaking frescoes and tattered silk banners of the Gonzaga with which this canto closes leave the poet stranded in the present, confronted by the pastness of the past.

Canto 4 has been the most elusive of this group of cantos for the critics, and yet its main theme is obvious enough if one considers the content of the many passages out of which it is made. Above all it is about danger, and specifically the danger that results from the beauty of women. We are shown Marguerite of Chateau Roussillon, about to throw herself from a castle window to her death after her husband has given her the heart of her lover, Cabestan, to eat. The swallows crying " 'Tis. 'Tis. 'Ytis!" remind us how her fate echoes that of Tereus whose rape of Philomela is avenged when his wife feeds him the flesh of his own son. Similarly there are echoes of the Greek myth of Actaeon—turned into a stag and hunted to death by his own hounds—in the Provençal story of Piere Vidal, who "ran mad, as a wolf, because of his love for Loba of Penautier" and was hunted by dogs (*P,* 30). Again the danger comes from the beauty of women. Actaeon's "sin" is to have seen Diana bathing naked and this reminds Pound of the story of Gyges, commanded by the Queen of Lydia to kill her husband since, in his pride at his wife's beauty, he had secretly arranged for Gyges to see her naked. The pool of Gargaphia, where Actaeon saw Diana, recalls another fatal pool in Ovid—Pergusa, where Persephone was picking flowers when Pluto, inflamed by her beauty, carried her away to Hell.

If we now turn to the opening lines of the canto, we see how they introduce the main theme:

Palace in smoky light,
Troy but a heap of smouldering boundary stones,
ANAXIFORMINGES! Aurunculeia!   [4/13]

Helen's beauty has reduced Troy to a heap of stones. "ANAXI-
FORMINGES"–"Lords of the lyre," is from Pindar's Second
Olympiad, which begins: "Hymns that are lords of the lyre, what
god, what hero, what man shall we sing of?" Pound's "Auruncu-
leia!," the bride praised by Catullus in his Carmen 61, seems to be
a response to the question implied by "ANAXIFORMINGES!"
and, as such, a way of advising the reader that he will be particu-
larly concerned with women in this canto. The women here are of
quite different types. Some of them have destructive power:
Procne; Helen; Salmacis the water nymph; the wife of Candaules,
who orders Gyges to kill her husband; Loba of Penautier, who
drives Piere Vidal mad; and Diana when she causes the death of
Actaeon. Others like Marguerite, Persephone, and Philomela are
themselves victims. Some, like Aurunculeia and the old woman of
Takasago (see appendix 1), are brides, while Danaë and the Virgin
Mary are "the god's bride." Pound's references to women as vic-
tims and as destroyers firmly establish the theme of the dangers
of love, but perhaps even more central to the canto is the opposi-
tion between the faithful wife and "the god's bride." The Noh
play, *Takasago,* like Catullus's epithalamion, celebrates married
fidelity, but the story of Danaë introduces the idea of passion as
an irresistible force before which mortals are powerless. By giving
emphasis to Danaë, Pound seems to be looking beyond the danger-
ous consequences of adulterous love, to acknowledge the ele-
mental passions which make adultery unavoidable. Like the
wind which cannot be owned or controlled, and over which King
Hsiang has no jurisdiction, Zeus's passion cannot be stayed by
Danaë's father.

Pound has a very personal reason for wanting to consider both
the dangerous consequences and the irresistible nature of adultery,
and once we realize this we can begin to appreciate the full force
of this canto. As he writes this canto, he is thinking not only of his
wife, but also of another woman whom he loves. Dorothy Pound
is associated not only with the references to Catullus's marriage

hymn and to *Takasago,* but also with the references to Provence, since she and her husband had spent the summer of 1919 making a walking tour of the area. In 1914 they had planned to spend part of their honeymoon in Europe, but because of the war it was five years before they could get to the continent. By insetting a reference to Gourdon in his picturing of the procession which leads Aurunculeia from her parent's house to her wedding, Pound links marriage and Provence, and the religious procession by the Garonne which he refers to near the end of the canto would be one that he and his wife had seen in Toulouse in the summer of 1919. We need to look closely at the cryptic closing lines of the canto to see how Pound is concerned not only with the Virgin Mary as "God's bride," but much more personally with two actual women. He writes:

> . . . upon the gilded tower in Ecbatan
> Lay the god's bride, lay ever, waiting the golden rain.
> By Garonne. "Saave!"
> The Garonne is thick like paint,
> Procession,—"Et sa'ave, sa'ave, sa'ave, Regina!"—
> Moves like a worm, in the crowd.
> Adige, thin film of images,
> Across the Adige, by Stefano, Madonna in hortulo,
> As Cavalcanti had seen her.
>   The Centaur's heel plants in the earth loam.
> And we sit here . . .
>   there in the arena . . .   [4/16]

The procession in honor of the Virgin is without dignity and "Moves like a worm in the crowd." In contrast, Stefano da Zevio's painting *Madonna del Roseto* is a particular favorite of his. Cavalcanti would have seen this painting in Verona, as Pound himself has. In Cavalcanti's Sonnet 35, he compares the face of his beloved to that of the Madonna of Or San Michele who is said to perform miracles for those who pray to her (see *T,* 95). Pound refers directly to this poem in Canto I; it is clear that, just as Cavalcanti compares his mistress to the Madonna of Or San Michele, Pound, in Canto 4, is making a connection between Stefano's Madonna and a beloved woman. The transition from religious devotion to human love alerts us to a particularly cryptic allusion to another woman besides his wife with whom Pound is in love. Once we catch this allusion, we can understand the tension in this canto between praise of married love and grim reminders of the consequences of adultery. The lines at issue conclude the canto: "And we sit here . . . / there in the arena . . . ," and refer to the Roman arena in Verona. We find a related and equally cryptic allusion in 29/145: "And another day or evening toward sundown by the arena / (les gradins) / A little lace at the wrist / And not very clean lace either." It is not until we get to 78/481 that we are given any information about whom Pound is with on this occasion: "So we sat there by the arena, / outside, Thiy and il decaduto / the lace cuff fallen over his knuckles" (see appendix 1). A few lines later Pound dates this "1920 or thereabouts." Stock tells us that Thiy is Bride Scratton, a married woman whom Pound had met at Yeats's, and that she and Pound "were very close at this period and saw a good deal of each other" (*Life,* 243). Stock suggests that it is her photograph which William Carlos Williams had seen in Pound's London apartment in March 1910, "with a lighted candle always burning before it" (*Life,* 83). After spending time with Pound in Paris and Italy, she returned to England, and in 1923 her husband divorced her, naming Pound as corespondent. Although Pound had been married since 1914, it seems that he had been in love with Bride Scratton as well as with his wife. (Although Canto 4 was written in October of 1919, chronology proves to be no problem in this case because the last two lines of Canto 4 were not added until the 1930 version in *A Draft of XXX Cantos.*)

Where Canto 4 focuses on passion as both inspirational and destructive, Canto 5 concentrates on the difficulty of accommodating intellectual inspiration to the complications and frustrations of an intractable reality—of keeping the vision of intellectual perfection intact in a sordid present. As the poet thinks of Ecbatan he turns his attention from Danaë on the gilded tower, "awaiting the god's touch," to the streets of the city where the crowd is "Rushing on populous business." These hurrying men, "toga'd . . . and arm'd," announce a shift from the private world of the lover and the writer in seclusion to the more public world of the writer who considers it his duty to write for the benefit of his society in some immediate and practical way. Danaë in the gilded tower is reminiscent of the Lady of Shalott, and the crowded streets of Ecbatan are, like Camelot, another world. Although Pound would be horrified at the suggestion, his transfer of allegiance from the private to the public world is not unlike Tennyson's, even though the problems that confronted Tennyson in mid-Victorian England are far less distressing than the spectacle of Europe after the First World War.

This canto, then, concentrates on the business of intellectual activity, particularly in a social setting. Beginning with the most direct and most intense visionary experiences of the "Intellectual Light," Pound moves to his own more fleeting visionary moments and then to a series of instances in which the pressures and problems of mundane reality become progressively more intrusive and finally completely overwhelming. The murders with which the canto closes become a metaphor for the extinguishing of the light of the intellect, not in the victim alone, but also in the society.

To see this canto as any more than a fairly random collection of fragments, we must look closely at the relationship between its parts and the logic of its progression. Pound moves from Danaë to the busy crowd, then from Ecbatan to Egypt and to the Nile which is first a real river with "Old men and camels / working the water-wheels," and then a symbol of eternity belonging with "Measureless seas and stars" and with the "Divine Light" of the Neoplatonists Iamblichus and Porphyry, the latter identified by his assertion, "Et omniformis [omnis intellectus est]." As the putative author of *On the Mysteries of the Egyptians, Chaldeans and Assyrians,* Iamblichus belongs here by "geographical logic," but Pound's real intention in referring to these Neoplatonists is to show that he endorses their conception of the nature and operation of the *nous.* From the philosophical he moves to the greatest of all literary presentations of the "Divine Light," to Dante's *Paradiso* and specifically here to canto 18 in which the saints, like points of fire, spell out the admonition, "LOVE JUSTICE YOU WHO JUDGE THE EARTH," whirling up like the cloud of sparks that fly up from a burning log when it is struck. Unlike Dante,

Pound is not granted a sustained paradisal vision, but he trusts that the Divine Light is always there even if he can only glimpse it fleetingly: "The fire? always, and the vision always, / Ear dull, perhaps, with the vision, flitting / And fading at will" (5/17). In its most sustained and accessible form the vision manifests itself for him as a "Titter of sound"—as the verbal music of those fragments of the poetry of the past which constantly come unbidden to the poet's mind, in this case the words of Catullus and Sappho. The abrupt change from the triumphant celebration of marriage in Catullus's two hymns to the despondency of Sappho's poem darkens the mood and moves the canto one step nearer to its pessimistic ending. In her poem Sappho imagines Arignota, now married and living in Lydia, homesick for the group of young women among whom she stayed before her marriage and particularly yearning for Atthis:

> Fades light from the sea, and many things
> "Are set abroad and brought to mind of thee,"
> And the vinestocks lie untended, new leaves come to the shoots,
> North wind nips on the bough, and seas in heart
> Toss up chill crests,   [5/18]

In this poem marriage means not fulfillment but deprivation, and has come to separate Arignota from her close friends and particularly from Atthis. "The talks ran long in the night," which follows the Sappho passage, links together Sappho, instructing her association of young girls in the myths and the rites of Aphrodite, with Savairic de Mauleon, to whose castle "came all who for courtesy wished honour and good deeds," whose court Pound describes as one of the "minute vortices" in the "darkness of decentralization" of the Middle Ages (*LE,* 95, 220). Pound tells the story of Gaubertz de Poicebot, a monk who became a troubadour and who, when the woman he loved refused him unless he became a knight, appealed to Savairic who "Gave him his land and knight's fee" (5/18). Here all the emphasis is on the disastrous end to that marriage, on how Gaubertz left his wife to go to Spain and how during his absence she was seduced by an English knight who took her away with him and then abandoned her eight months pregnant. Gaubertz finds her by chance in a brothel and "when he saw her, and she him, great was the grief between them and great shame. And he stopped the night with her, and on the morrow he went forth with her to a nunnery where he had her enter. And for this grief he ceased to sing and to compose" (*LE,* 96). The story of Peire de Maensac which follows, although it shows this troubadour's success in love, also shows the magnitude of the practical complications which arise from his love for another man's wife and from his skill in winning her love through his songs. His abduction of the wife of Bernart de Tierci leads to a full-scale war between her husband, backed by the Church, and the Dauphin of Auvergne who, by taking Peire's part, enables him to keep his Provençal Helen.

The two murders in the last part of the canto set the mood, in the most dramatic way possible, for the triumph of the sordid pressures of reality over the visionary. Pound takes his account of the murder of Giovanni Borgia and of the fortunes of the Renaissance Latinists mentioned here from William Roscoe's *The Life and Pontificate of Leo X.* Giorgio Schiavone, a bargeman on the Tiber, saw the murderers throw Borgia's corpse into the river, and the account that Schiavone makes of this to Giovanni's father, the Pope, is recorded by the Master of Papal Ceremonies, John Burchard, in his diary (see appendix 1). Pound follows Roscoe's translation of the diary to establish the mood for this part of the canto:

> John Borgia is bathed at last (Clock-tick pierces the vision)
> Tiber, dark with the cloak, wet cat gleaming in patches.
> Click of the hooves, through garbage,
> Clutching the greasy stone. "And the cloak floated."
> Slander is up betimes.   [5/18–19]

The slander here is what Roscoe maintains is the unjust assertion that Cesare Borgia was responsible for his brother's murder. Roscoe, who, like Varchi, is "one wanting the facts," contends that Giovanni was murdered by either a jealous lover or the "injured husband" of a woman whom he apparently was in the habit of visiting secretly, and that Cesare had no part in the events of that night.[3] In this sordid setting—"al poco giorno, ed al gran cerchio d'ombra" [To the short day and the great sweep of shadow]—the Latin poets of the time pursue their studies of classical poetry and produce their own polished Latin verses. "Ser D'Alviano" is the famous general Bartolommeo D'Alviano, who, much like Sigismundo Malatesta, "amidst the tumults of war, and the incessant occupations of his active life, had never ceased to cultivate and to encourage literary studies" (*Leo,* 3:285). He established a literary academy in the town of Pordonone and was the patron of Giovanni Cotta, Girolamo Frascatoro (see appendix 1) and Andrea Navagero (*Leo,* 3:285 n.). Roscoe tells us that Navagero "gave a striking proof of his aversion to a false and affected taste, by annually devoting to the flames a copy of the works of Martial; whom he probably considered, as the chief corruptor of that classical purity which distinguished the writers of the Augustan age" (*Leo,* 3:304). Hence Pound's "Navighero, / Burner of yearly Martials."

The depressive note of this last part of the canto is sustained by the pitiful spectacle of the poetaster Baraballo, "arrayed in the triumphal habit of a Roman conqueror," making an abortive attempt to ride on an elephant to the Capitol to be crowned with a laurel wreath to the great amusement of the Pope, his attendants, and the crowd (*Leo,* 3:334–36). (See appendix 1.) Even grimmer is the fate of Giovanni Mozzarello who, because he wrote excellent Latin and Italian verse, was made governor of the fortress of Mondaino by Leo X so that he would have enough income and leisure to continue writing without distraction. He died tragically while he was still young: "having been found . . . suffocated, with his mule, at the bottom of a well; a circumstance which confirmed the suspicions before entertained, that his death was occasioned by the barbarity and resentment of those persons over whom he was appointed to preside" (*Leo,* 3:325–26).

Where the references to the murder of Giovanni Borgia stress the sordidness of the crime, the references to the murder of Alessandro de'Medici by his cousin Lorenzaccio focus on the

3. William Roscoe, *The Life and Pontificate of Leo X,* 4 vols. (Liverpool, 1805), 1: 266–68. Subsequent references to *Leo* will be to volume and page number in this edition.

inevitability of his fate. Alessandro's perverse refusal to heed the astrologer's warnings conspires with the "risoluto / 'E terribile deliberazione" of Lorenzaccio to make this murder inevitable. Pound dwells at some length on the attempt of the historian, Benedetto Varchi, to determine whether Lorenzaccio murdered his kinsman "for love of Florence" or "for a privy spite," and when Varchi concedes that he has insufficient evidence to make a fair decision, Pound admires his scrupulousness, claiming that "the light of the Renaissance shines in Varchi when he declines to pass judgment on Lorenzaccio" (*LE*, 355). By the end of this canto we have moved from the mind illuminated by intimations of the divine to the mind bent on murder; from the vision of intellectual perfection to the intractable and sordid present; from the inspired poet to the conscientious historian.

Canto 6 is considerably more reassuring. It refers to the problems of men of action like Guillaume of Poitiers, Louis VII of France, and Theseus, and to the difficulties of Bernart de Ventadour and Sordello, two troubadours in love, but it is primarily intended to be a tribute to Eleanor of Aquitaine (see appendix 1) and Cunizza da Romano (see appendix 1). The nobility and beauty of these women have inspired not only the poets of their own day but also later writers like Pound himself, and this canto suggests that practical problems and frustrations can be transcended through the power of love and the poetic inspiration which can flow from it. This canto anticipates Canto 36 on Cavalcanti's celebration of the inspirational power of love in his "Donna mi prega." Even if they can be transcended for a while, the problems of action in the present remain to be handled, and Pound reminds us of this at the end of Canto 6. His reference to Theseus's narrow escape from poisoning at his father's court, with which the canto closes, prepares us for the poet's confrontation of his own problems in the next canto.

In Canto 7, Pound squarely confronts his problems as a writer in the present and voices his frustration at the intellectually enervating atmosphere of London and Paris. He first recalls the great writers of the tradition in which he hopes to establish himself. These are the writers who have impressed him by the minuteness and particularity of their observations and their ear for language—

Homer, Ovid, Bertrand de Born, Dante, Flaubert, and James. From Dante's panoramic vision to the claustrophobic nineteenth century interiors of Flaubert and James is a great leap. Pound imagines James moving *"Grave incessu,"* with heavy gait, through the tasteless, oppressive rooms of Edwardian "polite society," whose atmosphere he conveyed so exactly and which remain for Pound essentially unchanged. The people Pound sees around him seem themselves to be trapped in the world that James describes and held in a kind of enchantment—"Thin husks I had known as men, / Dry casques of departed locusts / speaking a shell of speech." James belongs too irrevocably to the last century to be able to serve as a guide to younger American writers like Pound and like Eliot, whose "Portrait of a Lady" is echoed in:

> We also made ghostly visits, and the stair
> That knew us, found us again on the turn of it,
> Knocking at empty rooms, seeking for buried beauty;
> And the sun-tanned, gracious and well-formed fingers
> Lift no latch of bent bronze, no Empire handle
> Twists for the knocker's fall; no voice to answer.   [7/25]

Eliot had found Paris in 1910 and 1911 depressing and disorienting, and his temporary return to Boston—in which his "Portrait" is set—was at a period of considerable confusion about his writing and his career. Eliot returned to Europe in 1914 and settled in London where he met Pound. Pound moved from London to Paris in December 1920, but, as we see from this canto, Paris provided little relief from his feeling that his heroes of the past, like Lorenzaccio, are "more full of flames and voices" than his dessicated contemporaries.

In this canto the women are not sources of literary inspiration, as Eleanor and Cunizza had been for the poets of their time, and Pound's opening line "Eleanor (she spoiled in a British climate)" prepares us for this. He mentions the death of beautiful women—of "Ione" and of the woman in Liu Ch'e's poem (see *P,* 112, 108)—and also associates women with the stifling of passion and vitality. Dido, mourning her murdered husband, tries to turn away from the possibilities of love in the present—"Drowning, with tears, new Eros"—and offers another instance of the dead hand of the past, Pound's main concern in this canto. Of another once-beautiful woman Pound writes: "Still the old dead dry talk, gassed out— / It is ten years gone, makes stiff about her a glass, / A petre-faction of air." She reminds us a little of the woman in Eliot's "Portrait" and even more of the subject of Pound's own "Portrait d'une Femme." The curious and miscellaneous reminiscences of Pound's lady, even though of little intrinsic value, still had the power to fascinate the poet, but this is no longer the case with her counterpart in this canto who has herself become a kind of curio, encased in glass. Sordello found his inspiration in a flesh-and-blood woman who was both beautiful and strong-willed, a woman en-dowed—Pound claims—with "charm and imperial bearing, grace . . . [and] that vigour which is a grace in itself" (*GK,* 107–08). Pound must rely for inspiration on something less substantial: the possibility of passion is held in his mind and manifests itself in the apparition of "Nicea," the beautiful, naked woman whose shape moves before him as he walks the cold Paris streets—"we alone having being." When, at the end of the canto she turns to face him, he recognizes her as Aphrodite, "Eternal watcher of things, / Of things, of men, of passions. / Eyes floating in dry, dark air, / E biondo, with glass-grey iris." Aphrodite at the end of Canto 1 was "mirthful," but here she is inscrutable.

Cantos 8–30

The Repeat in History: The Renaissance

The block of four "Malatesta Cantos" which follows is strategi-cally placed and prepares us for the strong emphasis on the Italian Renaissance in this sequence of the poem. Pound realizes that the unremitting problems and hardships of Sigismundo's career make him a far more appropriate hero than Valla who, one of Pound's sources says, when he ceased to be subversive, "Took a fat living from the Papacy" (III/250). By contrast, Sigismundo's whole life was one long political and military struggle, and Pius II, when he finally defeated him, confiscated most of his lands. In spite of his constant shortage of money, and in the midst of wars, Sigismundo nevertheless managed to be a generous and discriminating patron, and Pound considers his "Tempio Malatestiano" in Rimini "perhaps the apex of what one man has embodied in the last 1000 years of the occident." He reminds us that the Tempio was built "outside the then system, and pretty much against the power that was, and in any case without great material resources" (*GK,* 159). It was also, appropriately, unfinished for lack of funds: "And there was grass on the floor of the temple, / Or where the floor of it might have been" (21/98).

By emphasizing the waning of the creative power of the Renaissance as early as the fifth canto, Pound prepares us for the deepening gloom and mounting disillusion in Cantos 1–30. Sigismundo's example and achievement prove to be the high point of the sequence and, by comparison, Pound's tribute to the Medici in Canto 21 is far more cursory and far less enthusiastic. He clearly cannot discount Lorenzo il Magnifico's contributions to culture, yet we sense a certain disapproval of the Medici wealth. Pound is torn between admiration for their shrewdness and enterprise and his regret that Sigismundo did not have their resources at his disposal:

> And he begat one pope [Leo X] and one son
>   and four daughters,
> And an University, Pisa; (Lauro Medici)
> And nearly went broke in his business,
> And bought land in Siena and Pisa,
> And made peace by his own talk in Naples.
> And there was grass on the floor of the temple,
> Or where the floor of it might have been . . .   [21/98]

Pound chooses Niccolò d'Este's execution of Parisina and Ugo as the central incident of Canto 20, but the canto as a whole is more concerned with the poet's own struggle than with Niccolò's remorse. Canto 24, however, is devoted to Niccolò's life from the trip to Greece and Jerusalem that he made when he was twenty-nine, through the execution of Parisina and his third marriage, to his death. Niccolò produced nothing comparable to Malatesta's

Tempio, and the decoration of the *Salone dei Mesi* in the Palazzo Schifanoia mentioned at the end of the canto was arranged by his illegitimate sons Leonello and Borso who succeeded him and under whom the court at Ferrara became a great cultural center. Pound's attention seems first to have been caught by the incident of Parisina's execution and then he becomes fascinated by Niccolò in spite of the latter's obvious shortcomings. He was notorious for the large number of illegitimate children he fathered, and Pound includes a reference to this in his brief description of his hero as, "Affable, bullnecked, that brought seduction in place of / Rape into government, ter pacis Italiae auctor" (24/112). Pound finds Niccolò a sympathetic figure despite his wrongheadedness and suggests that a decisive act, even if it is brutal, is preferable to the inactivity of those who make nothing and "set nothing in order," whose "dead concepts" he contrasts to "the solid, the blood rite, / The vanity of Ferrara" (25/118). When, in the detention camp at Pisa, Pound confronts the prospect of his own death, he remembers Niccolò who "By Ferrara was buried naked" (82/526).

In Canto 25, on the Venetian Republic, Pound emphasizes the impersonality and officiousness of the Venetian government by council and contrasts the Council Major's patronage of Titian to the highly personal involvement of a ruler like Sigismundo with the artists under his patronage. Sigismundo sends instructions to let his "*Maestro di pentore*," Piero della Francesca, "work as he likes, / Or waste his time as he likes, / . . . / never lacking provision" (8/29), whereas the Venetian Council requires Titian to repay all the money that he has received during the period when he suspended work on his "Battle of Spoleto" (25/120). Titian habitually failed to finish his paintings on schedule, and this, the greatest of his secular paintings, took him twenty-five years to complete. Without personal involvement between patron and artist, patronage becomes no more than a financial transaction.

Canto 26 serves as the organizing center of the Italian references in this sequence. The central event is the arrival in Venice in 1438 of the Byzantine Emperor and the Patriarch of Constantinople with their entourage—among them Gemistus Plethon—who are on their way to participate in the Council of Ferrara-Florence. They have come to Italy to secure a promise of papal aide in their

defense of their empire against the Turks and to this end are pre-
pared to agree to the unification of the Greek and Roman churches,
even though this will be tantamount to their submission to the
Pope. Their mission is finally a failure. The unification is rejected
by the Byzantine people and the promised military aid proves
ineffectual—fifteen years later Constantinople falls to the Turks.
Even though politically little is achieved, culturally the visit of the
Byzantines has a positive outcome since it results in Gemistus's
meeting with Cosimo de'Medici which leads to the founding of the
Platonic Academy in Florence. For the purposes of the poem also
the visit is fortuitous, since on this occasion most of the personali-
ties of the period who have played important parts in the poem to
date are in Venice at the same time. Cosimo de'Medici, currently
in exile from Florence, has been made ambassador of the Venetians
"for his great wisdom and money" (26/124). Niccolò d'Este has
come to see the Emperor, and the party later goes to his court in
Ferrara. Francesco Gonzaga has come with Niccolò for the joust-
ing (26/123); later his grandson will marry Niccolò's grand-
daughter, the same Isabella who will be the patron of the greatest
artists of her day and whose motto—"Nec Spe Nec Metu"—con-
cludes Canto 3. Sigismundo is briefly in Venice on "government
business" before returning to his troops in the field; he and his
brother "Novvy" are making war on the papal troups with the
covert support of the Venetians who will give them money to en-
gage soldiers rather than sending soldiers outright. In the mean-
time, Nicolo Sagundino, spokesman for the Venetians at Rome, is
under pressure to arrange a peace between the Malatesta and Pius
II as quickly as possible. Sigismundo's uncle Carlo is also men-
tioned, the father of Parisina who was beheaded by Niccolò thir-
teen years earlier. Sigismundo as well as Cosimo was impressed by
Gemistus's Neoplatonism and after the philosopher died in the
Peloponnesus, Sigismundo had his body brought to the Tempio to
lie in one of the sarcophagi. (Pound is by this point much more
interested in the philosophical influence of Gemistus than in the
linguistic acuity of Valla.)

   Canto 26 also makes several points on the important subject
of patronage. The canto begins with a reference to Pound himself
as a young and aspiring poet, in Venice, with no patron and almost

no money. His case is contrasted to that of Matteo de'Pasti who can rely on his patron Sigismundo to help him prove his innocence when he is accused of treason. Alessandro Sforza is also presented as a patron who appreciates his protegés and we learn that he entrusted Pisanello with the responsibility of buying horses for him on the strength of his ability to paint them so well. Mozart's dealings with the Archbishop of Salzburg—with which the canto closes—were, on the other hand, completely unsatisfactory, and because he was not paid enough to live on, Mozart asked to be free to leave.

Pound chooses to close the first sequence of *The Cantos* with a passage which focuses on Cesare Borgia. He reproduces part of a letter written to the new "Duke of the Romagna" by Hieronymus Soncinus, informing him that he has brought to Cesare's press at Fano the famous typecutter, Francesco Griffo of Bologna, who had designed the italic and cursive Greek type for the Aldine Press at Venice, and that he has also engaged other expert typecutters, printers, and compositors who can print not only in Latin and Italian but also in Greek and Hebrew. The date, "7th July 1503," together with the closing reference to the death of Pope Alessandro Borgia in August of the same year, invites us to consider the setting for this publishing activity, and we find that this is a fateful time both for the cities of the Romagna and for Cesare Borgia. In the last four years he had taken by force Imola, Forlì, Cesena, Rimini, Pesaro, Facenza, and Urbino, but in 1503 the Pope, his father, suddenly died and by November of that same year he had been arrested. Yet the Romagna was never again to be as it was, and formerly independent city-states like Rimini now fell under papal rule. It is ironic that Cesare's unlooked-for destruction should have come so suddenly and so soon after this optimistic and forward-looking communication from Soncinus, yet Pound seems to be looking beyond this to make a more serious point— to show how the transmission of culture continued even under the most unpropitious circumstances, uninterrupted by the political chaos of the times. Pound intends the reader to contrast the lack of concern for culture of those with power in the twentieth century with the automatic support for the arts of a ruler even as unscrupulous and self-seeking as Cesare Borgia who has no compunction about seizing Rimini yet considers it his duty to set up a press to print, among other things, "a codex once of the Lords Malatesta."

The Hell of the Present

When we turn to those cantos which deal with the "Hell" of the present, we find not generous patrons but "obstructors of knowledge, / obstructors of distribution" (14/63). We have already seen how the Hell Cantos are written as a direct attack on such people, and in other cantos Pound shows us in more detail exactly what abuses he is most distressed by. Canto 12, for example, shows what kind of people become wealthy in the twentieth century. Baldy Bacon gets rich by hoarding copper pennies and then selling them back at interest and by making crooked insurance deals. He makes money from other people's misfortunes and even engineers the misfortunes himself. José María dos Santos becomes "a great landlord of Portugal" because of his shrewdness in realizing that a cargo of wet grain, considered worthless by everyone else, was ideal pig-food. His scheme is certainly enterprising and harmless enough—it even shows Chicago that you do not have to be corrupt to be rich—but he is clearly not in the same category as someone like Sigismundo Malatesta, and an "aristocracy" of such men is unlikely to make much contribution to the level of culture in their own time. To remind us that the rare breed of enlightened modern patrons is not yet completely extinct, Pound mentions John Quinn ("Jim X"), the New York lawyer who had given generous support to Gaudier, Lewis, Joyce, and Pound, among others. Pound transfers to him his own outrage at the usurers—"the ranked presbyterians, / Directors, dealers through holding companies, / Deacons in churches, owning slum properties, / *Alias* usurers in excelsis" (12/55)—and relates how, at a banker's meeting, he decided to relieve the boredom by telling a "dirty joke." The "Honest Sailor" of the story serves, among other things, as a kind of totally debased modern Odysseus-figure, rather as Eliot's original long version of "Death by Water" offers a wasteland counterpart to an Odyssean voyage.

The present as it appears in Cantos 18 and 19 is largely made up of crooked financial deals, monopolies, and racketeering, and here we find Pound's supreme villains, the war profiteers and arms manufacturers. Foremost among these is Sir Basil Zaharoff ("Zenos Metevsky"), a man of great wealth and international power who owes both to the sale of munitions and to whom war is simply an opportunity to sell arms to both sides. Canto 41 ends with more instances of this macabre practice:

> 120 million german fuses used by the allies to kill Germans
> British gunsights from Jena
> Schneider Creusot armed Turkey
> Copper from England thru Sweden . . . Mr. Hatfield
> Patented his new shell in eight countries.
> > ad interim 1933   [41/206]

In Canto 22 Pound makes the point that determination and honest effort alone will not lead to success. His grandfather "sweat blood / to put through that railway," but his lumber business was broken up by Weyerhaeuser's crooked dealings. Integrity is a liability—to succeed, Pound suggests, one must cheat on a grand scale or come up with some clever gimmick like Pa Stadtvolk's gutter hooks in Canto 28. Pound is always pleased to number scientists among his present day heroes and in Canto 27 he pays tribute to the heroism of Dr. Spahlinger, the inventor of an anti-tuberculosis serum, and Pierre Curie:

> Ten million germs in his face,
> "That is part of the risk and happens
> "About twice a year in tubercular research, Dr. Spahlinger . . ."
> "J'ai obtenu" said M. Curie, or some other scientist
> "A burn that cost me six months in curing,"
> And continued his experiments.   [27/129]

Now that society is so complex, sound leadership is crucial, yet politicians are either ineffective or ludicrous. In the Middle Ages, the poet believes, society was so cohesive and communities were so small that the whole community could work together spontaneously to create something of lasting beauty. He says of the building of the Cathedral of Ferrara that "All rushed out and built the duomo, / Went as one man without leaders / And the perfect measure took form" (27/130). In contrast, Russian communism which could have offered exciting possibilities for the improvement of civilization and the arts proves to be a complete disappointment. The Graces hover over Tovarisch, but he does not respond. He has a chance to build a great new culture—"carved stone upon stone. / But in sleep, in the waking dream, / Petal'd the air," but he "rose, and talked folly on folly, / And walked forth and lay in the earth" (27/131). Helios invites him, but he will not build a civilization to replace that ruined in Provence, "where loose stone hangs upon stone."

Canto 28 presents a series of portraits to illustrate the deadness and lethargy that Pound feels characterizes Europe in the present. We are shown several embarrassing Americans: the vacuous "Emersonian," Mr. Lourpee; Mrs. Kreffle—who doesn't pay her bills—and her listless daughter; the New York drama critic unwittingly lodged with his family in a bordello; the old woman from Kansas sitting in the waiting room of the station at Chiasso as though waiting for the train for Topeka. Such people seem to be trying to keep what is worst about the American character intact in Europe and this tendency is apparently institutionalized in a certain "Great moral secret service plan," which seems to be a kind of secret police in Paris, made up of American veterans who will round up and deport offending Americans like Frank Robert Iriquois, who is expelled on a narcotics charge. Pound also comments on the degeneration of the artistocracy in his reference to the "Second Baronet," who is surprised that one should read books, and to "Prince Oltrepassimo," who owned Myron's *Discobolus* which he kept shut away where the public could not see it and whose body now lies in state, with a hole in one sock and with children running into the chapel and a cat stepping over him. Even in the field of aviation, one of the few endeavors which still offer some opportunity for heroism, courage alone will not merit recognition—one must also be an "official pet" or notorious for scandalous reasons or "a placard for non-smokers or non-alcohol" or for "the code of Peoria" (28/140).

In his descriptions of the "Hell" of the present and in his accounts of the "repeat" of present problems in the Renaissance, Pound's approach is predominantly factual and usually more objective than subjective. The more personal passages are those which belong in the third category, those in which the poet makes some contact with the "divine or permanent world," and in these the poet's struggle is presented in an immediate and dramatic way. These passages reveal the poet's confusion and indecision about how best to deal with the intractable reality of his own present, and for this reason they are complex and often difficult, yet, at the same time are the most dynamic part of this sequence.

The Paradisal and Its Complications

Cantos 17-27 were published as a group in 1928 and in five of these cantos Pound is particularly concerned with the complications of the paradisal. In Canto 17 we are given the two poles of the paradisal—its most concrete manifestation in marble and its most evanescent as states of mind, here, as so often in the poem, represented by the apparition of pagan deities. We expect that sexual love will also be an important component of the paradisal, yet we find that in this section of the poem, as in Cantos 1-7, Pound approaches this subject with a good deal of ambivalence. He does allude to personal relationships in Cantos 21 and 23, but in a carefully veiled way, and before this, in Canto 20, sexuality is presented as highly dangerous. Canto 25 makes a summarizing statement about the paradisal, but it is too general to be entirely effective, and the poet's frustration at "the female" is voiced strongly in Canto 29. It is clearly difficult for him to reconcile his mythic assertions about sexuality with the realities of his personal experience and, with the honesty which we expect of Pound, he does not allow himself to gloss over the disparity between the two.

In Canto 17 we are given an insight into Pound's state of mind when he was in Venice in 1908, and, more generally, we see what the city represents for him. The architecture and sculpture of Venice make a statement about human artistic creativity and Pound finds "in Venice more affirmations / of individual men / . . . than any elsewhere" (104/743). He finds this inspiring but also somewhat unsettling; this spectacle of sculptural skill and ingenuity acts as an incentive but suggests no definite direction. Venice belongs to the past—it is a *fait accompli*—and to be creative himself, Pound must go elsewhere. There is little room for the present in this city and throughout the canto Pound stresses its "unreality." Two levels of reality alternate in the canto so that it falls into six parts. On one level are the "landscapes of the gods" which are seen by daylight and on the other are scenes of the city illuminated by "light not of the sun" so that Venice is made to seem magnificent and yet strangely artificial and insubstantial. The poet, symbolically metamorphosed into a vine stock, sees Diana on "The green slope, with white hounds / leaping about her" and then sees Dionysus himself and gods and nymphs "under the almond-trees" with the sea in the distance. Hermes and Athene, the protectors of Odysseus, are here also, preparing us for the linking of Odysseus and Pound which is implicit in the third of these scenes. Here the poet is on the shore itself, watching "Zothar" and her dancers performing rites in honor of Isis and seeing Persephone in "the bright meadow" before she has been snatched away by Pluto. "Gray light, with Athene," is an allusion to the mist which the goddess creates around Odysseus when he is laid sleeping on the shore of Ithaca by the Phaeacians and which makes the place unreal and unrecognizable so that he is not aware, at first, that he has finally returned to his homeland.

Odysseus is set ashore in the cove of Phorcys, "The Old Man of the Sea" at the head of which is the cavern of the Naiads. Nereus is also known as "The Old Man of the Sea," and Pound has created his female counterpart when he writes of the "Cave of Nerea." Her "cave" is described in the first of three passages on Venice, and to reach it the poet must pass "Marble trunks out of stillness," and go "on past the palazzi." The "cave" is, in fact, a part of the architecture of the city—the dimly lit interior of St. Mark's Cathedral:

> salt-white, and glare purple,
> cool, porphyry smooth,
> the rock sea worn.
> No gull-cry, no sound of porpoise,
> . . . .
> Sand as of malachite, and no cold there,
> the light not of the sun. [17/77]

Pound writes in *Jefferson and/or Mussolini* of "the spirit that filled the Quattrocento cathedrals with the slabs of malachite, porphyry, lapis lazuli" (30), and when he says that the "Cave of Nerea" is "like a great shell curved," and mentions its "glare purple" and porphyry, we remember that, for Oscar Wilde also, "the pearl and purple of the sea shell is echoed in the church of St. Mark in Venice."[4] Looking at the mosaics which cover the interior of the domes, Pound notices how, " 'In the gloom the gold / Gathers the light about it' . . ." [17/78].

At the end of his life he would return to Venice, but now the city is a place to come to, not a place to stay; one must go elsewhere to get on with the serious business of living and writing. Yet it is necessary to return to Venice at times to get one's bearings. Sigismundo came there "after that wreck in Dalmatia," and "Borso, Carmagnola, the men of craft, *i vitrei,* / Thither, at one time, time after time." In 1908 Pound too, overwhelmed with doubts about the feasibility of making a career of poetry, had found himself reanimated by the sun of Venice to which, in "Alma Sol Veneziae," he had written:

> Thou that hast given me back
> Strength for the journey,
> Thou that hast given me back
> Heart for the Tourney,
>
> O Sun venezian,
> Thou that thru all my veins
> Hast bid the life-blood run.   [*CEP,* 246]

He remembers this in this canto where he becomes the son of the Sun-God, "brother of Circe" and sees "the sun for three days, the sun fulvid, / As a lion lift over sand-plain; / . . . / Splendour, as the splendour of Hermes" (17/79).

He does recommit himself, in the next two cantos, to the painful task of anatomizing his own times, but in Canto 20 he returns

4. Oscar Wilde, *The Critic as Artist,* ed. Richard Ellmann (New York, 1968), p. 371.

to the complications of the paradisal. This canto is very complex, but is crucial to our understanding of the nature of the poet's struggle at this time. The main concern of the canto is the danger of hedonism, both sensual and intellectual. The doomed sensualists are Parisina and Ugo, and the "intellectual hedonist" is Pound the young student of Romance and classical literature whose fondness for the poetry of the past threatens to make him an escapist. At the beginning of the canto some of Pound's favorite lines from the poetry of Bernart de Ventadour, Cavalcanti, Propertius, and Ovid are compared to the song of the sirens—"Ligur' aoide",— and he dramatizes the escapist state of mind which he falls into when he is absorbed in the study of Provençal poetry by describing an idyllic pastoral landscape outside of time. This is a hedonist's paradise—ideal both for the aesthete and for the sensualist— where one "would be happy for the smell of that place / And never tired of being there, either alone / Or accompanied" (20/90). Here one could easily become a lotus-eater or give oneself over to passion without thinking of its possible dangers since here the warning song of the nightingale is "too far off to be heard."

The poet, however, is both aware of and troubled by the dangerous consequences of hedonism, as we see from his decision to focus on the fate of Parisina and Ugo and on Niccolò, delirious with remorse at his own brutality. Niccolò's delirium provides an extreme correlative to the poet's own sense of confusion and Pound continues to link the escapism of the aesthete with that of the sensualist by having Niccolò confusedly identify himself with the heroes of some of the very works of classical and Romance literature that Pound himself has studied and written on in the past. Niccolò, in his delirium, sees himself as Roland betrayed and as King Sancho inflamed with love for his own sister, and compares Parisina to Helen and the fall of the house of Este to the fall of Troy.

The lotus-eaters in the section which follows Niccolò's delirium are hedonists who are confirmed in their escapism, and Pound cleverly makes them simultaneously aesthetes and sensualists. Although the attitudes and gestures of the lotus-eaters are described with great precision, it is very hard to see quite how they fit together or to know how to visualize the complete scene, and we understand the reason for our difficulty once we discover that Pound is describing an actual picture, and a highly unusual one at that. His figures, "Floating, each on invisible raft, / On the high current, invisible fluid," are modelled on the pairs of lovers from the Second Circle of Dante's Hell as Blake has pictured them in "The Circle of the Lustful: Francesca da Rimini." Pound's languid lotus-eaters are very far from Dante's tormented souls who shriek and moan as they are driven before the blast of the black wind, yet it is not Pound but Blake who has commuted their sentence and who shows them in a state of voluptuous ease so that, with only a few exceptions, they do seem, as Pound says, "Swift, as if joyous" (see appendix 1). We cannot visualize Pound's lotus-eaters successfully until we discover Blake's engraving and when we do that we cannot dissociate them from the souls of the

Figure 3. William Blake, *The Circle of the Lustful: Francesca da Rimini.*
"Floating, each on invisible raft,
On the high current, invisible fluid." [20/92]

lustful, among them Paolo and Francesca in their forked flame—
"nel fuoco d'amore"—whom Pound has earlier in the canto com-
pared to Parisina and Ugo.

To this extent, the lotus-eaters are sensualists, but the poet
wants us to think of them as aesthetes also. The incense which en-
velops them smells like "hay in the sun," recalling the "hay-fields
under sun swath" of the poet's idyllic "Provençal" landscape, and,
once they speak, we do not think of them as "the lustful":

> Lotophagoi of the suave nails, quiet, scornful,
> Voce-profondo:
> > "Feared neither death nor pain for this beauty;
> If harm, harm to ourselves."   [20/93]

Pound, like Tennyson, although he cannot accept the lotus-eaters'
reasons, allows them to justify their desire to escape by recounting
the hardships of their voyage. He ends by comparing the attrac-
tion of their philosophy of life to the seductive beauty of the great
poetry of the past when he describes both as "Ligur' aoide," but it
is clear that the poet is determined to stop his ears against the song
and to commit himself to action.

The strange, somnolent Dionysiac procession at the end of the
canto suggests a continuation of the drugged state of the lotus-
eaters, but what begins as claustrophobic and enervating finally
becomes more sinister. Between two gilded, baroque columns we
see "Vanoka, leaning half naked, / waste hall there behind her,"
and the "waste hall" suggests the void which finally awaits the
hedonist—both the sensualist and the literary aesthete who allows
his enchantment with the literature of the past to divert him from
the task of writing about his own times. By showing Isotta and
Sallustio in this procession, Pound also seems to suggest that the
Malatesta have now served their purpose in his poem and must be
relegated to their place in the romantic past; that to dwell on them
further would be to choose to become a "lotus-eater" himself.

Between Niccolò's delirium and the description of the lotus-
eaters we find a brief and cryptic passage in which the poet voices
both his present confusion and his expectation that it will be the
"basis of renewals." The jungle imagery and vivid colors suggest
that the confusion stems from an overabundance of energy and we

assume that it bears some relation to Niccolò's own confusion after he has acted rashly in passion and anger. To reject the detachment of the lotus-eaters and to commit oneself to acting with passion is to run the risk of acting rashly and unwisely, but this is a risk that Pound is willing to take.

For Pound, as for Niccolò, the confusion has a good deal to do with the complications of love as we see in Canto 21, where allusions to the poet's relationship with Bride Scratton are followed by a passage which specifically echoes the "confusion and renewals" passage of Canto 20. In May of 1920 Pound and his wife were in Venice and then went on to Sirmione and, in June, to Paris. It seems that he was concurrently spending time with Bride Scratton since he says that in this year he was with her in Verona. We are advised of her presence by: "and we sit here / By the arena, *les gradins* . . . ," after which the scene changes to Venice. "Voices of the procession, / Faint now, from below us," recalls the religious procession by the Garonne from Canto 4 and so suggests Dorothy Pound, as does "Grow with the Pines of Ise"—a reference to the twin pines of *Takasago* which represent married fidelity. When he writes: "In the dawn, as the fleet coming in after Actium," Pound's allusion to Cleopatra indirectly suggests Bride, whom he chooses to call "Thiy" after another Egyptian queen. (See appendix 1.) As in Canto 17 we move from Venice to a "landscape of the gods" where we find Diana's hounds on the slope, Athene, and Diana herself (Titania). This time the gods appear at night and their presence is troubling. The moon creates "confusion"; by moonlight "Yellow wing," "Green wing," "Pomegranate," and "White horn" all look similarly "pale." Again, as in Canto 20, he trusts that confusion is "source of renewals," but at this point the confusion prevails. The complications of Pound's personal relationships mean that the unqualified celebration of sexual energies —through allusions to pagan deities—represents an oversimplification. For this reason the gods have now become "discontinuous."

Canto 25 makes a further comment on this matter, but first, in Canto 23, we find an allusion to Pound's relationship with another woman. The central episode of the canto is an idyllic interlude with the poet standing with his beloved at a window on a hill overlooking the sea, watching men on the beach below emptying sand from their boat. The hillside with its olive trees and view of the

Figure 4. Stefano da Zevio, *Madonna del Roseto*.
"Under the arras, or wall painted below like arras
And above with a garden of rose-trees." [23/108]

ocean suggests that Pound is in Rapallo and not in the apartment on the seafront where he and his wife stay, but in Olga Rudge's apartment in Sant' Ambrogio, on the hill above Rapallo. As he looks at the view from the window he recalls standing at another window with a woman—presumably Olga Rudge, but possibly Bride Scratton—and looking at a deceptively similar view where, though inland, the "hill-gap, in mist" looked "like sea-coast." It seems that on this other occasion they were in Verona since "As we had lain there in the autumn / Under the arras, or wall painted below like arras, / And above with a garden of rose-trees," is a very exact description of the background to Stefano da Zevio's *Madonna del Roseto.* When Pound says that they were "under" this, he must be referring to the location of their room with respect to the Palazzo Laveozzola Pompei in which the painting at that time hung (*Era,* 358).

In Canto 25 Pound returns to the subject of passion to make some general recapitulation of his position. Drawing from Cantos 17 and 21 he begins with Venice at night:

> and the palace hangs there in the dawn, the mist,
> in that dimness,
> or as one rows in from the past the murazzi
> the barge slow after moon-rise
> and the voice sounding under the sail   [25/117]

He chooses to generalize his presentation of passionate love by focussing on the Roman poet Sulpicia rather than a specific beloved woman. She is more real than the "discontinuous gods" and yet frees the poet from being too personal. Her call to her lover to "Put away fear" and her reassurance that "god does not harm lovers" challenge the sterility of those who have created their own circle of hell by concession to empty proprieties and by their refusal to be imaginative or creative. It is here that the poet suggests that even Niccolò d'Este can be more readily excused than they when he writes: "the dead concepts, never the solid, the blood rite, / The vanity of Ferrara." Finally the poet makes the transition from physical passion to the realm of the intellect, of "thought . . . the deathless": "Form, forms and renewal, gods held in the air, / Forms seen, and then clearness, / Bright void, without image." The poet, having recognized the limitations of mythic statement is now "Casting his gods back into the νους."

Pound's confusion about the discrepancy between the simplicity of the ideal of "inluminatio coitu" and the very real complications that can arise as a result of it is far from resolved, as we see when we turn to Canto 29. Here, as we have already noted, Pound gives in to a Lewisian rhetoric and, quite out of character, demeans the female as "a chaos, / An octopus / A biological process," and as fit only to provide men with inspiration and incapable of creating anything intellectual herself. The only places where things can be properly made, he says, are in men's minds or women's wombs. Behind the superciliousness we sense considerable frustration, but he then turns to write more characteristically about two occasions when he was with Eliot, first at Excideuil when Dorothy Pound was one of the party and then in Verona when Pound was with Bride Scratton. The canto ends with another scene of Venice by night.

The "Compleynte to Artemis" with which Canto 30 begins is in part an announcement that he has chosen to set aside his personal confusions for the time being and to concentrate on more definite matters. Artemis here is the cool, dispassionate intellect, untrammeled by "weak" emotional considerations. By attacking pity rather than just sentimentality, Pound is announcing his resolve to choose the intellectual rather than the emotional approach in his poem. Pity seems to him a tacit acceptance of the evils which have injured the object of pity: his job is to root out the evils themselves. He seems to see compassion and reform as mutually exclusive and reaffirms his decision to turn his back on his own feelings and to stick to facts.

Eleven New Cantos *and the* Fifth Decad

In these cantos we find that Pound has, in fact, chosen to subordinate his personal struggle to his concern with the struggle against usury. *Eleven New Cantos* moves from the good sense of Jefferson and Adams to Jackson and Van Buren's fight against the Second

United States Bank, and closes with a celebration of Mussolini's policies, which seem to Pound to be the only serious attempt to curtail the power of the usurers in his own time. The *Fifth Decad* celebrates the founding of the Sienese Communal Bank, the *Monte dei Paschi,* and praises the achievements of Leopold II and Ferdinand III of Tuscany, offering these as a precedent for Mussolini's policies and suggesting that the Duce is part of a tradition of economically responsible government in Italy. In both sequences Pound attempts to judge the strength of the usurers and their opponents, and in both he ends on a pessimistic note.

Pound keeps so singlemindedly to his researches into the fight against usury in America and Europe that only four cantos are devoted to other matters and only two—Cantos 39 and 47—are personal and nonliterary. His dogged anatomizing of usury and social decline has served to keep any anxieties about personal relationships or personal objectives well in the background. Cantos 39 and 47 suggest that at this period he has subconsciously chosen to hide any personal anxieties from himself, not only for the purposes of his poem, but perhaps also in general. He chooses to treat the subject of love generally rather than personally and intimately. Canto 36, for example, he devotes to *"Donna mi prega"* which, as we have seen in chapter 1, interests him as a complex metaphysical speculation on the operation of love. In Cantos 39 and 47, sexuality is ritualized. In both he emphasizes the need to leave Circe and travel to Hell in what seems to be a justification of his subordination of personal to social matters.

The ritual which concludes Canto 39 is wholly positive, but the rest of the canto is troubling. At first we see the poet in his home setting, at Olga Rudge's apartment in Sant' Ambrogio, but he is in an unsettled state of mind and the opening word of the canto forewarns us of this: "Desolate is the roof where the cat sat, / Desolate is the iron rail that he walked / And the corner post whence he greeted the sunrise." The sound of the olive press on the ground floor of the building suggests to him the clacking of a loom (*Disc.,* 115), and this, together with the song of a worker in the nearby olive groves, conjures up a vision of "the ingle of Circe." The poet adopts the persona of Odysseus looking back on the time he spent as Circe's captive, strongly aware, in retrospect, of the emptiness of sexuality for its own sake and of how distasteful and even dangerous it now seems: "All heavy with sleep, fucked girls and fat leopards, / Lions loggy with Circe's tisane, / Girls leery with Circe's tisane / . . . / kaka pharmak edōken [she had given them dreadful drugs]." Although at first Circe offers men honey and wine, they later come to eat acorns, and Odysseus, realizing that Circe does turn men into beasts by depriving them of their will to struggle and achieve, refuses Circe's proffered drug and refuses "to go into the pigsty." The ingle of Circe breeds its own kind of desolation—we see time wasting away and the blurring of distinctions between seasons where no work is done and no harvest gathered: "Spring overborne into summer / late spring in the leafy autumn."

Yet for Odysseus, made invulnerable to the goddess's destructive power by virtue of the properties of moly, Circe is not sinister but beneficent. She is beautiful and gracious, but also dignified and commanding. She is firm in insisting that he make the journey to Hell, but her precise instructions save him and most of his crew from danger, not only in the descent into Hell, but also during the passage between Scylla and Charybdis and the encounter with the Sirens. Since the canto opens in Olga Rudge's apartment, it seems most likely that there is some connection in the poet's mind between the woman and the goddess—that he sees Olga Rudge in part as a Circe-figure. This would account for the highly positive borrowings from the *Paradiso:* "Che mai da me non si parte il diletto [the delight of which has never left me]," and "Fulvida di folgore [Blazing with brilliance]," which Pound uses here mainly in isolation from their original contexts, intending them to apply to Circe and to "Odysseus's" relationship with her. Pound at this stage was living with his wife, but regularly visiting Olga Rudge, and this perhaps gives particular point to "Circe's" complaint—"Always with your mind on the past . . ."—a complaint that Homer's Circe does not make. Whatever the personal resonances of this Circe episode, the poet chooses, in the second part of the canto to set the personal aside and to present ritualized sexuality. He begins with "Sumus in fide / Puellaeque canamus" from Catullus's hymn to Diana. The virginal Diana is Circe's antithesis and Pound dedicates his rite not only to her but to Flora and

Venus also, making it a composite celebration of spring and fertility ritual rather than one particular festival. Earlier, Pound had written of the *Pervigilium Veneris,* a Greek feast "transplanted into Italy" (*SR,* 18), which he felt was carried over into Provençal poetry. In this canto he suggests the persistence of the tradition by using Greek, Latin, Italian, and Middle English. The most moving part of the ritual is rendered in modern English. "Beaten from flesh into light / Hath swallowed the fire-ball" still has an aloofness in keeping with its archaism, but this disappears in the final lines of the canto: "Dark shoulders have stirred the lightning / A girl's arms have nested the fire, / Not I but the handmaid kindled / . . . / I have eaten the flame." As beautiful as this is, it is nevertheless generalized and distanced from the personal by being a fertility ritual, just as the speaker of the final lines has lost her individual identity and has become "the handmaid."

Canto 47 seems somewhat more personal but largely because of the elegiac note which Pound strikes in it. He is oppressed by the sense of his own mortality and has given a foretaste of this mood in Canto 43 where he writes: "wave falls and the hand falls / Thou shalt not always walk in the sun / or see weed sprout over cornice / Thy work in set space of years, not over an hundred" (43/210). This mood seems almost certainly the result of his sense of having failed to help correct the economic and social abuses of the times. The knowledge which he had hoped to learn from his descent into "Hell" proves to have been elusive and indefinite— "Knowledge the shade of a shade." Despite his sense of failure, he still feels that he could not have chosen any other path and insists "Yet must thou sail after knowledge / Knowing less than drugged beasts" (47/236). His feeling of ineffectuality and his sense of time running out makes him identify with the vulnerability of Adonis. Odysseus, like Dante, can return with wisdom from Hell while still alive, but Adonis must die before he goes down into the underworld. He brings fertility to the land, but only at the price of his own life.

Pound strongly emphasizes the difference he sees between male and female sexuality, and now, rather than criticizing the female as "chaos," he seems to envy her more complete participation in "the process." He suggests that women can create almost effortlessly through procreation, while men must try to create strenuously, and always with the knowledge that their achievements are not an intrinsic part of the natural order and therefore in one sense less substantial. He sees "the process" less as consolation than as a reminder that he is working alone. He suggests that all men share in the vulnerability of Adonis and he contrasts this to the permanence and timelessness which seems to him intrinsic to women's sexuality: "Two span, two span to a woman, / Beyond that she believes not. Nothing is of any importance. / To that she is bent, her intention / To that art thou called ever turning intention" (47/237). Through her sexuality, woman is a fixed point to which man is irresistibly drawn, and through her ability to bear children she seems to be granted a reprieve from death. The "two span to a woman" could refer to the double life span she is vicariously allowed through her offspring. Compared to her, man seems limited and trapped in time: "By this gate art thou measured / Thy day is between a door and a door." This "gate" is both the grave and the womb-door by which man is measured in the act of love and from which he takes the measure of his physical body at birth. Man's "day" stretches from the "door" of the womb to the "door" of his grave in "Mother Earth." Pound seems to be registering in these lines the same consciousness that we see in Dylan Thomas's "Twenty-Four Years": "In the groin of the natural doorway I crouched like a tailor / Sewing a shroud for a journey."[5] This elegiac mood becomes common in the *Pisan Cantos* and we find a particularly close parallel to Canto 47 in "How drawn, O GEA TERRA, / what draws as thou drawest / till one sink into thee by an arm's width / embracing thee" (82/526). Pound generalizes the idea of woman in this canto until she is identified with "Mother Earth." Man's labors are like those of the farmer with "Two oxen yoked for ploughing." Man also labors with oxen in "drawing down stone" for building, and in the works of stone he leaves behind him he can make some stand against oblivion, despite the ephemerality of his physical existence:

> the floating martin
> . . . has no care for your presence,
> His wing-print is black on the roof tiles

---

5. Dylan Thomas, *Collected Poems* (London, 1962), p. 99.

And the print is gone with his cry.
So light is thy weight on Tellus
Thy notch no deeper indented
Thy weight less than the shadow
Yet hast thou gnawed through the mountain,
                    Scylla's white teeth less sharp   [47/237–38]

The lines on ploughing in the canto are taken from Hesiod's *Works and Days,* a strangely timeless work since times and seasons are still the same for farmers as they have always been. Ploughing with oxen continues in Pound's Italy much as it was in Hesiod's Greece—"Thus was it in time" (47/237). Yet finally, in this canto, the "works and days of hands" take second place to man's direct participation in "the process" through his sexuality:

Hast thou found a nest softer than cunnus
Or hast thou found better rest
Hast'ou a deeper planting, doth thy death year
Bring swifter shoot?
Hast thou entered more deeply the mountain?

The light has entered the cave. Io! Io!
The light has gone down into the cave,
Splendour on splendour!
By prong have I entered these hills.   [47/238]

After this, the poet's identification with Adonis is less troubling and the final emphasis of the canto is on the rebirth of vegetation, on calm and healing:

When the almond bough puts forth its flame,
When the new shoots are brought to the altar,
                    Τυ Διώνα, Και Μοῖραι
                    TU DIONA, KAI MOIRAI
Και Μοῖραι' Ἀδονιν
KAI MOIRAI' ADONIN
                    that hath the gift of healing,
that hath the power over wild beasts.   [47/239]

Although in Bion's "Lament for Adonis," the fates are weeping for the dead youth, Pound omits the weeping, simply juxtaposing Dione, the Fates, and Adonis. The main emphases of the rest of the canto make it clear that it is not Adonis, who was after all killed by a wild boar, but "Dione" or Aphrodite who has "the gift of healing" and "the power over wild beasts." Aphrodite's avatar is Circe—Circe as the embodiment of positive sexuality, as she is to Odysseus when he is under the protective influence of moly. In one sense the moly itself has "the gift of healing" and "the power over wild beasts," but Pound's emphasis in this canto is not on Circe as a dangerous force, and the figures of Odysseus and the goddess are gradually eclipsed by those of the poet and his lover. Of the power of "Aphrodite" who draws both man and animal irresistibly to their mating Pound writes:

> To that she is bent, her intention
> To that art thou called ever turning intention,
> Whether by night the owl-call, whether by sap in shoot,
> Never idle, by no means by no wiles intermittent
> Moth is called over mountain
> The bull runs blind on the sword, *naturans*
> To the cave art thou called, Odysseus.   [47/237]

And it is clear that sexual love brings to the poet "the gift of healing:"

> By prong have I entered these hills:
> That the grass grow from my body,
> That I hear the roots speaking together,
> The air is new on my leaf,
> The forked boughs shake with the wind.
> Is Zephyrus more light on the bough, Apeliota
> more light on the almond branch?   [47/238]

The dominant theme in Canto 48 is one of loss, and the mood, as in Canto 47, becomes elegiac. The positive parts of the canto have to do with precise definition and with the value of expertise. There was some guarantee that those who were given power would use it conscientiously in the days when people had to prove their fitness to occupy positions, and Pound recalls how Athelstan required a man to have made three trading voyages before he would make him a thegn, and how, to qualify for consideration as a trustee of the Salem Museum, a man had to have "doubled / both Good Hope and The Horn" (48/241). Always an advocate of precise observation and careful attention to detail, Pound is impressed at having heard how Pacific islanders can "spread threads from gun'ale to gun'ale / in a certain fashion / and plot a course of 3000 sea miles / lying under the web, watching the stars" (48/242), and he includes his daughter's account of the occasion of a new priest's first mass in Gais as another instance of precise observation.

Yet finally the note of loss comes through most strongly in this canto. The death in San Remo of the ex-sultan, Mahomet VI of Turkey, marks the end of the once-great Ottoman Empire, hurried to its extinction by the First World War, and the fact that in St. Peter's at the beatification of Paula Frassinetti, "80 loud speakers were used," seems to Pound a telling comment on the loss of the Eleusinian spirit from contemporary religion. The First World War itself is on Pound's mind, as it so often is when he is oppressed by thoughts of the decay of his own times, and he dwells for a moment on Fritz Von Unruh's account of a pit at Verdun overflowing with corpses where "the sergeant jammed 'em down with his boots / to get the place smooth for the Kaiser." This pit of corpses takes us back to the "lake of bodies" in Canto 16 and, inevitably, to the corpse of Gaudier. It also anticipates the thousand dead "in the eel-fishers basket" on the last page of this sequence. The second part of Canto 48 becomes more directly personal yet feelings of loss and of regret remain. His obvious enjoyment of his daughter's excitement at the festivities in honor of the priest's first mass suddenly gives way to a more complicated and troubled mood. Mary's account of the occasion was part of a letter written from Gais, but is followed by a request made when she was visiting her father and mother:

> . . . I liked it,
> all the houses were full of lights and
> tree branches in the windows

covered with hand-made flowers and
the next day they had mass and a procession
Please may I go back there
and have a new pair of Sunday shoes?"   [48/242]

In chapter 3 of *Discretions,* Mary de Rachewiltz describes the
painful occasion on which she asked "Please may I go back there?"
and upset her mother with the reminder that Gais was "home" to
her daughter and that Mary's foster mother, Frau Marcher, was
"Mamme." Pound captures beautifully the artlessness and direct-
ness of the child who states her preferences with no intimation of
the pain she will cause. The canto ends with other images of loss
also. The area around Montségur and Excideuil, remembered as it
was when Pound was there in 1919 with his wife and Eliot, is a
place of endings where little trace remains of the earlier cultures
that had flourished there. The ruins of the temple-citadel of
Montségur are a cenotaph for the hundreds of Albigensians mas-
sacred nearby, and at San Bertrand de Comminges only a village
stands where a great town had flourished in the time of the
Roman Empire:

From Val Cabrere, were two miles of roofs to San Bertrand
so that a cat need not set foot in the road
where now is an inn, and bare rafters,
where they scratch six feet deep to reach pavement
where now is wheat field, and a milestone
and altar to Terminus . . .
. . . .
Savairic; hither Gaubertz;
                        Said they wd. not be under Paris
                                              [48/243]

This trip, made as soon as it was possible to travel in France after
the war, was also a much belated wedding journey, reminding the
poet in retrospect of another kind of loss. As the canto ends, the
emphasis is not so much on personal loss as on the disappearance
of the whole way of life of prewar Europe. He closes the canto
with a curious, poignant detail salvaged quite randomly from com-

plete oblivion—an elderly lady's memory of "an old man with a basket of stones" at the Lido in Venice whose job it was to anchor the long beach costumes when it was windy.

The closing lines of Canto 49—"The fourth; the dimension of stillness. / And the power over wild beasts"—provides a strong echo of the conclusion of Canto 47—"that hath the gift of healing, / that hath the power over wild beasts"—and we find that the "Seven Lakes Canto" is clarified if we are sensitive to its kinship with Canto 47. Both are concerned with approaches to the paradisal. In the earlier, through the experience of sexual love, the poet receives "the gift of healing," and, in the later, through meditation on art and poetry, he tries to enter for a while "the dimension of stillness."

The object of the poet's meditation is a manuscript book of eight paintings of traditional scenes from the Sho-Sho [Hsiao-Hsiang] lake region of China, each of which is accompanied by a pair of poems, one in Chinese and one in Japanese. Details of the manuscript and the translation of the Chinese poems from which Pound worked are given in Daniel Pearlman's *The Barb of Time* and in *Paideuma* by Hugh Kenner (2, no. 1), Angela Palandri (3, no. 1) and Sanehide Kodama (4, no. 2). Not only the subjects of the scenes but also the order in which they appear are established by tradition so that they move seasonally from spring to winter, but Pound either is unaware of this or has chosen to rearrange their order when he comes to write about them in his poem. When he writes, "and by no man these verses," he is reminding us that not one, but many poets, both Chinese and Japanese, have written poems on these scenes, but he is not implying that his own version will be a series of objective descriptions without an identifiable viewpoint. We notice, on the contrary, that a dominant mood is quickly established and sustained in a way that unifies the sequence of scenes. Although it is interesting to see the translations of the poems that Pound was working with, a study of these does not add to our appreciation of the effect that he wants to create in this canto and can even be distracting in a way that a study of his sources otherwise rarely is. The reason for this is the marked difference between the separateness of each of the poems of the source from each other—a separateness underlined particularly strongly by their individual titles and their relationship to separate paintings—and the opposite effect of continuity that Pound creates in his canto.

Even a westerner uninitiated into the specifics of oriental aesthetics can immediately recognize the importance of the "dimension of stillness" in paintings like those of the eight scenes of Sho-Sho. The spaces made in the painting by mists, brilliance of the sky, light on water, or even distance suggest a Zenlike meditative state and give both emphasis and stillness to those details of the scene which, by contrast, are thrown into relief. It is not, however, this particular quality of stillness that Pound has tried to capture in this canto where a sense of separateness or isolation comes through most strongly. Traditionally the scene of night rain comes toward the end of the sequence of scenes, but, by putting it at the beginning of the canto, Pound established a mood which dominates the sequence of descriptions:

> Rain; empty river; a voyage,
> Fire from frozen cloud, heavy rain in the twilight
> Under the cabin roof was one lantern.
> The reeds are heavy; bent;
> and the bamboos speak as if weeping.   [49/244]

To the stillness has been added a strong feeling of loss and of isolation. In comparison to the stillness of healing in Canto 47 when the poet says, "The air is new on my leaf," the effect of the heavy rain and the cold is claustrophobic. The "voyage" was made by someone else, away from this place where the speaker is now left alone. Although it took place in the past, it is still on his mind— "Under the cabin roof was one lantern"—and is recalled again in "Sail passed here in April; may return in October." The number of references to the cold, repeated at intervals throughout the passage, color our reactions even to passages that were associated in the original poems with warmth, good weather, and expansiveness:

> a cold tune amid reeds.
> Behind hill the monk's bell
> borne on the wind.

> Sail passed here in April; may return in October
> Boat fades in silver; slowly;
> Sun blaze alone on the river.   [49/244]

Here the "cold tune amid reeds" makes the wind that follows cold also and the "sun blaze" on the water suggests only light and not warmth. "Sparse chimneys smoke in the cross light," makes us think of cold weather, although the poem from which this detail is taken has a spring setting, and this line is followed by a snow scene:

> Comes then snow scur on the river
> And a world is covered with jade
> Small boat floats like a lanthorn,
> The flowing water clots as with cold. And at San Yin
> they are a people of leisure.   [49/244]

The small boat seen from the shore reminds us of how, in Canto 47, "The small lamps drift in the bay / And the sea's claw gathers them," and intensifies a little more the sense of vulnerability. The poet's viewpoint in this section of the canto–far removed from the detachment of the "two Chinamen" in Yeats's "Lapis Lazuli" –is, as the comment about the people of San Yin reminds us, that of a peasant who lives by these lakes and will never travel to any other place or be free from the endless manual labor that is his life.

"In seventeen hundred came Tsing [Yong Tching] to these hill lakes," anticipates the new voice that is introduced with:

> State by creating riches shd. thereby get into debt?
> This is infamy; this is Geryon.
> This canal goes still to TenShi
> though the old king built it for pleasure.   [49/245]

Implicit here is that Confucian vision, more farseeing than the peasant's, which realizes that the actions of the Emperor have an impact throughout the empire and that if the ruler is concerned, as the "old king" Kang Hsi was, for the good of his people, what seems to have been done for his pleasure will be found to benefit the people also.

The Japanese poem included in the canto is very obtrusive in its capital letters but is probably a complete enigma to the reader. It is different from most of Pound's other quotations in Chinese or Greek in that there is no hint in the surrounding text, or anywhere else in the poem, of what the Japanese means. Paradoxically its inscrutability turns out to be an important part of its meaning. To the non-Japanese-speaking reader the poem is undeniably there, typographically dominating the whole canto, yet its significance is concealed from him. Since the poem is about the beneficent influence on the lives of the people that results from their leaders working in harmony, the reader's inability to understand the poem is a correlative to the peasant's failure to understand the significance for him of the Emperor's exercise of his power.

The "Sun up" poem that follows is Pound's version of a folk song, the "Kei Wun Ka" or "Beating Soil Song," and even if the original is intended as a celebration of the simple life, it does suggest a life limited to fieldwork, while "Imperial power is? and to us what is it?" seems to emphasize the obtuseness of the common people. The dimension of stillness in the first part of the canto seems, in retrospect, somewhat embattled, certainly without exhilaration. Although in the *Pisan Cantos* the poet, with the help of Confucius, will attain stillness, both in the Chinese History Cantos and in *Rock-Drill* and the Sacred Edict Cantos of *Thrones,* Pound's study of China will not be a quest for stillness but a laborious task of digging to uncover the roots of a healthy society. China does not reveal the dimension of stillness to him again until he studies the religion and culture of the Na Khi, whom he writes about in Cantos 101 and 104 and in *Drafts and Fragments.* "And the power over wild beasts" has no real referent within this canto and so leads us back to Canto 47, where the impersonal rhythms of regeneration within the natural world are eclipsed by the sacramental experience of human sexuality.

The canto in which Pound writes with most certainty and most intensity is Canto 45, the "*Usura* Canto," and, as his most heartfelt canto in this sequence, it is—in an important sense—his most personal. Although it is thoroughly archaic in diction, syntax, and references, we have learned to expect that he will often veil his most painfully personal feelings in such a style, and he chooses to again in the "Pull down thy vanity" section of Canto 81. We have noticed in chapter 1 Pound's concern in Canto 45 for the victims of *Usura,* and he seems to have recanted his earlier denunciation of "Pity." In fact, this canto shows us more clearly than anything else exactly what he means by his campaign against usury. As we see here, his only real concern is that the arts be allowed to flourish for the benefit of the whole society, and that ordinary people have decent food and shelter, be free to work and raise their families, and have access to some life-affirming form of religion. He enumerates all of these carefully in this canto. *"Usura"* itself is a vague concept; it appears not as a substantial manifestation but as an explanation for the hardships and inequities of people's lives. The more it is specified in the canto, the less real it seems. At first it is only a condition so that things happen or are prevented from happening "with Usura" or "by Usura." Later it acts—gnawing thread, cankering azure, slaying the child in the womb—but in such a way that it has become a kind of mythical beast. In the parts of the canto that deal with the arts it is entirely eclipsed by the great works of art, architecture, and sculpture that Pound celebrates even as he is saying that they "Came not by Usura." The more acute his distress at the problems of Western civilization and the farther from solution they appear, the more specific he tries to be about "the usurers" and the more his irritation and frustration give way to rage.

Since the early 1930s Pound had devoted a prodigious amount of time and energy to disseminating his economic ideas, writing articles for any publication that would accept them and—an indefatigable correspondent—sending letters and even questionnaires to anyone who might conceivably be receptive to his suggestions for fiscal reform. As the economies of Europe and America collapsed and the hardships of unemployment became increasingly widespread, he worked with a mounting sense of urgency. As the general suffering increased, those remedies which, he was convinced, would end the suffering continued to be ignored and his frustration and anger grew. The perversity of those with the power to correct the situation seemed to him unforgiveable, but he could do nothing more than reiterate, tirelessly, the same diagnosis and the same remedies.

Even in the early 1930s the need for economic reform seemed of the utmost urgency to Pound, haunted as he was by the horrors of the First World War. As the decade moved toward its close and the possibility of another war suggested itself with increasing ominousness, it was not surprising that he found the frustration and the tension almost unbearable. His worst fears for Western civilization seemed about to be realized, but the only people with the power to avert a catastrophe showed no interest in his warnings or the solution which he was sure would save them. In 1939 he travelled to Washington, but his ideas did not receive the attention that he had hoped and he realized that, with Roosevelt in power, neither the monetary reforms, nor the foreign policy that he, the poet, wanted to see would be adopted.

In his letters and prose tracts he had no choice but to hammer away at the same basic ideas, but in his poem this would not serve. By the time that Cantos 42–51 were published in 1937 he had made his main points about economics, war, and culture repeatedly and in detail. Further repetition would make the poem labored and obsessive. We can see from the beginning of Canto 52, and would most likely see even more clearly from the expurgated passages, why, in his next sequence of cantos, he chose to write about Chinese history and John Adams. His hatred of the usurers threatened to get out of control and had reduced him to anti-Jewish outbursts and rantings about "gun-swine" and "bank-buzzards." To keep the rhetoric and the anger of his prose pieces from dominating his poem, he chose, in Cantos 52–71, to take a broader perspective and to consider present problems from the vantage point of the past. By keeping the frenzy of propaganda separate from the more contemplative world of his poem, he saved his poem, but put his own sanity in jeopardy. The poem gained from the separation, but the state of mind of the propagandist was more vulnerable when it was no longer under the influence of the poem's contemplative calm. It is clear that, from Pound's viewpoint, he had no alternative but to continue with his campaign and to use the radio to reach as many people as possible. Both from a sense of desperation and from a sense of integrity he decided that he must continue with his warnings. To Pound the propagandist the prospect of another war was so unthinkable that he decided that, if war did come, it could only be because there were people who wanted it to happen and had made sure that it did. The poet, however, could take a broader view, and in the Chinese History Cantos and the Adams Cantos he reminded himself that such struggles had always taken place. His overview of the course of China's past helped to keep present problems in perspective, and the wisdom of Confucius and the example of John Adams were fixed points from which he drew strength and which reassured him that his humanitarian ideal was preserved, inviolable, beyond the sordidness of the present.

Cantos 52-61: The Chinese History Cantos

The Chinese History Cantos are the most straightforward, immediately accessible and conventionally organized part of the poem, yet in some important ways they are the least successful. The first and last parts of this "decad" are effective, but the middle section —roughly a half of the sequence—is very uneven; in it we see Pound treating his material in a mechanical way and showing, in his style, his uneasiness about this.

Clark Emery has drawn our attention[6] to a passage from one of the notes to *Confucius* which states what Pound considers to be the most fundamental truth that can be derived from a study of Chinese history—the truth that he writes the Chinese History Cantos to illustrate:

> The dynasties Han, Tang, Sung, Ming rose on the Confucian idea; it is inscribed in the lives of the great emperors, Tai Tsong, Kao Tseu, Hong Vou, another Tai Tsong, and Kang Hi. When the idea was not held to, decadence supervened. [*C,* 188]

Confucius insisted on the importance of studying the histories to learn about the operation of moral laws in the state and showed in the *Ta Hio* what he had learned, as Pound reminds us in a note to his 1945 translation of this work:

6. Clark Emery, *Ideas into Action: A Study of Pound's Cantos* (Coral Gables, Fla., 1958), p. 40.

> Confucius . . . had two thousand years of documented history behind him which he condensed so as to render it useful to men in high official position. . . . His analysis of why the earlier great emperors had been able to govern greatly was so sound that every durable dynasty, since his time, has risen on the Confucian design and been initiated by a group of Confucians. China was tranquil when her rulers understood these few pages. [*C,* 19]

The twelfth century Confucian, Chu Hsi, following his master's teachings, made his own digest of Chinese history, the *Tong Kien Kang Mou,* which was translated by Father Joseph de Mailla to serve as the first part of his *Histoire Générale de la Chine*—Pound's source in these cantos.

It has been suggested that Pound deliberately chose de Mailla as a source because he wanted to give the Jesuits credit for transmitting Confucian thought to Europe and hence for helping to shape the thinking of the intellectual leaders of the Enlightenment and, ultimately, of John Adams.[7] This is an interesting possibility but there does not seem to be sufficiently persuasive evidence, either in these cantos or in the Adams Cantos, to support this view. Throughout the Chinese Cantos, the poet's attention is fixed firmly on China itself and, where cultural exchange between East and West is an issue, the emphasis is all on the transmission of learning *into* China. The emperor Kang Hi was willing to allow the Jesuits to introduce European scientific and artistic ideas into his court, but mistrusted their religious and moral teachings. In a way that is appropriate to the centripetal force of these cantos, he made it a condition of their remaining at the court that they promise never to return to Europe again.

Were Pound's main concern the transmission of Confucian thought to the West, de Mailla himself would surely emerge as the hero of this sequence as John Adams obviously does in the next, yet the purpose of the Chinese Cantos is clearly to present the history of the rulers of China rather than to serve as a tribute to

---

7. David Gordon, "Confucius, Philosophe: An Introduction to the Chinese Cantos 52–61," *Paideuma* 5, no. 3 (Winter 1976): 387. See also Hugh Kenner, *The Pound Era,* p. 231.

Father de Mailla—whose name in fact is never mentioned—or more generally, to the Jesuit missionaries in China. Even in the cantos on the Jesuits, Kang Hi and his son are the main focus of Pound's attention. Kang Hi's concern for his native language prompted him to have Chu Hsi's Chinese history translated into Manchu by a panel of the best scholars he could find who were fluent in both languages. We learn from Pound's source that it was this undertaking of Kang Hi's that gave de Mailla the idea of making his own translation of the same work into French.[8] Nor should we assume that Pound is making a particular point about the importance of Chu Hsi in these cantos as though de Mailla's history were no more than a translation of the *Tong Kien Kang Mou*. Chu Hsi, whose name is not mentioned in these cantos either, died in 1200, and the *Histoire Générale* takes us up to 1780, so that more than half of the material that Pound takes from his French source has nothing to do with Chu Hsi.[9]

The fact that Pound makes no reference to de Mailla's other sources strongly suggests that his interest lies with the content of his source and not with its compiling, its compiler, or its influence in Europe. In addition, we notice that Pound makes no serious attempt to give any sense of the style of the *History*. He includes occasional passages in French but an equal number in Latin, and these direct our attention not so much to de Mailla's prose as to Pound's orthographical note at the beginning of *Cantos LII–LXXI* in which he explains that he uses the French form of Chinese names since "Our European knowledge of China has come via latin

8. Joseph de Mailla, *Histoire Générale de la Chine*, 13 vols. (Paris, 1777; reprinted Taipei, 1969), 1: xxv.

9. For his account of the Kin and Yuen dynasties, de Mailla uses the official histories commissioned by Chun Chi, father of Kang Hi. His account of the Ming dynasty is based upon the writings of the three most reliable historians of the period and of Hong Vou, founder of the dynasty. He uses the official record of the wars against the Eleutes, commissioned by Kang Hi and printed with his own preface, and gives an eyewitness account of the last twenty years of this reign. Although he was in Peking during the reigns of Yong Tching and Kien Long, anti-Christian feeling made it too dangerous for him to write about this period, and his editor, Hautesrayes, adds his own account of these rulers, working from Bertin's *Mémoires Concernant les Chinois*.

and french and at any rate the french vowels as printed have some sort of uniform connotation." In the Adams Cantos, Pound takes pains to preserve the sense of Adams's style and succeeds most impressively; in the Chinese Cantos, especially toward the beginning, it is some approximation of a Chinese style, not of de Mailla's French, that he aims for:

> Grow pear-boughs, be fearless
> let no man break twig of this tree
> that gave shade to Chao-Kong
> he had shadow from sun here;
>   rest had he in your shade.   [53/269]

The Chinese History Cantos begin very strongly, and Canto 52 is particularly striking in its demonstration of the poet's ability, after his outburst against the usurers, to curb and redirect his energies, to find a pivot, and to "hold fast in the middle." He begins by recalling Siena, Duke Leopold, and the Monte dei Paschi bank, and then, after his tirade against the subsequent corruption of banking, returns to Siena again when he writes:

> Between KUNG and ELEUSIS
> Under the Golden Roof, la Dorata
>   her baldacchino
> Riccio on his horse rides still to Montepulciano
>   the groggy church is gone toothless
> No longer holds against *neschek*
>   the fat has covered their croziers
> The high fans and the mitre mean nothing   [52/258]

In the Town Hall of Siena, in the Sala del Mappamondo, are two frescoes by Simone Martini: *Guidoriccio da Fogliano victorious over the castles of Montemassi and Sassoforte of Maremma,* and the *Madonna Enthroned with the Child, Angels and Saints*—the *Maestà.* The Madonna sits under a great red canopy, "her baldacchino," and the upper part of her elaborate Gothic throne looks like a "Golden Roof." This together with her golden halo and gold-bordered cloak earns her the epithet "la Dorata," while, as the recipient of the gifts and devotions of the angels and Saints, she is also "l'Adorata." With the "Confucian" figure of the Commander of the Sienese militia on one wall and the Madonna on another, Pound suggests that, in this room, one can stand "between KUNG and ELEUSIS." Yet the Confucian and the Eleusinian also come together within the *Maestà* itself. The worship of the Virgin and the Christ Child, like the rites in honor of Persephone and Iakchos, is intended to ensure the fertility of the land and the prosperity of its people, yet the Council of Nine, in commissioning this painting, shows that it is not content to leave the matter of the welfare of the Republic wholly in the realm of the mysteries. With a Confucian directness and practicality, the artist spells out for the rulers of Siena their duty to govern wisely. On the platform below the figures he has inscribed verses spoken by the Virgin. To the angels who offer her flowers she says that good counsels are more pleasing to her than the roses and lilies of heaven and warns anyone who by deception intends to serve his own interests at the expense of the good of the people. She reminds the saints to withdraw their aid from the rulers of Siena if ever they allow the weak to be oppressed. In addition, the Christ Child holds a scroll on which is written "DILIGITE IUSTITIAM QUI IUDICATIS TERRAM," the words spelled out in points of fire by the Spirits of the Just in Canto 18 of the *Paradiso.* In Cantos 42–44 Pound has celebrated the exemplary achievements of Sienese government and particularly the founding of the Monte dei Paschi bank. In 43/218 he notes that in 1622 the members of the general council appointed to organize the Monte met together "in the hall of World Map" where they would have been watched over by Simone Martini's Virgin. Yet now, Pound feels, the "groggy church" plays no part in safeguarding the welfare of the people by encouraging good government, and Catholicism with its "old buffers keeping the stiffness" is no longer in touch with the "radiant world" of Eleusinian energies or with the rhythms of the natural world. Pound at this point turns away from the present problems of the West to the China of the past and discovers in the *Li Chi* or *Book of Rites* a striking instance of a scrupulous attention to the workings of the "process" which can provide an "unwobbling pivot" for a harmonious society.

Figure 5. Simone Martini, *Guidoriccio da Fogliano victorious over the castles of Montemassi and Sassoforte of Maremma.* "Riccio on his horse rides still to Montepulciano." [52/258]

Figure 6. Detail of figure 5.

Photo credit: Grassi

Figure 7. Simone **Martini**, *Madonna Enthroned with the Child, Angels, and Saints.*

"Under the Golden Roof, la Dorata
her baldacchino" [52/258]

His source is the fifth chapter of the *Li Chi*—the *Yueh Ling* or *Proceedings of Government in the Different Months*—which is divided into four sections of three parts corresponding to the four seasons, each of three months. For each month the position of the stars is described, the presiding deity named, and the appropriate musical note, number, taste, smell, and sacrifice indicated. Seasonal changes in the behavior of animals and growth of plants are noted. The emperor's correct garments, equipage, and food are specified, and also the rites which he must perform as he fulfills his duty to advise his ministers by example, by moral precepts, and by practical instructions. His orders are to be transmitted by the ministers to the people, and an account of the correct tasks and occupations to be pursued during that month is given. Each part ends with a warning of the disorders that would follow were

Figure 8. Detail of figure 7.

the correct procedures neglected: not only civil and military crises, but also natural catastrophes. This idea that the natural process itself would be turned aside from its true course if Emperor, ministers, and people failed to put themselves actively in harmony with it represents the most emphatic possible assertion of the need for the conduct of the state to be grounded on a proper attention to the times and the seasons.

The extremely detailed and comprehensive nature of the injunctions of the *Yueh Ling* make the section of Canto 52 that deals with them stand somewhat apart, as a fixed point, but it also sets up resonances with important passages elsewhere in the poem. We are reminded, for example, of Canto 47:

> Begin thy plowing
> When the Pleiades go down to their rest,
> Begin thy plowing
> 40 days are they under seabord,
> Thus do in fields by seabord
> And in valleys winding down toward the sea.
> When the cranes fly high
> think of plowing. [47/237]

The injunction that the "Inspector of dye-works, inspector of colour and broideries / see that the white, black, green be in order / let no false colour exist here / black, yellow, green be of quality" (52/259–60) stands as the corrective to the situation described in Canto 45 where, under the influence of *Usura*, "None learneth to weave gold in her pattern; / Azure hath a canker by usura; cramoisi is unbroidered / Emerald findeth no Memling" (45/230).

Pound uses the section from the *Yueh Ling* as a dedicatory rite in itself, an appropriate inauguration for this part of the poem. In the course of his telling of the history of China in the cantos which follow, we notice that he periodically makes other ritual gestures, telling over the names of the earliest of the legendary emperors—"Fou-hi by virtue of wood; / Chin-nong, of fire; Hoang Ti ruled by the earth, / Chan by metal. / Tchuen was lord, as is water" (53/264)—in the way that each conscientious emperor should recall the virtues of his ancestors so that he can emulate them.

Pound has committed himself to making a survey of the whole of Chinese history until 1780 and this leads to two particular problems—he must in many places cover a great deal in short space and he must write about periods of social disorder as well as periods of peace and prosperity. In both cases his style and his poem suffer. By the middle of Canto 54—the time of the fall of the Han dynasty—the style becomes prosaic, and slanginess and abbreviations appear increasingly, so that we feel that the poet is moving hurriedly, superficially, and mechanically through material that he does not particularly want to cover:

> OU TI had 'em centralized
> Yen Yen was frugal. Oueï prince went pussyfoot
> And the rites of *Tien,* that is Heaven
> were ploughing and the raising of silk worms
> OU TI ploughed his festival furrow
>   his Empress did rite of the silk worms
> Then OU went gay and SUNG ended.   [54/283]

> And the 46 tablets that stood still there in Yo Lang
> were broken and built into Foé's temple (Foé's, that is
>   goddam bhuddists.)
> this was under Hou-chi the she empress.
> OU TI went into cloister
>   Empire rotted by hochang, the shave-heads, and
> Another boosy king died.   [54/284]

In part the slanginess is a sign that he feels self-conscious about his perfunctory treatment of his material, but it also shows a certain irritation at having to cover material that he finds uncongenial and only too depressingly predictable: "Wars, / wars without interest / boredom of an hundred years' wars" (53/272). He is also in the habit of using slang and odd spelling when he feels very strongly about some matter and yet wants to avoid appearing too earnest, and at various points in these cantos the spectacle of bad government, corruption, brutality, and war moves him to anger.

Although Pound obviously considers Confucius greater than all of the great rulers of China, he chooses not to eulogize him, presenting his merits in a way which seems understated and yet shows a closeness of identification with his hero. This anticipates his sense of identity with John Adams in the next group of cantos. Kung lived in a time of great corruption, of heavy taxes, forced labor, starvation in years of bad harvest and of wars undertaken for the diversion of the nobility: "States of Lou were unhappy / Their Richards poisoned young princes. / All bloods, murders, all treasons" (53/272). While Kung was alive he had very little scope for action. His greatest concern was to alleviate the sufferings of the people by reforming the government, but he could find no one who would give him a position of power which would allow him to put his ideas into action. This is reflected in Pound's "minimal" description of Kung's life:

> And when Kung was poor, a supervisor of victuals
> Pien's report boosted him
> so that he was made supervisor of cattle
> In that time were banquets as usual, Kung was inspector
> > of markets
> . . . .
> Then Kungfutseu was made minister and moved promptly
> > against C. T. Mao
> > and had him beheaded
> . . . .
> > Kungfutseu retired
> . . . .
> He was seven days foodless in Tchin
> > the rest sick and Kung making music
> 'sang even more than was usual'
> . . . .
> Tchin and Tsi cut off Kung in the desert
> > and Tcheou troops alone got him out
> . . . .
> And Kung cut 3000 odes to 300
> . . . .
> in the 40th year of King Ouang
> Died Kung aged 73   [53/272–73]

The one other, somewhat more extended reference to Kung is very effective in establishing Pound's attitude toward his hero:

At Tching someone said:
>   there is a man with Yao's forehead
Cao's neck and the shoulders of Tsé Tchin
A man as tall as Yu, and he wanders about in front of
>   the East gate
>   like a dog that has lost his owner.
Wrong, said Confucius, in what he says of those Emperors
>   but as to the lost dog, quite correct.   [53/273]

In this anecdote Kung comes to life for the reader, and we see that even more important to Pound than Kung's modesty is his sense of humor. Through this one anecdote, Kung, unlike the other figures in these cantos, is taken out of his own time. Through Pound's close sense of identity with him, he becomes "contemporary," freed from the past. As Pound also emphasizes, Kung transcends his times by the force of his ideas. Though he was denied the power to act in his own time, his ideas generated a power far beyond any that he could have exerted alone. During his lifetime he was able to get positions of influence for some of his disciples, but after his death his ideas "went into action" with enormous force, so that Pound is justified in his observation that "every durable dynasty, since his time, has risen on a Confucian design." The kinship between Pound and his hero is really very close. Convinced as they are of the humanizing power of poetry and music, both are even more concerned to put their reforming ideas to work and yet totally frustrated in their attempts to find someone in power who will listen to them.

Up until Canto 58 the rushed and slangy writing continues, although in a few places, when he is writing of admirable figures, Pound's pace becomes less rushed and the writing is at times comparable to that of the opening cantos. When he writes of the first Taï Tsong, in Canto 54, Pound covers his reign in some detail, but the passage is marred by slang—"TAÏ TSONG had a letch for Corea"—and by the Emperor's Cockney accent—"I have spent money on palaces / too much on 'osses, dogs, falcons / but I have united the Hempire (and you 'aven't)" (54/286–87). The extended passage in Canto 55 on Ouang-Ngan-ché, who reformed the economy, "making to circulate the whole realm's abundance" (55/296), is not perfunctory and slangy like the rest of the canto, yet it still seems prosaic, while in Canto 56 the tone rises only with the description of the suicide of Ouang Chi:

> And in south province Tchin Tiaouen had risen
> and took the city of Tchang tcheou
> offered marriage to Ouang Chi,
> who said: It is an honour.
> I must first bury Kanouen. His body is heavy.
> His ashes were light to carry
> Bright was the flame for Kanouen
> > Ouang Chi cast herself into it, Faithful forever
> > High the hall TIMOUR made her.   [56/305]

Canto 57 is more slow-paced and largely free of slang, but short, with no major figures and no particular focus. From the passage in Canto 58 on the Second Taï Tsong, the first Manchu lord of China, until the end of these cantos, we see that Pound has renewed his interest in and commitment to his material and is writing with more care. Taï Tsong, who overthrew the corrupt Ming dynasty, particularly captures Pound's imagination, and the long section on this ruler is highly successful. Kang Hi and Yong Tching in Cantos 59–61 are also Poundian heroes, but his style when he writes of them is less direct and shows less engagement than in the section on Taï Tsong. This is partly because of the complications that are introduced by the presence of the Jesuit missionaries and their relationships with these rulers. In the Table at the head of *Cantos LII–LXXI*, Pound gives "Russian treaty" as the subject of the last part of Canto 59, and as the subject of Canto 60, "Jesuits," and these are the passages which cover the reign of Kang Hi. Pound's approval of the emperor is unqualified, but his attitude toward the Jesuits is ambivalent. He recognizes their dedication, intelligence, and integrity, but sympathizes with the point of view of the Chinese who see Christianity as inferior to Confucianism and who prohibit the Jesuits from making converts. Fathers Gerbillon and Pereira are clearly presented as the heroes in the difficult negotiations which lead to the Russo-Chinese boundary treaty and yet the clash of styles in Pound's tribute produces a strange effect: "and this was due to the frog and the portagoose / Gerbillon and Pereira / to Gerbillon in the most critical moment / that he kept their tempers till they came to conclusion" (59/327). Lapses into this kind of jocular slanginess are fairly frequent in these last cantos, but they do not spring from anger or animosity: "The European church wallahs wonder if this can be reconciled. / And the archbish of Antioch spent a year in Canton / mousing around" (60/330); "and 35 for the Portagoose boss who had sent him / i.e. he wuz honoured but cdn't spill proppergander / and the chink grandees took him down the canal" (61/337).

Kang Hi was at first prepared to allow the Jesuits complete freedom, but he was persuaded, after being petitioned to this effect by Tching Mao, a sea captain, to allow only those missionaries with permits to remain in the country, to forbid all prose-lytizing, to pardon only those Chinese converts to Christianity who would recant and pull down their churches, and to forbid the Jesuits who remained from ever returning to their native lands. Pound clearly had to decide whether he would be sympathetic toward the Jesuit or the Chinese point of view and, despite the obvious bias of his source, consistently sided with the Emperors. In summing up the achievements of Kang Hi's reign, Pound naturally mentions the introduction of European learning, but in a way that gives more credit to the emperor for permitting or "ordering" it than to the Jesuits for making it possible. Yong Tching, unlike his father, has little curiosity about the sciences or European inventions and strongly disapproves of Christianity which he bans completely. He is a conscientious and humane ruler, and Pound does not spend any time sympathizing with the trials of the Jesuits, Father de Mailla among them, during this reign:

> and he putt out Xtianity
> chinese found it so immoral
> . . . .
> . . . nothing personal against Gerbillon and his
> > colleagues, but
> Xtians are disturbing good customs
> seeking to uproot Kung's laws
> seeking to break up Kung's teaching.   [61/334]

Kang Hi and Yong Tching are important elsewhere in the poem also; when we read that Yong Tching spent "a million on canal reparations" (61/337), and Kang Hi "3 million a year on river embankments" (60/332), we remember being told in the "Seven Lakes Canto" that "In seventeen hundred came Tsing to these hill lakes," and "This canal goes still to TenShi / though the old king built it for pleasure." The scepticism of the peasant's question, "Imperial power is? and to us what is it?" is corrected by Yong Tching's wiser and more far-sighted understanding that, "Good of the empire of any part of the empire / concerns every mandarin / no matter where he is located / It is like a family affair" (61/337–38). These two rulers are important in the later cantos also as the authors of the first two versions of the *Sacred Edict* upon which Cantos 97 and 98 are based.

By the time that Pound was using the *Sacred Edict* as a source, he had become involved in a painstaking way with the study of the Chinese language, and the annotations in his personal copy of this work suggest that he was partly using it as a primer. His work with de Mailla's history had not required that he study Chinese, but, as we see from any page of Canto 85, by the time that he came to write *Rock-Drill* he was working closely with his Chinese text. During his years in St. Elizabeths he would spend an increasing amount of time on his study of Chinese.

Cantos 62–71: The Adams Cantos

The Adams Cantos are personal in a way that the Chinese History Cantos cannot be and, as a result, are more resonant and more substantial. On the simplest level, Pound, by concentrating on one man rather than making a panoramic survey of a vast sweep of time, allows the reader to come to know Adams much more intimately than any of the rulers of China. It also soon becomes clear that Pound himself identifies quite closely with Adams, and this personal involvement helps give these cantos their resonance and intensity.

In "The Jefferson–Adams Letters as a Shrine and a Monument," Pound says of these two statesmen that they "wrote an excellent prose which has not, so far as I know, been surpassed in our fatherland" (*SP,* 148), and we notice that, in his abbreviations and paraphrases of those passages that he has chosen from Adams's writings, Pound has deliberately preserved the cadence and movement of Adams's own prose. Although Pound's outrage is intense whenever the corruption that Adams remarks on reminds him of the chaos of the present, he only occasionally allows his own voice to interrupt Adams's. There are several instances of self-conscious slanginess on the second, third, and fourth pages of the first Adams canto, but Pound quickly drops this distracting mannerism and after this, with very few exceptions, only introduced colloquialisms for emphasis, or when someone other than Adams is speaking, or when he identifies the voice as that of "ego scriptor cantilenae"; or, in 69/407, when he acknowledges that the denunciations of Hamilton and his supporters are the poet's own, provided as a "vignette *in margine.*"

In these cantos Pound keeps to the order of the pieces in *The Works of John Adams.*[10] Cantos 62–65, because they are taken from Charles Francis Adams's biography of his father and from John Adams's *Diary* and *Autobiography,* show Adams in action. Cantos 66 and 67, which use his political essays as their source, show how he drew on his formidable knowledge of the law to demonstrate the legality of his countrymen's demands for guarantees of their basic rights and freedoms. Cantos 68 and 69, extracted from letters written between 1777 and 1787, show Adams on his vital diplomatic missions to France, Britain, and the Netherlands, tirelessly working to arrange treaties and, in Holland, to borrow the money which the new republic so urgently needed. Adams's presidential term is dealt with only briefly at the beginning of Canto 70 and then, on the second page of the canto, there is a drastic time shift as we move suddenly backwards from March 1801 to December 1773. This occurs because Pound has now reached the point in volume 9 of Adams's *Works* at which the "General Correspondence" section begins with a letter from August 1770. He provides only a brief transition with "And in the mirror of memory, *formato loco.*" Although in the remaining pages of this sequence Pound still keeps to the order of the letters in the re-

10. John Adams, *The Works of John Adams,* ed., with biography and notes, by Charles Francis Adams, 10 vols. (Boston, 1850–56). Subsequent references to *Works* are to the volume and pages of this edition. Location of passages in this work is made convenient in Frederick K. Sanders's *John Adams Speaking* (Orono, Me., 1975).

mainder of the *Works,* he has great latitude for choice and has chosen to select excerpts which present Adams in a predominantly reflective mood and give an overview of those opinions and judgments of Adams's that Pound considers most impressive. Canto 71 provides a very effective conclusion for these cantos, in large part because it makes so clear the closeness of Pound's identification with his hero and the extent of his admiration for and sympathy with his views and his ideals.

Pound naturally takes notice of Adams's anger at "swindling banks [that] have ruined our medium," and at the enormous power of an irresponsible press, but his interest in Adams's views goes far beyond this. He is clearly impressed by the way in which this "elder statesman" continued to affirm those principles and ideals upon which his whole political career had been based, yet understood too, from bitter experience, how rarely political ideals can be put into action in an unadulterated form. Adams looked back over his career with a sober awareness of the ways in which even the soundest of institutions could not prevent politicians who were motivated by greed and personal ambition from subordinating the public good to their own self-interest. He saw how the spirit of party, although necessary, was often destructive. "Histories are annihilated or interpolated or prohibited" (71/416) refers us to a letter to Jefferson in which we read, "parties and factions will not suffer improvements to be made. . . . No sooner has one party discovered or invented any amelioration of the condition of man, or the order of society than the opposite party belies it, misconstrues it, misrepresents it, ridicules it, insults it, and persecutes it. Records are destroyed. Histories are annihilated or interpolated or prohibited" (*Works,* 10:50). The destructive effects of factionalism were inevitable no matter what the political system, as Adams reiterated in another letter to Jefferson later in that same year. Asking how the laws of Zaleucus and Charondas came to be lost, he answered his own question in words to which Pound, remembering Erigena, would give his wholehearted support: "I say, the spirit of party has destroyed them; civil, political, and ecclesiastical bigotry. Despotical, monarchical, aristocratical, and democratical fury, have all been employed in this work of destruction of every thing that could give us true light, and a clear insight of antiquity" (*Works,* 10:84–85).

Adams was, of course, thinking of his own career when he wrote of how measures undertaken solely for the good of the country were attacked and denounced only because of party rivalry. In a letter of January 1815 to James Lloyd, to which Pound gives an important place in this canto, this is made particularly clear. "Little intercourse between the separate states" (71/417) refers to the way in which mutual ignorance of each other's "objects and qualities" has led to an "envy and hatred" between states which, "instead of being dissipated" by the American revolution, "has been cherished and perpetuated for political party purposes, and for the promotion of the sinister views and ambitious projects of a few restless and unprincipled individuals." Adams reflected how the two acts of his Presidency which seemed to him to have benefitted the American people most—his fight for a navy and his avoidance of war with France in 1800—were precisely those for which his administration has been most savagely attacked. The "headstone" for Adams which Pound provides (71/418) is his shorthand representation of Adams's emphatic assertion—"I will defend my missions to France, as long as I have an eye to direct my hand, or a finger to hold my pen. They were the most disinterested and meritorious actions of my life. I reflect upon them with so much satisfaction, that I desire no other inscription over my gravestone than: 'Here lies John Adams, who took upon himself the responsibility of the peace with France in the year 1800' " (*Works,* 10:109–11).

Pound also finds that Adams's views on religion and on human nature echo his own "Even Jesuits popes sorbonnists must have some conscience" (71/419) refers us to a passage from a letter of April 1817 to Jefferson which begins: "So far from believing in the total and universal depravity of human nature, I believe there is no individual totally depraved. The most abandoned scoundrel that ever existed, never yet wholly extinguished his conscience, and, while conscience remains, there is some religion" (*Works,* 10:254). "THEMIS CONDITOR" (71/417) points to a particularly Poundian passage: "Θέμις was the goddess of honesty, justice, decency, and right. . . . She presided over all oracles, deliberations, and councils. She commanded all mortals to pray to Jupiter for all lawful benefits and blessings. . . . Is not this Christian piety?

Is it not an acknowledgement of the existence of a Supreme Being, of his universal Providence, of a righteous administration of the government of the universe? And what can Jews, Christians, or Mahometans do more?" (*Works,* 10:75–76). Pound also wants us to note the generosity of Adams's tributes to Hancock, James Otis, and Samuel Adams, whom he had described as the "three most essential characters" in the making of the American Revolution (*Works,* 10:263) and his genuine admiration for Hancock's diligence and steadiness and for Otis's classical learning, public-spiritedness and integrity.

The canto ends with the opening lines of Cleanthes' "Hymn to Zeus" which Pound has previously translated (256) as, "Glorious, deathless of many names, Zeus aye ruling all things, founder of the inborn qualities of nature, by laws piloting all things." These lines have a double force: by following on from Adams's comments on Themis they emphasize the authenticity of the worship of the pagan gods, and, in their emphasis on the paramount importance of law, they look back to the achievement of Adams and forward to all of the many passages in the later cantos which deal with wise and just laws.

From Canto 62 on, there is no doubt that Pound has discovered that he has a greater admiration for and closer affinity with Adams than with Jefferson, so it is worth considering how his thinking about these two statesmen has changed since he wrote *Jefferson and/or Mussolini* in February 1933. Pound's main purpose in this piece was not to write a tribute to Jefferson—which would obviously have been redundant—but to defend Mussolini against the charge of authoritarianism by showing that, when a leader is truly public-spirited, the people have nothing to fear and everything to gain when he acts unilaterally. Pound's only interest was the welfare of the Italian people, and since Mussolini had already taken definite and effective measures to improve their living and working conditions, it seemed to Pound logical to assume that the Duce would proceed to that more thoroughgoing reform of the Italian fiscal system which, Pound felt, was the only effective guarantee of their continued welfare. He was, of course, taking Mussolini's good faith on trust, as he openly admitted: "Any thorough judgment of MUSSOLINI will be in a measure an act of faith, it will depend on what you *believe* the man means, what you believe that he wants to accomplish" (*JM,* 33).

Pound chose to compare Mussolini to Jefferson because he believed that the careers of both illustrated the wisdom of opportunism in a good cause and the benefits of decisive action. Jefferson was not, Pound says, "afflicted by fixations," and he "found himself in a condition of things that had no precedent in any remembered world. He saw like a shot that a new system and new mechanisms MUST come into being to meet it" (*JM,* 62). His was "the opportunism of the artist, who has a definite aim, and creates out of the materials present" (*JM,* 15). Both Jefferson and Mussolini are examples of the "OPPORTUNIST who is RIGHT, that is who has certain convictions and who drives them through circumstance, or batters and forms circumstance with them" (*JM,* 17–18). Pound claimed that the impediments to political action were no greater for Jefferson than they were for Mussolini as he tried to work for change in an Italy that was hidebound by extreme conservatism, regional parochialism, and inflexible traditionalism. Pound saw in both leaders an "indifference to mechanism as weighed against the main purpose" (*JM,* 64) and felt that in their case there could be no objection to the end justifying the means.

At this point we are a long way from the scrupulous attention to law and precedent that we find in John Adams and might wonder why Pound makes such a definitive switch from the "Opportunist" to the "Man of Law." Mainly Pound comes to see that the way of John Adams, although it is slower and less spectacular, is also more reliable and establishes a sound foundation upon which others, coming later, can build. In addition, a tribute in *Jefferson and/or Mussolini* to the impartiality of the historian and journalist William E. Woodward provides us with another possible reason for Pound's undervaluing of Adams at that time. Of Woodward's *George Washington: The Image and the Man,* Pound writes: "You will go far without finding any sounder estimates than his of Jefferson and John Adams" (*JM,* 78), so it comes as something of a surprise to read, in Woodward's first reference to Adams, "fat John Adams . . . was a friend and admirer of Washington—at times—but he was moody and changeable, as obese people frequently are. In one of his vitriolic moments he declared that George Washington would never have amounted to much if he had

not married Mrs. Custis' money."[11] This page is headed, "Asper-
sion by Fat John Adams." Woodward does give Adams credit for
defending the soldiers involved in the Boston Massacre, but insists
that he was vain and snobbish, saying that, had Britain decided, as
Governor Bernard of Massachusetts at one point suggested, to
create an American order of nobility, "we may be . . . sure that
John Adams, with his passionate love of titles, would have accepted
his." Where Woodward's references to Adams are sparse and usually
unfavorable, his comments on Jefferson are adulatory and at times
surprisingly Poundian in their imagery. We are told that "his
mental voltage was higher than that of any American of the eigh-
teenth century, except Franklin," that "such a personality in the
world of thought is like a prism of crystal in sunlight," and that
his ideas "have the subtle permanence of cameos."[12]

In *Jefferson and/or Mussolini* Pound had said, "Let us deny
that *real* intelligence exists until it comes into action" (*JM*, 17),
and it was Jefferson's ability to be flexible and innovative and to
act swiftly that Pound particularly admired. By the time that he
writes the Adams Cantos, however, he has come to value more
highly the deliberateness and directness that he finds in Adams:

> . . . the clearest head in the congress
> > > 1774 and thereafter
> > pater patriae
> the man who at certain points
> > made us
> at certain points
> > saved us
> by fairness, honesty and straight moving
> > > > ARRIBA ADAMS
> > > > [62/350]

By the time that he writes *Guide to Kulchur* Pound, rather
than feeling that he must justify the extent of state authority in
Italy, is complaining that there is not enough of it; this leads him

11. William E. Woodward, *George Washington: The Image and the Man*
(New York, 1931), p. 103.

12. Ibid., pp. 238, 243, 287, 288.

to the assertion that "the tragedy of the U. S. A. over 160 years is the decline of Adamses. More and more we cd., if we examined events, see that John Adams had the corrective for Jefferson" (*GK,* 254). He persists in his conviction that Adams's steadiness is more valuable and more constructive than the brilliance of Jefferson, as we see when he writes in Canto 81:

> "You the one, I the few"
> said John Adams
> speaking of fears in the abstract
> to his volatile friend Mr Jefferson.   [81/518]

and, on the last page of the *Pisan Cantos:*

> John Adams, the Brothers Adam
>   there is our norm of spirit
>
> our 中 chung[1]
>
> whereto we may pay our
>   homage   [84/540]

Chung[1], the "unwobbling pivot," seems a particularly apt metaphor, not only for the steadying influence of Adams's values and example, but also for the way in which the Adams Cantos provide a central fixed point for the whole of the poem. They look backward to Cantos 31–34 and Canto 37 and forward not only to the Thomas Hart Benton and Andrew Jackson Cantos (88 and 89), but to all the many passages in the later cantos that deal with the theme of law. When Pound was writing Canto 50 he thought that it would be the midpoint of his poem and chose to begin it with Adams's words: " 'REVOLUTION' said Mr Adams 'took place in the / minds of the people / in the fifteen years before Lexington.' "

Pound does not dwell much on Adams's presidency but seems fascinated by his knowledge of the law and reliance on the tradition of English common law as his guide in establishing American rights and in drafting the Massachusetts Constitution. From Adams, Pound learns the importance of Coke. Taking Jeremiah Gridley's advice that he "must conquer the INSTITUTES," Adams "began with Coke upon Littleton"(63/352), and Pound, following

Adams's example, begins a study of the *Institutes* himself, using them as the basis for his three Coke Cantos. Here, on the second to last page of *Thrones,* Pound gives a digest of the First Charter of the Massachusetts Bay Colony, showing among other things the basis for those fishing rights which John Adams defended so strenuously. This passage takes us back to the beginning of the first Adams Canto and Charles Francis Adams's account of this same Charter, among whose grantees was one Thomas Adams. The opening lines of the canto, expressing Charles Adams's concern that he be excused for any of the shortcomings of his completion of his father's biography, refer us to a passage that could with equal sincerity be spoken by Pound: "All that he will venture to claim for himself is an earnest desire to be right, and an endeavor by no trifling amount of industry to become so. . . . Hence if it should turn out that he has fallen into any essential error, or been guilty of material injustice, he trusts that he may be acquitted of evil intention in the beginning, or inclination to persevere in it against evidence. Should any such be shown to him, he stands ready to acknowledge it with candor and to correct it with cheerfulness" (*Works,* 1:vi–vii).

Pound comes to identify very strongly with Adams as one who is wholeheartedly committed to the public good; who is consistent in his ideals and undeviating in his pursuit of them; who wants to avoid war but feels that it must be met if it is forced upon him; who is convinced of the importance of knowing the roots of sound institutions and of maintaining the precision of terms; who feels the importance of being close to the natural world; who believes in a divine power that goes beyond the boundaries of any one religion; who believes in the essential goodness of people, and who understands that, as a man of principle, he is bound to be abused and misunderstood. Standing at the center of the *Cantos,* the Adams Cantos are themselves a "record of struggle" and remind us, if we need reminding, of how unquestionably and fundamentally American this poem of Pound's is.

After Cantos 52–71 were finished, Pound had planned to change the emphasis of his poem from economics to matters of belief and philosophy—to write a paradiso (*L,* 331). He had no way of knowing at that time that his next sequence of cantos would be a purgatorio.

4 The Pisan Cantos

Inevitably, the *Pisan Cantos* begin with a lament for the death of Mussolini. In the background are the bodies of the Duce and Clara Petacci, hung head downward in the Piazza Loreto, but in the foreground the figure of the peasant whose loss, in Pound's eyes, is the real tragedy:

> The enormous tragedy of the dream in the peasant's bent
>   shoulders
>   Manes! Manes was tanned and stuffed,
>   Thus Ben and la Clara *a Milano*
> That maggots shd/ eat the dead bullock
> DIGONOS, Δίγονος, but the twice crucified
>   where in history will you find it?
> Yet say this to the Possum: a bang, not a whimper,
>   with a bang not with a whimper.   [74/425]

All of Pound's hopes had been pinned on Mussolini—not as he was, but as the poet had chosen to see him. From the mid-1930s on, Pound had subordinated all other concerns to the cause of economic reform and world peace. He had come to see Mussolini as the only world leader who was both capable of and committed to breaking the power of the usurers and willing to institute a sound monetary system based on the principles of Social Credit. Pound believed that this would not only improve the quality of life of the whole people, but also help to avert another European war, since,

178

if the usurers no longer stood to profit from countries' war debts, they would not try to encourage wars, as Pound claimed they now did. Since economic reform was the poet's main aim, and he believed the Duce to be his only hope of achieving it, he made little distinction between his own cause and the Fascist cause, and devoted the greater part of his energies to propaganda for both. Even after Mussolini's arrest and his subsequent liberation by the Germans and reinstatement as "leader" of the precarious "Republic of Salò," the poet continued his frenzied propaganda, writing radio speeches, slogans and letters, and even making one more radio broadcast.[1] Mussolini's death came as a great blow to Pound; it meant the end of any hope of economic justice, the ruin of all that he had worked for over the last ten years, the betrayal of "the dream in the peasant's bent / shoulders." Within four days, Pound himself was under arrest.

In his radio broadcasts, Pound was writing about a "war," but not about the Second World War. He had little knowledge of and even less interest in the events of the war; for him the real war was the war against the usurers, and the Second World War, like the first, was simply another phase in this conflict. Any careful consideration of the progress of the war and of the war aims of the countries involved was a waste of time because the only real issue was the economic one and all other considerations were merely red herrings, intended to distract attention from the machinations of the international bankers and their allies. He seemed to see the Second World War as a continuation of and almost a replay of the first—we even find him asking in 1943 "Who are out in the front line trenches, getting decimated?"[2]—and his highly theoretical approach was quite deliberate, as we see from comments that he made much later. In March 1960 he said: "as soon as [the first war] was over . . . one spent the next twenty years trying to prevent the second war . . . I think the *New Age* office helped me to see the war [not] as a separate event, but as part of a system, one

---

1. C. David Heymann, *Ezra Pound: The Last Rower* (New York, 1976), pp. 149–51.
2. From a radio speech for *Ente Italiano Audizione Radiofoniche*, May 12, 1943, quoted in Heymann, p. 124.

war after another." In retrospect, he saw what was wrong about the kind of propaganda he chose, but pointed out that his "method of opposing tyranny was wrong over a thirty year period; it had nothing to do with the Second World War in particular."[3]

Focussing all his attention upon his strange and highly unreliable paradigm of the European situation in the thirties and forties, Pound allowed himself to be led from one false assumption to another: Mussolini understood that the welfare of the whole people required that control of the nation's finances be taken out of the hands of private individuals, whose goals were purely selfish, and returned to the government. His economic ideas were sound and, since economic justice was all-important, his judgment in other areas had to be sound also, and any criticism of him had to come from people who either failed to understand his aims or were in league with the usurers. Since Mussolini had allied himself with Hitler, the Führer's ideas had to be economically sound also, and Churchill and Roosevelt, by declaring war on the Axis powers, showed that they were on the side of the usurers. Also, since wars are started by usurers, Churchill and Roosevelt must have been instrumental in starting this one.

Putting his faith implicitly in the public-spiritedness and astuteness of the idealized Mussolini that he had created in his own mind, Pound did not feel free to fault the Duce's approval of Hitler. Subconsciously he must have sensed that any objective scrutiny of Hitler's actions would reveal a set of aims and programs to which he would be violently opposed and which would also force him to question the political integrity of Mussolini. As a result he opted for complete evasiveness. He invented a Hitler whose main concern was the welfare of all of Europe and who saw monetary reform as an important means to this end. Having allowed himself to believe in this idealized Führer, Pound had no compunction about echoing some of Hitler's comments on the Jews as a race. In fact, his readiness to do so amounted to an insistence that Hitler's quarrel with the Jews was no more sinister than Pound's own desire to deprive international bankers of the power to influence world politics. Pound's extension of his criti-

3. Donald Hall, "Ezra Pound: An Interview," *The Paris Review* 28 (Summer/Fall, 1962): 40–41, 45.

cism from "Jewish bankers" to the whole race was, in large part, an act of bravado. In his sweeping derogatory comments about all Jews he was adopting a pose of self-confidence and certainty.

The radio gave Pound access to a great audience, but the ideas which he was trying to convey were accessible only to him:

> Every hour that you go on with this war is an hour lost to you and your children. And every sane act you commit is committed in homage to Mussolini and Hitler. Every reform, every lurch toward the just price, toward the control of a market is an act of homage to Mussolini and Hitler. They are your leaders, however much you think you are conducted by Roosevelt or told by Churchill. You follow Mussolini and Hitler in every constructive act of your government. [Rome Radio, May 26, 1942]

Once we understand how his bizarre logic runs, we can see how what appears to be treason is so completely divorced from the realities of the war that it has become wholly theoretical and irrelevant. He has moved from the realm of reason to the realm of feeling. He had, in the past, looked at plenty of evidence, but it was always evidence for his own position, never evidence against. By now, the very fact of the war was, to him, overwhelming evidence for his case against the usurers and made further explanations and reasons redundant. The words of his speeches were not there to explain and to convey ideas so much as to register the intensity of his moral outrage. He was propounding a "truth" which no longer needed to be proved, only to be reiterated obsessively. The two roles of Pound "the man of letters"—the propagandist and the poet—had come to seem like two different people. Mary noticed how, even at home, when he was reading to her and her mother, "it seemed as though he possessed two voices: one angry, sardonic, sometimes shrill and violent for the radio speeches; one calm, harmonious, heroic for Homer, as though he were taking a deep, refreshing plunge into the wine-colored sea after a scorching battle" (*Disc.*, 150).

In Rome, with complete freedom to broadcast whatever he wanted to say, Pound was in fact entirely trapped in evasions, distortions and obsessions of his own making. At Pisa, penned up in a cage in the Disciplinary Training Center, he found himself, paradoxically, free in ways that he had not been before. He was freed from his irresistible compulsion to act, to carry out his war against *Usura.* He was freed from all the distractions which before had saved him from having to examine himself and his motives. In the course of the *Pisan Cantos* he also learned to free himself from his compulsive objectivity and to rediscover his compassion, self-doubt, humility, contrition, and kindliness. Moreover, these cantos suggest that this process of self-discovery was undertaken readily, even with relief. The poet's movement toward self-confrontation and self-knowledge is so clearly the main organizing principle of the sequence that, for the most part, we will concentrate on this rather than on the less inclusive thematic patterns.

The dominant mood of these cantos, right from the beginning, is meditative, nostalgic, and reverential. Because of the restraints on his actions, time passes slowly and his thoughts become more far-ranging than they have been for a long time. He finds himself thinking a great deal about the events and friendships of the past; he pays close attention to the details of camp life and of the natural world that he can see near him, and he learns introspection. He cultivates a Confucian state of mind, thinks specifically rather than theoretically about pagan energies and "the process," and feels a strong affinity for the mood of the Noh.

Now that his dream of a new Italy has come to nothing, he sees that the only ideal city will be a city of the mind, and he chooses two cities of the past as symbols, Ecbatana—"the city of Dioce whose terraces are the colour of stars"—and Wagadu, from the African legend of "The Lute of Gassir." Wagadu is built and destroyed four times, each time under a new name. The legend looks forward to the time when the city will be rebuilt for the final time, never to be destroyed again:

> For in itself, Wagadu is not of stone, nor of wood nor of earth. Wagadu is the strength which lives in the hearts of men. . . . But if Wagadu should now be found again for the fourth time, then she will live so strongly in the minds of men that she can never be lost again, and so strongly that vanity, dis-loyalty, greed and disunity can never again harm her at all.

. . . [The fifth Wagadu] will be no more transitory than the rain of the South, and the rocks of the Sahara, because every man will have Wagadu in his heart, and every woman will shelter a Wagadu in her womb.[4]

Pound first mentions the "Lute of Gassir" on the third page of the canto and, three pages later, makes an explicit connection between Wagadu, Ecbatana, and Mussolini's Italy:

> 4 times was the city rebuilded, Hooo Fasa
> Gassir, Hooo Fasa   dell' Italia tradita
> now in the mind indestructible, Gassir, Hoooo Fasa
> With the four giants at the four corners
> and four gates mid-wall Hooo Fasa
> and a terrace the colour of stars   [74/430]

Later in this same canto he writes:

> "I believe in the resurrection of Italy   quia impossibile est
> 4 times to the song of Gassir
> now in the mind indestructible.   [74/442]

In fact the *Pisan Cantos* are, in large part, Pound's discovery of how much, previously disregarded, is "in the mind indestructible."

After the reference to the "city of Dioce" on the first page of these cantos, we find "The suave eyes, quiet, not scornful." The eyes, although enigmatic at this stage, introduce the central theme of this sequence which reaches its climax in Canto 81 with the apparition of eyes in the poet's tent. This apparition will initiate his affirmation that "what thou lovest well remains" and his self-castigation, "Pull down thy vanity." The eyes are important because of whom they belong to. We are already familiar with Pound's fascination with the eyes of women in paintings and of goddesses, particularly Venus, and in the first part of this sequence

4. "The Lute of Gassir," collected by Leo Frobenius in *Atlantis* (Jena, 1921), vol. 6, pp. 59–60, translation mine. Translated by Pound into Italian as *Il Liuto di Gassire* (Milan, 1961).

the goddesses and heroines of the past have an important place. However, as the *Pisan Cantos* progress, the goddesses give way to real women whom Pound has loved and the poem achieves an unprecedented depth and intensity of feeling.

The "suave eyes" of the first page are followed by a Confucian passage, and a few lines later we find:

> ΟΫ ΤΙΣ, ΟΫ ΤΙΣ? Odysseus
>
> the name of my family.   [74/425]

In fact, Pound is aware of how unlike Odysseus's fate his own has become and ΟΫ ΤΙΣ—Nobody—seems an appropriate name for him rather than an expedient alias. Five pages later he writes "ΟΫ ΤΙΣ / a man on whom the sun has gone down" (74/430), and then "between NEKUIA where are Alcmene and Tyro / and the Charybdis of action / to the solitude of Mt. Taishan." He dissociates himself even further from Odysseus when he reverses his earlier comment "nec ivi in harum" (39/194) and sees himself no longer under special protection but destined to share the fate which all other men meet at Circe's hands:

> ac ego in harum
> so lay men in Circe's swine-sty;
> ivi in harum *ego* ac vidi cadaveres animae
> [I too went into the pig-sty and saw the corpses
>
> of souls.]   [74/436]

Yet the Circe whose enchantment pens up the prisoners in the camp at Pisa is not, Pound says, Homer's "trim-coiffed Goddess," "benecomata Kirkê," but *Usura,* "neither with lions nor leopards attended / but poison, veleno? / in all the veins of the commonweal" (74/437).

Pound has been steadily moving away from an Odyssean ideal and toward a Confucian one, and the reason for this is given most succinctly in chapter 3 of *Guide to Kulchur.* Here he describes "The Homeric world" as "very human . . . A world of irresponsible gods, a very high society without recognizable morals, the individual responsible to himself" (*GK,* 38). He accuses both the Greek philosophers and Christ of lacking "a sense of social order," and finds Rome far more admirable than Greece because "Rome was the responsible ruler." Odysseus does not fit at all in the Confucian world of Pound's ideal "totalitarian" state. The poet believes that "the sense of responsibility, the need for coordination of individuals expressed in Kung's teaching differs radically both from early Christian absolutism and from the maritime adventure morals of Odysseus or the loose talk of argumentative greeks" (*GK*, 38). He insists that "The love of wisdom, or the responsibility that carries wisdom into details of action, is not a Greek glory but a Roman" (*GK*, 40). He does not break off all connections with Odysseus by any means, but these connections are often overshadowed by his emphasis on the importance of order and justice.

During the war years, Pound worked on translations of Confucius, and the partisans who came to arrest him found him busy with the *Book of Mencius.* When he left with them, he took his edition of Confucius's *Four Books* and a dictionary with him to the camp. Here he worked concurrently on his cantos and on English versions of the *Ta Hsio* and *Chung Yung* which he had already translated into Italian. At the end of the English version of the *Ta Hsio,* he includes a note urging the reader to continue to reread the work until it becomes clear how this has been the essential foundation for the great dynasties of China. The note is dated: "D. T. C., Pisa; / 5 October – 5 November, 1945."

Before his arrest, Pound considered himself Confucian in his political ideals and even convinced himself that Mussolini was a Confucian ruler, yet any relationships that he made between Confucius and Italian politics were made mechanically and without reflection. At Pisa, his response to Confucius's writings is more personal and more profound. Before, he had wanted political ideas that would go into action, but now, when action is no longer possible, he knows that he must reconcile himself to the pursuit of political and civic wisdom for its own sake. He has no doubts about the perennial wisdom of Confucius's writings as he asserts obliquely on the first page of this sequence in "washed in the Kiang and Han / what whiteness will you add to this whiteness, / what candour?" This is part of a quotation from Mencius which Pound gives in full in his *Confucius:* "After Confucius' death, when there was talk of regrouping, Tsang declined, saying: 'washed in the Keang and Han, bleached in the autumn sun's-slope, what whiteness can one add to that whiteness, what candour?' " (*C,* 194).

Pound values Confucius not only for what he teaches about statecraft and sound government, but also for his observations on personal conduct. The Confucian ideal of self-sufficiency and serenity in adversity is particularly consoling to him at Pisa. In Canto 74 he includes a paraphrase of the first three chapters of the *Analects:*

> To study with the white wings of time passing
> > is not that our delight
> to have friends come from far countries
> > is not that pleasure
> nor to care that we are untrumpeted?
> > filial, fraternal affection is the root of humaneness
> > the root of the process
> nor are elaborate speeches and slick alacrity.   [74/437]

In the same spirit he translates later from *Analects* (book 6, part 21): "the sage / delighteth in water / the humane man has amity with the hills" (83/529).

He is also attentive to Confucius's insistence on the need for self-examination and self-criticism. " 'Missing the bull's eye seeks the cause in himself' " (77/468) refers us to "Kung said: there is an analogy between the man of breed and the archer. The archer who misses the bulls-eye turns and seeks the cause of his failure in himself" (*C,* 127). In Canto 80 he writes:

> > as he had walked under the rain altars
> > > or under the trees of their grove
> > > or would it be under their parapets
> > in his moving was stillness   [80/512]

These altars are from *Analects,* book 12, part 21, where we read that the Master walked with Fan Ch'ih "below the rain altars" to advise his disciple who has asked "how to lift one's conscience in action; to correct the hidden tare, and separate one's errors?"

Confucius tells him: "Put first the action, second the success. Won't that raise the level of your conscious acts? Work on one's own faults, not on someone else's hatefulnesses, won't that comb out the hidden weeds? For one morning's temper to jeopard one's life and even that of one's relatives, isn't that hallucination?" (*C,* 247–48). Pound realizes that this is advice which he himself needs to follow, and he is now ready to "work on his own faults." The admonition against bad temper particularly sticks in his mind and we find it repeated in 98/693 and 99/698.

As we would expect, Pound includes many references to his immediate surroundings in these cantos. He pays attention both to the comings and goings of the other prisoners around him and to the changes of the sky and weather and the flora and fauna of the prison compound. After his first Confucian passage, he writes: " 'the great periplum brings in the stars to our shore,' " and this is a prelude to many subsequent observations of the clouds, the sun, the moon, and the stars. He talks of "the sun dragging her stars" (74/431) and later expands this to: "the sun in his great periplum / leads in his fleet here / sotto le nostre scogli / under our craggy cliffs" (76/452). The poet has all the time in the world to sit and think and study the sky. He looks at Orion and Canis Major (or Sirius alone): "man and dog / on the S. E. horizon / and we note that dog precedes man in the occident / and of course in the orient if the bloke in the / is proceeding rightwards" (80/499). Above all, as we shall see, he watches Venus, the morning and evening star.

The "green world" also is very close to him as he sits in his wire mesh cage, and his perspective becomes scaled down to the dimensions of the plant and insect life around him. From where he sits, "The ant's a centaur in his dragon world" (81/521). The simple life around him goes on, and this consoles him with some sense of permanence. He says: "A lizard upheld me."

The earth is Gea Terra, the mother of all living things, but it is also, when Pound feels depressed, "nether earth," the graveyard of its offspring and the gateway to the underworld:

χθόνια γέα, Μήτηρ,   [Nether Earth, Mother]
   by thy herbs menthe thyme and basilicum,

        from whom and to whom,
        will never be more now than at present
being given a new green katydid of a Sunday
emerald, paler than emerald,
            minus its right propeller
        this tent is to me and ΤΙΘΩΝΩΙ   [74/435]

Tithonus, the husband of Eos, the Dawn, was made immortal by
Zeus but was not given immortal youth. Pound is starting to feel
old. Above all, "mother earth" restores to him his sense of pro-
portion and his humility. Later he will admonish himself:

        Learn of the green world what can be thy place
        In scaled invention or true artistry,
        Pull down thy vanity,
                    Paquin pull down!
        The green casque has outdone your elegance.   [81/521]

    Intent as Pound is on his surroundings, he spends even more
time on nostalgic reminiscences. These thoughts are not only a
distraction from the discomfort and boredom of his present reality,
but also a way of preserving his sanity in this frightening predica-
ment. He clearly relies heavily on these moments from the past. In
Canto 74, after a great accumulation of memories, he writes:

        and that certain images be formed in the mind
                    to remain there
                        formato locho
            Arachne mi porta fortuna
        to remain there, resurgent ΕΙΚΟΝΕΣ   [74/446]

    He reflects now on moments of friendship and love which be-
fore, with his demanding program of research and propaganda for
reform, he had had little time to dwell upon. His nostalgic and
elegiac mood and his sense of kinship with the natural world so
close about him produce in him a state of consciousness very simi-
lar to the spirit of Noh drama. In Canto 74, he refers to three Noh
plays, *Hagoromo, Kumasaka,* and *Suma Gengi.* He had worked with

great enthusiasm between 1913 and 1916 to turn Ernest Fenollosa's literal translations of the Noh into polished versions and, in January 1917 the translations had been published as *'Noh' or Accomplishment,* with commentary by both Pound and Fenollosa on the art of the Noh.

Fenollosa's commentary begins with the observation that "The Japanese people have loved nature so passionately that they have interwoven her life and their own into one continuous drama of the art of pure living" (*T,* 268). He also notes his teacher Umewaka Minoru's statement that "the excellence of Noh lay in emotion, not in action or externals" (*T,* 238), and explains later that "the most striking thing about these plays is their marvellously complete grasp of spiritual being. . . . Their creators were great psychologists. In no other drama does the supernatural play so great, so intimate a part." The ghosts of heroes play a more prominent part than living people and even "spirits of the moonlight, the souls of flowers and trees, essences that live in wine and fire, the semi-embodiments of a thought . . . move before us in the dramatic types" (*T,* 280). As we shall see, Pound is now ready to reestablish contact with this world of spirits and essences, of ceremonial dignity and the contemplation of beauty.

Back in 1916, Pound the Imagist had been particularly fascinated by his observation that "the better plays are all built into the intensification of a single Image: the red maple leaves and the snow flurry in Nishikigi, the pines in Takasago, the blue-grey waves and wave pattern in Suma Genji, the mantle of feathers in the play of that name, Hagoromo" (*T,* 237). In a footnote, he says that these plays answer the question " 'Could one do a long Imagiste poem, or even a long poem in vers libre?' " In the commentary which he appends to *Suma Genji,* Pound, anticipating that the play might seem "undramatic" to some on a first reading, warns that the reader "will miss the feel of suspense if he is unable to put himself in sympathy with the priest eager to see 'even in a vision' the beauty lost in the years, 'the shadow of the past in bright form' " (*T,* 236–37). Here, in 1916, he had written of the "conscious effort" necessary to enable one to fall into this unusual frame of mind; now, almost thirty years later, he again finds himself reilluminating "the beauty lost in the years."

When the heroes of the Noh appear by daylight, they take the form of commonplace people, but when they reveal themselves in their former glory, it is by moonlight. Pound thinks of himself as "a man on whom the sun has gone down" and, in his pursuit of the memories of the past, himself seeks a moonlit world. He writes: "and the nymph of the Hagoromo came to me, / as a corona of angels" (74/430), and thus identifies with the fisherman, Hakuryo, who, finding the feather-mantle of a Tennin, a sky-spirit, will only return it on condition that she teach him her dance, "that can turn the palace of the moon." She agrees, saying "For the sorrows of the world I will leave this new dancing with you for sorrowful people" (*T,* 311). The words of the chorus, as Pound renders them, show how perfectly the mood of the Noh complements his own mood in these cantos:

> Nor is this rock of earth overmuch worn by the brushing of that feather-mantle, the feathery skirt of the stars: rarely, how rarely. There is a magic song from the east, the voices of many and many: and flute and sho, filling the space beyond the cloud's edge, seven-stringed; dance filling and filling. The red sun blots on the sky the line of the colour-drenched mountains. The flowers rain in a gust. . . . Wonderful is the sleeve of the white cloud, whirling such snow here. [*T,* 314]

Moved by the spirit of the Noh, the poet can conjure up "the beauty lost in the years," but, in the process, he inevitably reflects on the man he was and the man he has become, and in Canto 74 we begin to find for the first time in the poem Pound's thoughts about and criticisms of himself. By following these, we can trace the steps by which he comes to full self-knowledge. His complete self-assurance has gone and he says "I am noman, my name is noman" (74/426). He feels both contrition and the need to preserve his dignity. Quoting Bianca Capello, the mistress of Francesco de'Medici, Pound reminds us that his spirit is not broken: " 'Se casco . . . / 'non casco in ginnocchion' [If I fall, I do not fall on my knees]" (74/427). Yet, on the same page, he quotes from Villon's "*Epitaphe*": "under *les six potences* / Absouldre, que tous nous vueil absoudre" [under the six gallows / Absolve,

may you absolve us all]. The words "Linus, Cletus, Clement /
whose prayers" (74/428) are taken from the "Commemoration of
the Saints" in the Canon of the Mass where the penitent asks for
God's protection and for the benefits of the merits and prayers of
the Virgin and the Saints.

Feeling that he is "a man on whom the sun has gone down,"
he weeps "in the rainditch at evening" but he soon takes heart,
knowing that a man "first must destroy himself ere others destroy
him" (74/430). He can begin to face the truth about the man he
has become: "that had been a hard man in some ways" (74/431).
When Mr. Edwards, another prisoner, makes Pound a table "against
regulations," this one act of kindness leads the poet, no longer the
adversary of "Pity," to acknowledge that "the greatest is charity"
(74/434). In this "Dark Night of the Soul, "nox animae magna,"
he thinks of others besides himself:

> I don't know how humanity stands it
> > with a painted paradise at the end of it,
> > without a painted paradise at the end of it.
> > > > [74/436]

As the canto nears its close, Mary reappears as a consoling pres-
ence. Pound describes the Tyrolean village in which she grew up,
a sanctuary from the divisive forces of the twentieth century, a
place where "Herr Bacher's father made madonnas still in the tra-
dition / carved wood as you might have found in any cathedral /
and another Bacher still cut intaglios / such as Salustio's in the
time of Ixotta" (74/448). Memories such as this generate a pattern
which survives the threat of chaos and brings the poet back "out
of hell, the pit / out of the dust and glare evil" (74/449). The
"process" asserts its patterns even among the fragments of the
poet's shattered life and even at a time when he cannot impose
order himself through the force of his will. Pound illuminates this
with the image of the iron filings springing into the form of a rose
in the presence of the magnet. Yet with the patterns of the process
as a foundation, one can go on to construct the patterns of artistic
genius; to reassure himself of this, Pound devotes his next canto to
a transcription of the score of the violin part of "La Canzone de

li ucelli," once a choral arrangement by Janequin, rewritten by Francesco da Milano for the lute and rewritten again for the violin —for Olga Rudge's violin—by Gerhart Münch. Münch himself has come "out of Phlegethon," having visited Rapallo for just two days during a short leave. He had been called up to provide entertainment for the German troops (*Disc.*, 160).

The most important passages in the *Pisan Cantos*—those in which the poet writes about the women he loves—are of three related but somewhat different kinds. The simplest are brief, straightforward reminiscences in which the poet recalls some specific incident involving the beloved. Passages of a second kind are made up of a series of fleeting allusions which offer glimpses of the paradisal and describe, in one form or another, the *nous* out of which his goddesses and the beautiful women of the past materialize. This "sea crystalline and enduring" is very much connected, in the poet's mind, with the sea itself and especially with the waters off Rapallo and Zoagli, and the birth of Venus from the sea foam stands as the archetypal instance of the emerging of divinities from the *nous*. In the third type of passage there is a movement inland from the sea, and here the wind replaces the sea as the element which moves the poet and evokes in him the states of mind which, to him, seem equivalent to the presence of the gods. Now the events—created by the imagination rather than recalled by the memory—are less fleeting and more sustained. In passages of this third kind he takes his state of mind as a point of departure and creates a dramatic action which will dignify and amplify the mood, expressing his strongest and most intimate feelings in a veiled but also exploratory way. He constructs a setting which he calls the "land of Dione" which, rather than being "by / sea-bord," stretches inland from a cliff edge and incorporates parts of the landscape that he can see from inside the camp.

The wind and the quality of the air are important in passages of the second kind also:

ΧΑΡΙΤΕΣ [the Graces] possibly in the soft air
with the mast held by the left hand
in this air as of Kuanon
enigma forgetting the times and seasons

but this air brought her ashore a la marina
with the great shell borne on the seawaves
              nautilis biancastra
  By no means an orderly Dantescan rising
but as the winds veer
                tira libeccio [the south-west wind blows]
now Genji at Suma   , tira libeccio
      as the winds veer and the raft is driven
      and the voices   , Tiro, Alcmene
      with you is Europa nec casta Pasiphaë
           Eurus, Apeliota as the winds veer in periplum
Io son la luna" . Cunizza
           as the winds veer in periplum
  and from under the Rupe Tarpeia
  drunk with wine of the Castelli
  "in the name of its god" "Spiritus veni"
  adveni / not to a schema
. . . .

but as grass under Zephyrus
      as the green blade under Apeliota   [74/443–44]

Here, in response to the touch of the mild air, the poet's mood becomes euphoric. The air has a timeless quality; it is an "enigma forgetting the times and seasons," and reawakens thoughts of beauty—specifically of beautiful women or of deities. Yet these images of beauty are glimpsed only fleetingly and even tentatively: the Graces are only "possibly in the soft air," and, instead of the Goddess of Mercy herself, we have only "this air as of Kuanon." The image of Venus is primarily Botticelli's rather than the poet's and, instead of the women themselves, we have "the voices" of those who have written of them—Homer telling of Tyro and Alcmene in Hades, and Propertius of Europa and Pasiphaë. Before Pound prepared a version of Propertius's poem for *Homage,* he had translated it separately as "Prayer for his Lady's Life" which begins:

    Here let thy clemency, Persephone, hold firm,
    Do thou, Pluto, bring here no greater harshness

> So many thousand beauties are gone down to Avernus,
> Ye might let one remain above with us.   [*P*, 38]

"Genji at Suma" refers us to the triumphant ending of the
Noh play. Earlier in the play the chorus, speaking for the hero,
tells that he first came to Suma "knowing all sorrow of seafare,
having none to attend my dreams, no one to hear the old stories"
(*T*, 233), but when he finally appears in his divine form to per-
form "the blue dance of the sea waves," the chorus's description
establishes a mood that is very much in keeping with that of
Botticelli's painting and hence with that of the whole ΧΑΡΙΤΕΣ
passage:

> The flower of waves-reflected
> Is on his white garment;
> That pattern covers the sleeve.
> The air is alive with flute-sounds,
> With the song of various pipes
> The land is a-quiver,
> And even the wild sea of Suma
>
> Is filled with resonant quiet.
> Moving in clouds and in rain,
> The dream overlaps with the real;
> There was a light out of heaven,
> There was a young man at the dance here;
> Surely it was Genji Hikaru,
> It was Genji Hikaru in spirit.   [*T*, 235]

The fleetingness of the allusions in the ΧΑΡΙΤΕΣ passage is
appropriate to its content since, at this point, the paradisal mani-
fests itself unpredictably, "as the winds veer," and the spirits come
"not to a schema." The poet does not expect to be able to write
"an orderly Dantescan" *Paradiso* and must be prepared to content
himself with glimpses of perfect beauty. He has said as much a few
pages earlier:

> Le Paradis n'est pas artificiel
> but spezzato apparently

it exists only in fragments unexpected excellent sausage,
>   the smell of mint, for example,
>   Ladro the night cat;   [74/438]

The touch of the mild air enables the poet to move for a moment outside time, to escape from time as an inexorable continuum into a state of mind in which time is a series of perfect moments from the past. The ΧΑΡΙΤΕΣ passage is completed by one of these moments:

> Time is not, Time is the evil, beloved
> Beloved the hours βροδοδάκτυλος [rosy-fingered]
>   as against the half-light of the window
>   with the sea beyond making horizon
> le contre-jour the line of the cameo
> profile "to carve Achaia"
>   a dream passing over the face in the half-light
>   Venere, Cytherea "aut Rhodon"
>   vento ligure, veni [south wind, come]   [74/444]

The central image here is of Olga Rudge, seated in silhouette at a window, and she is shown in a similar pose in a photograph reproduced in *Discretions.* She herself has become Venus and eclipses Botticelli's goddess. She has been identified with Venus earlier also:

> she did her hair in small ringlets, à la 1880 it might have been,
> red, and the dress she wore Drecol or Lanvin
>   a great goddess, Aeneas knew her forthwith
> by paint immortal as no other age is immortal   [74/435]

Pound identifies her with Botticelli's Venus for a third time when he writes, later in Canto 74:

> her eyes as in "La Nascita"
> whereas the child's face
> is at Capoquadri in the fresco square over the doorway
>   centre background

>   the form beached under Helios
>   funge la purezza[5]   [74/446]

(Her eyes are like those of Venus, not in color, but in expression.)

Canto 74 closes with a celebration of the wind as *nous* and of that "property of the mind" which—in its ability to rise to the contemplation of divine energies at the touch of the wind—itself creates the *nous:*

>   How soft the wind under Taishan
>   where the sea is remembered
>   out of hell, the pit
>   out of the dust and glare evil
>   Zephyrus / Apeliota
>   This liquid is certainly a
>   property of the mind
>   nec accidens est but an element
>   in the mind's make-up
>   est agens and functions dust to a fountain pan otherwise
>   Hast 'ou seen the rose in the steel dust
>   (or swansdown ever?)
>   so light is the urging, so ordered the dark petals of iron
>   we who have passed over Lethe.   [74/449]

Canto 76 begins with the poet looking at the sky:

>   And the sun high over horizon hidden in cloud bank
>   lit saffron the cloud ridge
>   dove sta memor[i] a   [76/452]

The last line is from "Donna mi prega" and the words begin Cavalcanti's definition of love. In Canto 36, Pound has translated this passage:

>   Where memory liveth,
>   it takes its state

---

5. See Hugh Kenner, "The 5 Laws + Che Funge," *Paideuma* 1, no. 1 (Spring 1972): 83.

Formed like a diafan from light on shade'
. . . .
Cometh from a seen form which being understood
Taketh locus and remaining in the intellect possible
Wherein hath he neither weight nor still-standing,
Descendeth not by quality but shineth out
Himself his own effect unendingly   [36/177]

The cloud ridge, then, is not just a place where Pound can imagine
that his memories of the past are preserved; the sunlight on the
edges of the cloud forms a "diafan" and becomes an image of
what Cavalcanti has said about the birth of love. In his present
mood, the poet finds that the images of beautiful women come
into his mind as they used to when he walked through the country-
side around Rapallo. Now he can see in his mind's eye:

> . . . on the high cliff Alcmene,
>   Dryas, Hamadryas ac Heliades
>   flowered branch and sleeve moving
>   Dirce et Ixotta e che fu chiamata Primavera
>   in the timeless air   [76/452]

The "high cliff" could be the cloud ridge, but it anticipates the
cliff which is part of the "Land of Dione" described later in this
canto. Dante tells us in the *Vita Nuova*, 24, of Cavalcanti's lady,
Giovanna, that "for her beauty, as folk believe, the name Prima-
vera (Spring) was given to her: and even so was she called [*e cosi
era chiamata*]." When Dante sees Giovanna coming toward him,
followed by Beatrice, "Love" suggests to the poet that it is appro-
priate that Giovanna should precede Beatrice since "The first is
named *Primavera* solely for this coming to-day; for I moved the
giver of the name to call her *Primavera* which is to say *prima verra*
(she will come first) on the day that Beatrice shall reveal herself
after her liege's vision."[6] "Love" then seems to say to Dante, "He
who should subtly consider would call Beatrice, Love, for the

6. Dante Alighieri, *La Vita Nuova and Canzonieri of Dante Alighieri*,
text established and translated by Thomas Okey (London, 1906), p. 93.

great similitude that she hath unto me." Dante then composes the sonnet, "*Io me sentii svegliar dentro allo core,*" on this incident for his best friend Cavalcanti, and Pound will refer to this poem at the end of Canto 93.

Dirce is the woman who inspires Landor's poem of that name to which Pound will shortly refer the reader; Sigismundo builds the "Tempio" for Ixotta, Giovanna is Cavalcanti's inspiration, and Cunizza is Sordello's. Beatrice, whom we expect to follow Giovanna, is of course Dante's inspiration. On the final page of the *Vita Nuova,* he reveals that the memory of Beatrice has already led him to conceive his great plan for the *Commedia.* Pound's mind is on the women he himself loves, but he alludes to them only indirectly by recalling settings that he associates with them:

> Sigismundo by the Aurelia to Genova
>   by la vecchia sotto S. Pantaleone
> Cunizza qua al triedro,
> e la scalza, and she who said: I still have the mould,
> and the rain fell all the night long at Ussel
> *cette mauvaiseh venggg* blew over Tolosa
> and in Mt Segur there is wind space and rain space
>   no more an altar to Mithras
>
> from il triedro to the Castellaro
>   the olives grey over grey holding walls
> and their leaves turn under Scirocco   [76/452–53]

The Via Aurelia runs by Pisa, south to Rome and north to Genoa. Pound, remembering that Sigismundo took this same road to Genoa, follows the course of the road in his mind until it brings him to Rapallo. In *Discretions* we learn that one of Pound's favorite walks from Rapallo takes him "along the hill path, to the old Roman road [*la vecchia*] above the new Aurelia by the sea, al Triedro and Castellaro, over the San Pantaleo, past the church to the very edge of the hill from where one looks down on the cliffs of Zoagli" (*Disc.,* 117). The olive groves behind their "grey holding walls" are on the hill above Rapallo, at Sant' Ambrogio where Pound visits Olga Rudge several times a week. The rest of the time he spends with his wife in Rapallo, and the references to Provence—the rainy night at Ussel, the wind at Toulouse, and the ruins at Montségur—are recalled from the time when they were there together. This already tense and awkward arrangement was made immeasurably more painful when, in 1943, the apartment in Rapallo was commandeered by the Germans, and Pound and his wife had no choice but to move in "for the duration" with Olga Rudge. We understand why Pound finds it easier to write of these matters with the aid of myth. In *Discretions* Pound's daughter turns to myth herself to convey her reactions upon learning from her father that her mother was not married to him, that he had both a wife and a son, and that his wife had in fact lived close at hand. She writes: "I had a glimpse of the madness and the vision: Zeus-Hera-Dione," thinking of the two quite different consorts of the god, one a sky-goddess and one an earth-goddess. Zeus made Dione his consort by seizing her oracle of the sacred oak at Dodona and Mary sees Gais as "a new northern Dodona where we listen to the swish of the river under elms, to the rustling of an old oak tree" (*Disc.*, 187). She conjectures, with good reason, that "many shades of emotion will remain hidden, embedded in the Cantos as mythology" (*Disc.*, 190), and we see this particularly in the *Pisan Cantos*. Here, although there are many allusions to the goddesses, we realize, when we consider the poet's situation, that he is hardly likely to be thinking primarily of myth and that personal matters are bound to be uppermost in his mind. Imprisoned in the D. T. C., confronted with the very real possibility of execution for treason, the poet finds that his past comes to seem more precious to him than ever before. Above all, Olga, Mary, and Dorothy are constantly in his thoughts. Since his arrest he has not seen any of them, nor have they had any news of him (*Life*, 409). His wife was not able to visit him until October 3, 1945, and only the last of the *Pisan Cantos* seems to have been written after this date.

In the absence of those closest to him, Pound spends much of his time thinking about them and, as we have seen, in the *nous* passages he finds himself recalling isolated moments and incidents although these are held only briefly in the mind before other memories or intrusions from the present come to take their place.

Yet we find in these cantos passages of another kind also which show that his thoughts about the women he loves go far beyond simple reminiscence to involve him in a sustained exercise of meditation and self-examination. First he recalls past memories and then, through the power of the affections and of the imagination, he tries to hold in his mind the feelings that these reminiscences generate and to fix them for a while in the present by identifying them in some way with his present surroundings. This he does by endowing the surroundings with a special significance of his own devising which is hospitable to the "quality of the affections" that he feels. Gradually he can dissociate his strong feelings from those settings in the past with which he had associated them and can hold them "in the mind indestructible" and even create for them new settings in the features of the landscape that he sees around him. The mountains, fields, and orchards that he can see from the camp are made into sacred places, charged with divine energies, worthy settings for the apparition of pagan deities, which Pound chooses as an appropriate tribute and as a dramatic correlative to those strong emotions of his which he most wants to celebrate. As the months pass, he "appropriates" the Pisan landscape—and the sky-scape—and transforms them into a kind of counterpart to the Earthly Paradise of the end of the *Purgatorio*—a setting splendid enough for the climactic moment in which the beloved woman reveals herself to the questing poet.

In Canto 76 we see how, among personal reminiscences and *nous* passages, the poet begins to introduce details of the "Land of Dione" which is beginning to take shape in his imagination. If we look at the following sequence of passages from this canto, we can see how the three kinds of passages keep their distinctive characteristics and yet complement and comment on each other. Instead of showing the goddess as she is portrayed in Botticelli's *Nascita,* the poet writes of her appearance to Anchises which occurs among the mountains of Ida so that this passage which deals with the *nous* at the same time contributes to the general movement inland from the sea:

> or Anchises that laid hold of her flanks of air
> drawing her to him
>   Cythera potens, Κύθηρα δεινά

> no cloud, but the crystal body
> > the tangent formed in the hand's cup
> > as live wind in the beech grove
> > > as strong air amid cypress　　[76/456–57]

Shortly after this, the poet, taking an incident from his past as a point of departure, embellishes and mythicizes it until he arrives at a setting which seems appropriate to his present state of mind. We assume that he has a specific occasion in mind when he writes:

> > Lay in soft grass by the cliff's edge
> with the sea 30 metres below this
> > > and at hand's span, at cubit's reach moving,
> the crystalline, as inverse of water,
> > clear over rock-bed　　　　　　　　[76/457]

Here again the crystal is associated with the air, rather than the water, this time with the "30 metres" of air between the palm of his hand stretched out over the cliff edge and the surface of the sea below. Soon the setting ceases to be recognizable as the cliffs of Zoagli and becomes stylized with flowers and animals which seem to belong on a tapestry:

> > ac ferae familiares
> the gemmed field *a destra* with fawn, with panther,
> > corn flower, thistle and sword-flower
> > to a half metre grass growth,
> lay on the cliff's edge
> > > . . . nor is this yet *atasal*
> > nor are here souls, nec personae
> > neither here in hypostasis, this land is of Dione
> and under her planet
> > to Helia the long meadow with poplars
> to Κύπρις
> > the mountain and shut garden of pear trees in flower
> here rested.　　　　　　　　　　　[76/457–58]

This "Land of Dione" exists in the present. The poet has no power to summon up the images of those he loves, as he does when he is remembering the past; he must wait here until the spirits of those he wishes to see appear to him of their own volition and while he waits, he rests. The goddesses are not present either; Dione is represented by the planet Venus and we are told only that the meadow is Helia's and the mountain and orchard Aphrodite's. It seems most likely that, not only the mountain, but also the meadow with its poplars and perhaps also the orchard are taken from Pound's own present surroundings.

The poet's situation as he waits for *atasal*—for union with the spirits that he yearns to see—is much like that of Dante in the *Purgatorio* as he waits in the Earthly Paradise for Beatrice to appear to him. As the "Land of Dione" is "under" the planet, Venus, so, in the *Purgatorio,* Matelda comes to lead Dante to Beatrice "in the hour, I think, when Cytherea, who seems always burning with the fire of love, first shone on the mountain from the east" (2. 27. 94–97).

As the poet rests, he thinks about his daughter and about Gais, which had seemed to be a kind of "Earthly Paradise." It proved not to be secure against the effect of war, though, as Pound's anecdote shows. When Mary was working as a secretary in a convalescent home for German soldiers, she met a local farmer's son from near Gais who had been blinded in the war, and he told her that "when he came back from leave / he was sad because he had been able to feel / all the ribs of his cow" (76/458).

In the camp, Pound feels desolate: "A lone ant from a broken ant-hill / from the wreckage of Europe, ego scriptor," but the rising of the evening star brings him new strength. As the planet rises above the horizon, it takes on a variety of colors before it is high enough to be seen as white light alone, undistorted by the effects of the earth's atmosphere at the horizon:

> The rain has fallen, the wind coming down
> out of the mountain
> Lucca, Forti dei Marmi, . . .
>
> . . . .
>
> . . . and within the crystal, went up swift as Thetis
> in colour rose-blue before sunset
> and carmine and amber,

spiriti questi? personae?
> tangibility by no means *atasal*
> but the crystal can be weighed in the hand

formal and passing within the sphere: Thetis,
Maya, 'Αφροδίτη,
> > no overstroke
> no dolphin faster in moving
> > nor the flying azure of the wing'd fish under Zoagli
> when he comes out into the air, living arrow.

and the clouds over the Pisan meadows
> > are indubitably as fine as any to be seen

from the peninsula

. . . .

O white-chested martin, God damn it,
> as no one else will carry a message,
> > say to La Cara: amo.   [76/459]

The echoes of the "Land of Dione" passage—"spiriti questi? / personae? / tangibility by no means *atasal*"—are included here in a section which is very specifically set in the present. The wind is now blowing from the northeast, from the direction of Lucca, and the poet is clearly watching the ascent of Venus and the Pisan clouds. As he looks at the evening sky, he thinks of the sea, first generally—when Venus seems to move "swift as Thetis"—and then of the sea under the cliffs of Zoagli. Maya is included here as one of the Pleiades and Thetis because she is a sea-goddess. A daughter of Proteus, Thetis uses her inherited gift of metamorphosis to frustrate the advances of Peleus until her own father tells her lover how to overpower her. She visits her favorite bay on the coast of Thessaly, riding naked on a dolphin, and Pound seems to be imagining her swimming in the bays of the Gulf of Tigullio and also to be thinking of Olga Rudge. In Canto 74 the poet remembers how "the bathers like small birds under hawk's eye / shrank back under the cliff's edge at il Pozzetto / al Tigullio" (74/439), and Mary tells how she used to go swimming with her mother early in the morning at the Pozzetto or in a little bay between Rapallo and Zoagli (*Disc.,* 170). Pound is almost certainly speaking of Olga Rudge when he asks the martin to carry his love message to "La Cara."

The poet then turns to reminiscence, but first he accuses himself and weeps as he recognizes that he has probably shown too little pity for others and then only "at moments that suited my own convenience" (76/460). Heaven and Hell are no longer "artificial" but are states of mind that he must live through in the present. He remembers Venice where he came as a young man and took lodging by "the Squero where Ogni Santi / meets San Trovaso" and where, in the thirties, he would spend the summers with Olga Rudge in her apartment, "the hidden nest" (76/462). Again he weeps and again reminds us of the splendor and the cruelty of Aphrodite "ΠΟΙΚΙΛΟΘΡΟΝ', 'ΑΘΑΝΑΤΑ," richly throned, immortal. As the canto ends, he shows his capacity for pity, and we are reminded of how much his efforts for fiscal reform have sprung, from the beginning, from a real sense of compassion for the sufferings of ordinary people:

> po'eri di'aoli [poor devils]
> po'eri di'aoli sent to the slaughter
>   Knecht gegen Knecht
>   to the sound of the bumm drum, to eat remnants
>   for a usurer's holiday to change the
> price of a currency
> . . . .
>   woe to them that conquer with armies
>   and whose only right is their power.   [76/462–63]

Pound's mind wanders in Canto 77 without a clear direction and, for the time being, he sets aside the subject of love. Demeter, when she appears, is simply the good earth and Aphrodite is the morning star who "faces Apollo" (77/471). In Canto 78, he gradually returns to the personal. It seems likely that he is particularly thinking of his wife in this canto, and is speaking to her when he says:

> Cassandra, your eyes are like tigers,
>   with no word written in them
> You also have I carried to nowhere

> to an ill house and there is
> > no end to the journey   [78/477]

Dorothy Pound has told Hugh Kenner that her husband wrote the
"lynx chorus" in Canto 79 for her, and Kenner wonders whether
"all those sharp-eyed cats that prowl through the *Cantos* com-
memorate Dorothy Pound."[7]

The poet then recalls how he set off on foot from Rome to
see Mary in Gais and to tell her, finally, about his wife and son. He
had left as soon as he heard that Italy had surrendered to the
Allies, and made his way to Gais by train and on foot. When he
arrived, exhausted and covered with dust, Mary's foster-mother
did not recognize him until he greeted her: " 'Gruss Gott,' 'Der
Herr!' 'Tatile ist gekommen!' " (78/478). Toward the end of the
canto, Pound's mind seems to be again on his wife:

> > Cassandra your eyes are like tigers'
> no light reaches through them
> . . . .
> To be a gentildonna in a lost town in the mountains
> > on a balcony with an iron railing
> > with a servant behind her
> > as it might be in a play by Lope de Vega
> and one goes by, not alone,
> > > No hay amor sin celos
> Sin segreto no hay amor
> > > eyes of Doña Juana la loca,
> Cunizza's shade al triedro and that presage
> > in the air
> which means that nothing will happen that will
> > be visible to the sargeants
> Tre donne intorno alla mia mente   [78/482–83]

"No hay amor sin celos," but the jealousy which springs from the
painful, three-sided relationship in Rapallo must go beyond the
usual jealousies of love. Yet outward appearances were preserved

---

7. Hugh Kenner, "D. P. Remembered," *Paideuma* 2, no. 3 (Winter
1973): 491.

and Dorothy Pound, by nature a very dignified woman, probably did seem like "a gentildonna in a lost town in the mountains" from a play by Lope. Hugo Rennert, a professor of Pound's at the University of Pennsylvania, had edited for the first time Lope's *Sin Secreto no hay Amor* and Pound, recalling this now, is probably thinking somewhat ruefully of how far his own experience has borne out the assertion of Lope's title. The eyes of Doña Juana *la loca* present a drastic and tragic image. Her husband's infidelity was the focus of and spur to her madness and his sudden death plunged her into complete insanity. The gloom is immediately relieved, though, by the apparition of Cunizza, associated as she always is for Pound with great love overflowing into compassion. She forewarns of some new development in Pound's thoughts about the "Tre donne intorno alla [sua] mente."

It seems clear now that one of the three women is Olga Rudge and another is Dorothy Pound. The third woman whom Pound has loved is mentioned two pages earlier when he recalls how he sat by the Roman arena in Verona with "Thiy and il decaduto." "Thiy," as we have already seen, is Bride Scratton.

The three altars which are to be paid as a fine (*multa*) in Canto 79 are exacted as restitution for the suffering which their love for Pound has brought to all three. Each of the three altars is to be given a set of two golden cups which are to be like the one whose perfect form was fabled to have been modelled from Helen's breast and which was in the temple of Pallas Athene at Lyndos on the island of Rhodes. Pound seems to be commenting on the appropriateness of having such a cup on Athene's altar in his aside that "Athene cd/ have done with more sex appeal" (79/486).

The spirit in which Pound makes this aside is, by and large, sustained throughout the canto. He seems in good spirits, and as the morning sun comes up, puts self-reproach behind him, at least for a while:

> and when the morning sun lit up the shelves and battalions
> of the West, cloud over cloud
>   Old Ez folded his blankets
> Neither Eos nor Hesperus has suffered wrong at my hands
>   [79/488]

(He uses Eos here, as he does elsewhere, rather than Phosphor, to refer to Venus as the morning star.)

In the last part of the canto he turns again to the "Land of Dione" which is now established in detail and which is the setting for the "lynx chorus" and the triumphal procession of Aphrodite. When the morning sun lights up the clouds, "Old Ez fold[s] his blankets," and looks out on the landscape that he has transformed into the "Land of Dione." The details of the scene are elaborations and extensions of the meadow of Helia and the mountain and "shut garden of pear trees" mentioned in Canto 76. The "long meadow with poplars" is now "the field of lynxes" and instead of, or in addition to, the pear orchard we find "the orchard of Maelids," the "close garden of Venus," and the "orchard / That is named Melagrana / or the Pomegranate field." At first the lynx chorus promises to be thoroughly Eleusinian in its invocation of Iacchus and address to Kore, but it becomes clear that the Eleusinian deities are finally overshadowed by Aphrodite. The pomegranate is significant, not only in its connection with Kore, who ate six of its seeds "in the under world," and with Dionysus from whose blood it was said to have sprung, but also because Pound associates it with Aphrodite herself. This transference seems quite deliberate since "Melagrana" is first an orchard, "or the pomegranate field"—and so associated with the cultivated or Eleusinian part of the landscape—and then we are told that "this forest is named Melagrana." The poet's description of the pomegranate suggests that it symbolizes passion:

> This fruit has a fire within it,
> Pomona, Pomona,
> No glass is clearer than are the globes of this flame
> what sea is clearer than the pomegranate body
> holding the flame?   [79/490]

This seems intended to recall the ending of Canto 39:

> Dark shoulders have stirred the lightning
> A girl's arms have nested the fire,
> Not I but the handmaid kindled

Cantat sic nupta
I have eaten the flame.   [39/196]

In the forest, Aphrodite's roses twine themselves around the other trees in preparation for her triumph. Part of the forest is oak-wood, suggesting Zeus's sanctuary and oracular oak at Dodona where he was worshipped with Dione. The poet asks, "Will the scrub-oak burst into flower? / There is a rose vine in the underbrush," and when he says, "Will you trade roses for acorns" he is perhaps suggesting an opposition between Aphrodite and Circe also. The pine, like the apple- and fig-tree and the vine, is sacred to Dionysus, and now, in the forest, "The smell of pine mingles with rose leaves."

At last Aphrodite appears as the sun rises:

The Graces have brought Ἀφροδίτην
Her cell is drawn by ten leopards
O lynx, guard my vineyard
As the grape swells under vine leaf
Ἥλιος is come to our mountain
there is a red glow in the carpet of pine spikes
. . . .
This Goddess was born of sea-foam
She is lighter than air under Hesperus
        δεινὰ εἶ, Κύθηρα
terrible in resistance
        Κόρη καὶ Δήλια καὶ Μαῖα
trine as praeludio
        Κύπρις Ἀφρόδιτη
a petal lighter than sea-foam
        Κύθηρα
                aram
                nemus
                vult

O puma, sacred to Hermes, Cimbica servant of Helios.   [79/491–92]

(For a note on Cimbica, see appendix 1.) The poet has brought his sea-born goddess to land and surrounds her with the gods and god-

desses of the earth, with Dionysus and with Kore, Delia and Maia—
Persephone before she was carried into Hades, Artemis as Delia
after the land of her birth, and Maia as Bona Dea, the earth god-
dess of the Romans. The poet has already written of the open
pomegranate that "The sea is not clearer in azure," and now the
goddess herself, "lighter than air under Hesperus," is "a petal
lighter than sea-foam."

Before the arrival of Aphrodite, "the mountain forest is full of
light" because " "Ηλιος is come to our mountain," and the "lynx
chorus" closes with the puma, "Cimbica servant of Helios." The
"sun god" is a strengthening and reassuring presence whenever he
appears in the poem and, unlike Κύθηρα δεινά, is detached from
mortal confusions and complications: "seeing the just and the un-
just, / tasting the sweet and the sorry, / Pater Helios turning"
(113/786). His presence in the lynx chorus complements the basic
optimism of the poet's mood that expresses itself at times in wry
and charming snatches of humor:

> Manitou, god of lynxes, remember our corn.
> Khardas, god of camels
>   what the deuce are you doing here?
> I beg your pardon . . .
> "Prepare to go on a journey."
>   "I . . ."   [79/488]

He is in good spirits, and yet he realizes that the "Land of
Dione" is a place where he can rest but not remain—that he must
persist in the way of thinking that has led him to this state of
mind. He has begun to consider his relationships with the women
he loves from their point of view and to appreciate the different
ways in which they have suffered on his account. This new under-
standing will eventually lead to the climactic moment of the *Pisan
Cantos*—the "vision of eyes" in Canto 81—that brings him reassur-
ance and a new peace of mind, but before he can be granted this
vision, he must make a painful act of contrition.

In Canto 80, the extent of his exhaustion and powerlessness
gradually makes itself felt, and once he confronts his despair he is
capable of the penitence which must precede his recovery. On the
first page of the canto he states as an article of faith "Amo ergo

sum," and again, "senesco sed amo," but, in the reminiscences that follow, we find that he concentrates, not on the women he loves, but on the friendships of his years in London and Paris during that happier time, "before the world was given over to wars" (80/506). In Canto 45 he has told how, under the sway of *Usura,* no great works of art are produced and "with usura . . . / is thy bread ever more of stale rags / is thy bread dry as paper, / with no mountain wheat, no strong flour"; we are intended to recall these lines now as we read his reminiscences of the quite different state of things that he found in Spain and Paris during his youth:

>   an era of croissants
>   then an era of *pains au lait*
>
>   . . . .
>   "Come pan, niño!"
>   that was an era also, and Spanish bread
>   was made out of grain in that era
>
>   . . . .
>   Madri', Sevilla, Córdoba,
>   there was grain equally in the bread of that era
>
>   . . . .
>   (and the mortal fatigue of action postponed)
>   and Las Meniñas hung in a room by themselves
>   and Philip horsed and not horsed and the dwarfs
>   and Don Juan of Austria
>   Breda, the Virgin, Los Boracchos
>   are they all now in the Prado?
>   y Las Hilanderas?   [80/493]

In recalling this happier time he surely intends to find comfort, but although the pleasure is there, it cannot do more than temporarily keep at bay the horror of his present situation. He is relieved to find that, like Teiresias in Hades, he "Still hath his mind entire" (80/494), but he cannot overcome his frightening sense of disorientation:

>   put me down for temporis acti [bygone days]
>   ΟΥ ΤΙΣ [No Man]

ἄχρονος [without time]
now there are no more days   [80/499]

For someone who had identified himself so much through action,
the "mortal fatigue of action postponed" and the confusion that
comes from complete ignorance about what is to happen to him
makes him feel that he is losing his identity and living "outside
time." He tries to reestablish his sense of time by looking at the
moon and the stars, but now they seem to share the ominous
quality of Tennyson's "Cold fires"—"glaring Eos stared the moon
in the face," and

        Death's seeds move in the year
                        semina motuum
           falling back into the trough of the sea
           the moon's arse been chewed off by this time
semina motuum   [80/500]

Instead of bringing comfort, nature seems not only to "wear the
colors of the spirit" but even to answer his mood:

        fog rose from the marshland
           bringing claustrophobia of the mist
    beyond the stockade there is chaos and nothingness
                                [80/501]

He amasses more and more reminiscences before he finally
turns his attention again to the sky. Now Venus is so close to the
crescent moon that Pound asks: "(Cythera, in the moon's barge
whither? / how hast thou the crescent for car?" (80/510), and he
notices how, in the dawn sky the planet loses its brilliance:

in the moon barge βροδοδάκτυλος Ἠώς

    with the veil of faint cloud before her
        Κύθηρα δεινὰ as a leaf borne in the current
    pale eyes as if without fire   [80/511]

She is still "Κύθηρα δεινὰ" and Pound knows that he is impli-
cated in her cruelty as we see in the confession that he is about to

make. As so often, Confucius shows him the way that he must take and, as we have seen, in Pound's reference to the "rain altars" he is recalling Kung's admonition—"Work on one's own faults, not on someone else's hatefulnesses, won't that comb out the hidden weeds?" Pound has decided to follow this course, but sees that the only measure that will serve now is an act of complete humility. By now his strength is failing and he writes, "Je suis au bout de mes forces," and asks:

> hast'ou swum in a sea of air strip
> > through an aeon of nothingness,
> when the raft broke and the waters went over me,
> > > > > > [80/513]

When he finds a copy of Speare's *Pocket Book of Verse* "on the jo-house seat," he can feel a kinship with Lovelace writing from prison and Whitman reconstructing a child's first revelation of the enormity of death, but it is in the pages of the Missal that he finds help in framing the prayer for pardon which will save him from despair:

> Immaculata, Introibo
> > for those who drink of the bitterness ;
> Perpetua, Agatha, Anastasia
> > > saeculorum

> repos donnez à cils
> > senze termine funge Immaculata Regina
> > > Les larmes que j'ai creées m'inondent
> Tard, très tard je t'ai connue, la Tristesse,
> I have been hard as youth sixty years   [80/513]

The mood of the rest of the canto is of "calm after tempest" and, as the sun rises, he feels a sense of fellowship with the prisoners around him who, like him, are "men of no fortune."

His thoughts turn to England and, although his first impulse is to deplore the economic and political decay of the country, pleasant personal memories intrude so that nostalgia takes over. Since the presence of his wife presides over the rest of this canto, it also stands, in part, as a tribute to her. He remembers how they visited an old abbey in Yorkshire, the inheritance of a cousin of Dorothy's, a Talbot—hence the punning on the name[8]—where they climbed across a roof to see a copy of one of the great Charters of Confirmation of the Magna Carta kept in a case in a turret room:

> To watch a while from the tower
>   where the dead flies lie thick over the old charter
> forgotten, oh quite forgotten
> but confirming John's first one,
> and still there if you climb over attic rafters.   [80/514]

His thoughts about England's decline are made not in anger, but in a tone of elegiac regret:

> . . . look at the fields; are they tilled?
> is the old terrace alive as it might be
> with a whole colony
>   if money be free again?
> Chesterton's England of has-been and why-not,
> or is it all rust, ruin, death duties and mortgages
> and the great carriage yard empty
>   and more pictures gone to pay taxes
> . . . .
> and the old kitchen left as the monks had left it
> and the rest as time has cleft it.   [80/514–15]

He remembers how strongly he responded to the sense of the closeness of the past in England and how, in 1911, riding from Southampton across Salisbury Plain to spend Christmas with Maurice Hewlett, he could see in his mind's eye the spirits of those who had travelled these roads in the past at Christmastime:

> and for that Christmas at Maurie Hewlett's
> Going out from Southampton
> they passed the car by the dozen

8. Kenner, "D. P. Remembered," *Paideuma* 2, no. 3 (Winter 1973): 492.

> who would not have shown weight on a scale
>> riding, riding
>>> for Noel the green holly
> Noel, Noel, the green holly   [80/515]

He thinks of Mary Stuart and the murder of Rizzio, of the bloody reigns of the Tudors and of the Wars of the Roses, but in lines that emphasize his attraction to the drama of it all:

> Tudor indeed is gone and every rose,
> Blood-red, blanch-white that in the sunset glows
> Cries: "Blood, Blood, Blood!" against the gothic stone
> Of England, as the Howard or Boleyn knows.
>
> Nor seeks the carmine petal to infer;
> Nor is the white bud Time's inquisitor
> Probing to know if its new-gnarled root
> Twists from York's head or belly of Lancaster: [80/515]

He can recapture the romance that the country held for him as a young man and now, setting aside the anger in which he had left for France in 1920, he makes his peace with England:

> and the Serpentine will look just the same
> and the gulls be as neat on the pond
> and the sunken garden unchanged
> and God knows what else is left of our London
>> my London, your London   [80/516]

At the center of Canto 81 we find the most important visionary moment of the whole poem, and the canto has an appropriately auspicious opening, presided over by the morning star:

> Zeus lies in Ceres' bosom
>> Taishan is attended of loves
>>> under Cythera, before sunrise
>>>>   [81/517]

The poet thinks back over time he has spent in Spain and then, among other reminiscences, we are given hints which prepare us for the great revelation which is to occur. We find an allusion to his relationship with his wife and Olga Rudge in:

> "Some cook, some do not cook
>   some things cannot be altered"
> Ἰυγξ . . . . . ἐμὸν ποτὶ δῶμα τὸν ἄνδρα
> [Little wheel . . . man to my house]   [81/518]

From the time of their marriage, Pound and his wife agreed that she would not have to cook (*Era,* 399), and the reference probably extends to Olga Rudge also, who, her daughter says, had "no flair" for cooking, unlike Pound himself, who was an excellent cook (*Disc.,* 49). The quotation marks around these lines raise the possibility that these may even have been Dorothy Pound's own words on the subject. In the fragment from Theocritus, the girl who is speaking is trying to charm her faithless lover to return to her by using her magic wheel.

Just before his tribute to Waller, Dowland, and Arnold Dolmetsch, Pound writes:

> AOI !
> a leaf in the current
>   at my grates no Althea   [81/519]

(For a discussion of AOI, see appendix 1.) He has been reading Lovelace's "To Althea, from Prison" in Speare's anthology and wishes that his "Althea" were there to visit him. From an earlier typescript version of the crucial passage leading up to and including the "Pull down thy vanity" section, we see that the reference to Althea is personal rather than literary. In place of the passage which now begins "Ed ascoltando al leggier mormorio," Pound had originally written:

> Whose world, or mine or theirs
>   or is it of none?

> So thinking of Althea at the grates
> Two rose-like lips pressed down upon my own.[9]

Nor surprisingly, he cancels the lips and includes instead his vision of eyes. At first he writes: "Your eyen two wol sleye me sodenly / I may the beauté of hem nat susteyne" (81/520), but his fear that the eyes will be merciless is immediately shown to be unjustified. In Chaucer's "Merciles Beaute," from which the quotation comes, the plea for pity in part 1 is followed by a realization of the woman's mercilessness, and in part 3 the lover escapes from the power of love. There is a reversal also in the canto, but of a different kind:

> there came new subtlety of eyes into my tent,
> whether of spirit or hypostasis,
> but what the blindfold hides
> or at carneval
> nor any pair showed anger
> Saw but the eyes and stance between the eyes,
> colour, diastasis,
> careless or unaware it had not the
> whole tent's room
> nor was place for the full Εἰδὼς
> interpass, penetrate
> casting but shade beyond the other lights   [81/520]

When the eyes appear to the poet he can only see clearly "the eyes and stance between the eyes"—only that part of each face which would be covered by a blindfold or a carnival mask. The eyes seem to have an accompanying form, but this is indistinct and incomplete, "casting but shade beyond the other lights." When the eyes first appear, Pound is unsure of their full significance. At first he cannot distinguish this vision from his earlier visionary apprehensions of goddesses or of the beautiful women of the past like Cunizza, Dirce, Isotta, or Cavalcanti's Giovanna "che fu chiamata Primavera" (76/452). Hence his use of the Neoplatonic

---

9. Princeton University manuscript collection, AM 19845.

"hypostasis." When he wonders if they are "of spirit or hypostasis" he is trying to decide whether the eyes are embodiments of the spirits of particular individuals or whether they are a mythic and therefore less specific manifestation of a universal "Idea" or "Form" whose place is in the *nous,* or "second hypostasis." But when he looks at the color of the eyes, he sees that they belong neither to goddesses nor to long-dead women:

> sky's clear
> night's sea
> green of the mountain pool
> shone from the unmasked eyes in half-masks's space.
> What thou lovest well remains   [81/520]

There are three pairs of eyes and they belong to three women who are very much alive. We learn from Mary that her mother has "violet-blue eyes, clear and luminous," and that Dorothy Pound's eyes are "steel-blue" (*Disc.,* 117, 259); Bride Scratton's eyes must have been green. The love, without anger, of these three women gives Pound the strength he needs to enable him to make his great affirmation:

> What thou lovest well remains,
>   the rest is dross
> What thou lov'st well shall not be reft from thee
> What thou lov'st well is thy true heritage
> Whose world, or mine or theirs
>   or is it of none?
> First came the seen, then thus the palpable
>   Elysium, though it were in the halls of hell,
> What thou lovest well is thy true heritage
> What thou lov'st well shall not be reft from thee.
>   [81/520–21]

While Dante is granted his vision of eternal love in Paradise, Pound's glimpse of Elysium comes to him "in the halls of hell," yet with such certainty that he knows it to be an eternal truth. For as long as he continues to write his poem he will never come to question his faith that "What thou lov'st well shall not be reft from thee," and this will make all his doubts, no matter how painful, finally bearable.

Now when he turns to the natural world, it is not, as before, for consolation, but to find in it an admonition:

> The ant's a centaur in his dragon world.
> Pull down thy vanity, it is not man
> Made courage, or made order, or made grace,
>   Pull down thy vanity, I say pull down.
> Learn of the green world what can be thy place.
>
> [81/521]

What seems to begin as a general moral exhortation is soon seen to be a specifically personal self-castigation:

> "Master thyself, then others shall thee beare"
>   Pull down thy vanity
> Thou art a beaten dog beneath the hail,
> A swollen magpie in a fitful sun,
> Half black half white
> Nor knowst'ou wing from tail
> Pull down thy vanity
>   How mean thy hates
> Fostered in falsity,
>   Pull down thy vanity,
> Rathe to destroy, niggard in charity,
> Pull down thy vanity,
>   I say pull down.   [81/521]

Yet here, as we see again so clearly in *Drafts and Fragments,* even when he speaks "de profundis," he does not belie the complexity of the truth by falling into an easy fatalism and tries "To confess wrong without losing rightness." If on one hand his energy and his aspiration led him into vanity, on the other they led to much that was positive for others as well as for himself:

> But to have done instead of not doing
>   this is not vanity

To have, with decency, knocked
That a Blunt should open
            To have gathered from the air a live tradition
or from a fine old eye the unconquered flame
This is not vanity.
            Here error is all in the not done,
all in the diffidence that faltered . . .   [81/521–22]

Canto 82 begins cheerfully enough with more reminiscences, but a reference to Clytemnestra's murder of Agamemnon prepares us for the despair which is to follow. We find another sinister reference in:

Be glad poor beaste, love follows after thee
 . . . .
                     f f
                  d

                     g
                        write the birds in their treble scale
Terreus! Terreus!   [82/525]

The birds, perched on the wire around the compound, are like notes on a stave and seem to be martins like the one he formerly asked to carry a message to "La Cara," since, later in the canto, they have "white downy chests black-rimmed." As they look very similar to swallows, this leads him to think of Tereus and the "poor beaste" could well be the nightingale whose song as she laments her rape is, paradoxically, an incentive to love for those who hear her. Immediately before this, we read:

            (Cythera   Cythera)
            With Dirce in one bark convey'd   [82/525]

Cythera here is primarily the planet Venus in her double aspect as both morning and evening star. The parentheses remind us there is in fact no separation; they also suggest the horns of the crescent moon, and this idea is reinforced by the reference to "bark" in the next line, reminding us of the moon's "barge." Dirce is the woman in Landor's poem of that title: "Stand close around, ye

Stygian set, / With Dirce in one boat conveyed! / Or Charon, seeing, may forget / That he is old and she a shade."[10] The evening star in the boat of the crescent moon, shining out in the surrounding darkness, recalls not the Dirce of myth, but this beautiful but now dead woman.

Pound has been reading Whitman's "Out of the Cradle Endlessly Rocking" in the anthology he has salvaged, and the song of the bird and the sea's message of death have made as strong an impression on Pound as they had on Whitman. The lines which Pound chooses to quote tell us a good deal about the impact of the poem on him. "O Throat, O throbbing heart" is followed by the lines:

> And I singing uselessly, uselessly all the night.
> O past! O happy life! O songs of joy!
> In the air, in the woods, over fields,
> Loved! loved! loved! loved! loved!
> But my mate no more, no more with me!
> We two together no more.[11]

The other line which Pound singles out—"O troubled reflection"—refers to the moon reflected in the sea. In Whitman's poem, the moon presides over the tragedy of the she-bird's death and the moon herself is a depressing presence since she reflects the increasing despair of the he-bird and of the poet. At first she is a "yellow half-moon late risen and swollen as if with tears," reminding us of Pound's comment in Canto 79: "The moon has a swollen cheek" (79/488). Then the grieving bird says of the moon: "It is lagging— O I think it is heavy with love, with love," and finally the poet sees her as "The yellow half-moon enlarged, sagging down, drooping, the face of the sea almost touching." The moon is given no power and no dignity, and we see Pound following this approach when he writes: "the moon's arse been chewed off by this time"

---

10. Walter Savage Landor, *The Poetical Works,* ed. Stephen Wheeler, 3 vols. (Oxford, 1973), 3: 234.

11. Walt Whitman, "Out of the Cradle Endlessly Rocking," *The Pocket Book of Verse,* ed. M. E. Speare (New York, 1940), pp. 228–34.

in 80/500. Whitman's boyhood intoxication with his new under-
standing of the sea's "low and delicious word death" is the im-
petus for "the thousand responsive songs at random, / My own
songs awaked from that hour." Although Pound's response in-
cludes fear of "the loneliness of death" (82/527), it also shows the
same hypnotic attraction as Whitman's:

> How drawn, O GEA TERRA,
>   What draws as thou drawest
>   till one sink into thee by an arm's width
> embracing thee. Drawest,
>   truly thou drawest.
> Wisdom lies next thee
>   simply, past metaphor.   [82/526]

He describes himself as "drunk with 'ΙΧΩΡ of ΧΘΟΝΙΟΣ / fluid
ΧΘΟΝΟΣ, strong as the undertow / of the wave receding" and his
choice of sea imagery to describe the attraction of the depths of
the earth particularly echoes Whitman's choice of the sea, "the
fierce old mother incessantly moaning," as the bearer of the mes-
sage of death. Instead of "leaves of grass," Pound chooses herbs:
"Where I lie let the thyme rise / and basilicum / let the herbs rise
in April abundant" (82/526). He thinks of Niccolò d'Este, buried
naked, and it seems to him that man and earth are "two halves of
the tally." Then, surely thinking of the prospect of insanity rather
than the possibility of hell, he writes: "but that a man should live
in that further terror, and live." For a moment he confronts the
thought of his own death and he weeps:

> the loneliness of death came upon me
>   (at 3 P.M., for an instant)   [82/527]

Three martins still sit "on the middle wire," like Whitman's birds
in that they have become a part of his confrontation with death.

Like Whitman after his revelation of death, Pound can proceed
to his songs, and Canto 83, which follows, shows the poet at his
most expansive and feeling most at one with himself. The rain
brings peace: "in the drenched tent there is quiet / sered eyes are

at rest." He quotes Confucius's "the sage / delighteth in water / the humane man hath amity with the hills" (*C,* 217). Gemistus Plethon, Pound tells us, "stemmed all from Neptune," and he traces the Neoplatonist's influence to the bas reliefs of Simone Ferucci in the "Tempio Malatestiano" which show children playing in water and around a fountain. The bas-relief of Sigismundo is actually in the chapel of the "Madonna dell'Acqua." Right at the beginning of the canto we are prepared for the light which will follow the rain: Pound quotes from Richard Grosseteste, who claims that the whole universe is created from light, and from Scotus Erigena: "omnia, quae sunt, lumina sunt" [all things that exist are lights].

For a while at least, the poet has found peace. He recalls again the Palazzo Capoquadri "with Maria's face there in the fresco," and the grass growing on the roof of San Giorgio, across the street from his window, where the wax is blessed in August before the day of the Palio. After the reference to the rain altars and to the frustration of Pound "the caged panther" at his inability to act, the Dryad comes as comforter, and after the rain life begins afresh:

> and now the new moon faces Taishan
> one must count by the dawn star
> > Dryad, thy peace is like water
> There is September sun on the pools   [83/530]

The sun comes as a benediction and a reaffirmation of vitality and of the process.

Pound then makes a personal affirmation of great significance; he adapts Mencius's celebration of the "passion-nature" (one's emotions and desires):

> this breath wholly covers the mountains
> > it shines and divides
> it nourishes by its rectitude
> does no injury
> overstanding the earth it fills the nine fields
> > to heaven

> Boon companion to equity
>> it joins with the process
>>> lacking it, there is inanition
>
> When the equities are gathered together
> as birds alighting
> it springeth up vital
>
> If deeds be not ensheaved and garnered in the heart
> there is inanition   [83/531]

The second book of Mencius is called the *Kung-Sun Ch'âu,* and in chapter 2 of part 1 Mencius says of the "passion-nature":

> It is exceedingly great, and exceedingly strong. Being nour-
> ished by rectitude, and sustaining no injury, it fills up all be-
> tween heaven and earth. . . . It is the mate and assistant of
> righteousness and reason. Without it *man* is in a state of
> starvation. . . . It is produced by the accumulation of righ-
> teous deeds; it is not to be obtained by incidental acts of
> righteousness.[12]

In his introductory note to this chapter, Legge says that Mencius's recognition of the importance of the "passion-nature" has earned him his place in Chinese philosophy. He goes on to explain Mencius's main points:

> The moral and intellectual powers ought to be supreme and
> govern, but . . . the active powers may not be stunted, for
> then the whole character will be feeble. But . . . they must
> not be allowed to take the lead. They must get their tone
> from the mind, and the way to develop them in all their com-
> pleteness is to do good. Let them be vigorous, and the mind
> clear and pure, and we shall have the man, whom nothing
> external to himself can perturb. [*Mencius,* p. 185]

---

12. James Legge, ed. and trans., *The Chinese Classics,* vol. 2, *The Works of Mencius,* p. 190. Subsequent page references to *Mencius* will be to this edition.

His painful experience in the D. T. C. has meant for Pound the rediscovery of his own emotions, and he can now appreciate the wisdom of Mencius's comments on the "passion-nature." His decision to use "this breath" to refer to the "passion-nature" seems puzzling at first, even though on one level it is obviously a way of linking the "passion-nature" to the "brightness of 'udor," the sunlit morning mist. Legge's note on the character which he translates as "passion-nature" helps to explain "breath," since the upper part of the character means "cloudy vapour" and the lower part "rice," the whole character suggesting "steam of rice" or "steam" generally. Mencius then uses it metaphorically to refer to the energy given off from the emotions and desires, from one's "animal vigour or courage" (*Mencius,* p. 188 n.). "As birds alighting" refers us to chapter 3 of *The Great Digest* and to a passage which Pound has already alluded to cryptically in Canto 79 in "the yellow bird / to rest" (79/487). Confucius explains one of the Odes in which a "twittering yellow bird . . . Comes to rest in the hollow corner of a hill" by saying: "Is man, for all his wit, less wise than this bird of yellow plumage that he should not know his resting place or fix the point of his aim?" (*C,* 39). The birds alighting represent the certainty of aim which is necessary before a man's deeds can be fruitful. In Canto 74 we find: "only that bird-hearted equity make timber / and lay hold of the earth" (74/426), and this also refers to the "yellow bird" passage and to part 4 of chapter 2 which immediately precedes it and which Pound translates: "Hence the man in whom speaks the voice of his forbears cuts no log that he does not make fit to be the roof tree [does nothing that he does not bring to a maximum, that he does not carry through to a finish.]" (*C,* 39). To know one's resting place one must be in touch with one's own emotions. Pound can now see how he has mistaken his aim in the past and has worked against himself. Now he sees the wisdom of "Giovanna's" advice not to work so hard and finds Mencius making the same point. The three characters *wu*[4]*, chu*[4]*,* and *chang*[3], meaning "do not assist to grow," occur in Mencius's further explanation of the operation of the "passion-nature." He says that if one persists in virtue for its own sake, the "passion-nature" is automatically nourished, but one does more harm than good by trying to force the development of this nature in any other way. He relates the anecdote of "a man of Sung" who was disappointed by the slow growth of his corn and, in the course of trying to make it longer by his own efforts, only succeeded in pulling it up.

Having decided that his aim will be true if he follows the promptings of his emotions, Pound now returns to reminiscences and, thinking of Venice, weeps at the thought that he may have seen it for the last time:

> Will I ever see the Giudecca again?
> > or the lights against it, Ca' Foscari, Ca' Giustinian
> or the Ca', as they say, of Desdemona
> or the two towers where are the cypress no more
> > or the boats moored off le Zattere
> or the north quai of the Sensaria DAKRUŌN ΔΑΚΡΥΩΝ
> > > [83/532]

A wasp is building a mud nest on his tent roof and, when later he sees one of its young crawl out of the nest and down "from mud on the tent roof to Tellus," he imagines that it has gone to carry greetings to the underworld, "to them that dwell under the earth," and to "sing in the bower / of Kore . . . / and have speech with Tiresias, Thebae" (83/533). For now, Pound is spared that journey to Hades and the infant wasp goes instead of him. His world is a sunlit world presided over by "Christo Re, Dio Sole."

He devotes the rest of the canto to intimacies, to memories of Stone Cottage in Sussex where, staying with Yeats in the winter of 1913, he overheard the poet downstairs composing "The Peacock" out loud, and where he spent his honeymoon in April of 1914. Thoughts of his wife lead him to recall the vision of eyes from Canto 81. There he had asked "Whose world, or mine or theirs / or is it of none?" showing how the revelation of the selfless and forgiving love of the three women had helped him to begin to take into consideration their feelings and their point of view. Earlier he had accused himself of having considered the feelings of others too little or "Only at moments that suited my own convenience," and in Canto 81 he shows how he has been able to move beyond self-absorption. Now he finds himself thinking only of the three women and turns to make an unprecedentedly intimate appeal to the reader to see their eyes through his eyes—to understand the way in which his relationships with them have been his "world:"

> A fat moon rises lop-sided over the mountain
> The eyes, this time my world,
>> But pass and look *from* mine
>>> between my lids
>>>> sea, sky, and pool
>>>> alternate
>>>> pool, sky, sea,
>> morning moon against sunrise
> like a bit of the best antient greek coinage   [83/535]

Artemis is completely eclipsed by these women and the moon is now a coin, albeit a handsome one, with nothing of the woman about it.

The poet's feeling of growing old makes him think of the continuity of the family and he closes the canto with thoughts of his daughter and his mother. Both are protected from the hell of the present, not only his mother by her memories of a better past, but also Mary because she has been raised in a culture in which the best traditions of the past are kept alive. In "Rémy de Gourmont" in *Pavannes and Divisions* he had commented on the "poignancy" of Anacreon's

> Λέγοισιν αἱ γυναῖκες
> Ἀνακρέων γέρων εἶ

[The girls say to me, "You are old Anacreon"], and now, because he is thinking of his daughter, he renders the couplet in German:

> Mir sagen
> Die Damen
> Du bist Greis,
>> Anacreon

and that a Madonna novecento

cd/ be as a Madonna quattrocento
This I learned in the Tirol
       and as perfect
where they paint the houses outside with figures
and the deep inner courts run back triple   [83/535]

In his mother's time "it was respectable, / it was social, apparently, / to sit in the Senate gallery," and public speaking was still an art:

. . . if Senator Edwards cd/ speak
and have his tropes stay in the memory 40 years, 60 years?
in short/ the descent
has not been of advantage either
    to the Senate or to "society"
                or to the people
    The States have passed thru a
           dam'd supercilious era
Down, Derry-down/
    Oh let an old man rest.   [83/536]

We sense his tiredness in the last canto of the sequence also as he turns his attention to the chaos of the world outside the prison compound that he must now soon face. Other prisoners were checking out and he knew that he would shortly be taken to America himself, but he seems to have arrived at a stoic attitude toward the prospect of facing his own dangerous personal predicament. In this canto he thinks a good deal about lost causes and about having to settle for dignified defeat and failure with courage rather than positive achievement. He begins with an elegy for the poet J. P. Angold, whose concern with economics in both his prose and poetry had particularly impressed Pound. Angold had been a contributor to Orage's *New English Weekly* and was killed while serving with the R. A. F. in 1943. Pound then recalls his trip to America in 1939 when he had tried, with no success, to get his economic ideas across to senators and congressmen and to warn about the danger of trusting England or taking England's part in the event of a European war. He saw Roosevelt as an insuperable obstacle to economic reform and quotes Senator Bankhead of Alabama on the President:

> "an' doan you think he chop an' change all the time
> stubborn az a mule, sah, stubborn as a MULE,
> got th'eastern idea about money.   [84/537]

By contrast, Jacob Coxey has maintained his commitment to the cause of economic justice. In 1894 he had led "Coxey's Army" to Washington to draw attention to the plight of the unemployed and to influence Congress to act on a noninterest bond bill which he had proposed. Now, in October 1945, at the age of 91, he is still making public statements about "bonds and their / interest" (84/537). Unlike him, Sinclair Lewis never considered the economic roots of American social decline, and, for all Charles Beard's interest in the interaction of economic and political forces, in *The Rise of American Civilization* he has only "given one line to the currency" (84/538). Pound assumes that writers like himself who do concentrate on economic theory "will be about as popular as Mr John Adams / and less widely perused."

"Carson the desert rat's" lost cause is a mining venture in which he has invested $80,000 with nothing to show for it at the end but "experience." Pound's great aunt, we are told, also lost her money when she bought a "too large hotel" but was not discouraged and "at least saw damn all Europe" and "in general had a run for her money" (84/539). Among others who have shown courage are men who have been executed for their allegiance to causes that have failed. Wei, Chi, and Pi-kan are mentioned as being "full of humanitas (manhood) / or jên^2," and book 18 of the *Analects* begins with Confucius's praise of the courage and integrity of these three men under a corrupt ruler. The Viscount of Wei retires in protest, the Viscount of Chi tries to remain in office and is made a slave, and Pi-kan, who protests this, is executed. Pound draws an analogy between these men and those Fascists who were executed after the recent Allied victory—Mussolini; Pierre Laval, head of the Vichy government; Vidkun Quisling, Laval's Norwegian counterpart; and Philippe Henriot, Minister of Propaganda for Pétain's government[13]—and praises the integrity that they show in maintaining their convictions, even in defeat. This same kind of integrity prompts one man to break off his association with Imperial Chemicals once a European war seems likely so that he will not make a profit from a "blood-bath."

Arnaut asks that Dante remember his pain "quand vos venetz al som de l'escalina"—when he reaches the summit of Purgatory and can pass through the fire and the Pass of Pardon to the Earthly Paradise. Arnaut is on the highest cornice of Mount Purgatory, so, by including this reference to him, Pound reminds us that his own time in Purgatory is drawing to its close. The reference to the "escalina," the stair of the Mountain, is followed by:

$$\dot{\eta}\theta o\varsigma \text{ gradations}$$
These are distinctions in clarity

ming² 明 these are distinctions   [84/539]

The cornices of Purgatory correspond to "gradations" of sin and in "$\dot{\eta}\theta o\varsigma$ gradations" Pound seems to be reminding us that *ethos* means "accustomed place" as well as "character," and thus referring us back to the plan of Purgatory where the locations of the sinful are determined by their moral character. The "distinctions in clarity" suggest ethical distinctions as well as the distinctions which one is enabled to make by the "light of the intelligence." Ming², "the total light process . . . hence, the intelligence," is a paradisal character, and even in Paradise there are distinctions between the ten heavens.

Yet this does not seem to be an appropriate time for thoughts of Paradise, and Pound turns again to this world and to his determination to use John Adams for an ethical fixed point, for his "norm of spirit," his "unwobbling pivot." He does however, in passing, draw our attention to Micah 4 : 5 where, when the prophet describes the establishment of the kingdom of Heaven on earth, he

13. Francis J. Bosha, "Pound's Henriot," *Paideuma* 4, no. 1 (Spring 1975): 99–100.

seems to suggest that other religions as well as Judaism will have their rightful place:

> For all people will walk every one in the name of his god, and we will walk in the name of the LORD our God for ever and ever.

The poet then turns to the politics of his own times:

> So that looking at the sputtering tank of nicotine and
>   stale whiskey
>   (on its way out)
> Kumrad Koba remarked:
>   I will believe the American.
>   Berlin 1945
> the last appearance of Winston P.M. in that connection
>   [84/540]

This odd reaction to the Potsdam Conference and the poet's wish, a few lines later, to find some connection between the idealism and integrity of John Adams and the motives of Stalin are clearly willfully perverse, and yet they spring less from a strong enthusiasm for Stalin than from his antipathy to Churchill (and Roosevelt). He bears a grudge against these two leaders—in defiance of all logic—because they let the war happen. To him this is inexcusable, not because he wanted Germany to rule the world, but because of his horror of war. He approves of Stalin's favoring of Truman over Churchill, partly because of the slight to the Prime Minister, and partly because Truman is acceptable to him because he is presiding over the ending rather than over the beginning of a war.

A more appropriate passage to include on the last page of this sequence—and one even closer than the Potsdam anecdote to the poet's feelings on the subject of war—would be the verses that precede the quotation from Micah 4:5 that he does include:

> 3. And he shall judge among many people, and rebuke strong nations afar off; and they shall beat their swords into plow-

shares, and their spears into pruning-hooks: nation shall not lift up a sword against nation, neither shall they learn war any more.

4. But they shall sit every man under his vine and under his fig tree; and none shall make *them* afraid: for the mouth of the LORD of hosts hath spoken *it.* [Micah 4:3–4]

And perhaps, by including the verse that follows these, he intends the reader to dwell on these verses anyway.

The final couplet of the canto brings us back to Pound's present reality, to the chill of an autumn morning, and to the prisoner's gratitude for even some small relief from his discomfort:

> If the hoar frost grip thy tent
> Thou wilt give thanks when night is spent.   [84/540]

5 J'Ayme Donc Je Suis

"Beyond civic order:
                    l'AMOR."

At first, in St. Elizabeths, Pound had to struggle to survive the mental strain of his uncertainty about his fate. After he was declared unfit to stand trial, he still had to fight the depressing effect of his imprisonment, his surroundings, and his lack of privacy. He kept himself busied with as many projects as possible, partly because it was his nature to be constantly active, and partly because it distracted him from his many problems. His economic views remained the same and much of his activity was devoted to arranging—or persuading others to arrange—for those views to be disseminated.

Pound's imprisonment in St. Elizabeths was very different from his imprisonment at Pisa, and in the asylum there was little incentive to or opportunity for self-examination. He needed great privacy before he could be introspective; here he had almost none. Any kind of reflection was potentially dangerous and it was safest to live from day to day as much as possible. Thoughts about the future could only be frustrating or depressing, and nostalgia threw into relief the unpleasantness of his situation and was a temptation to self-pity. In addition, the very fact of his imprisonment seemed to make any self-criticism at least redundant if not masochistic. The specters of the insane all around him were a constant warning to him not to do anything that would undermine his powers of endurance.

Yet, in spite of all the dangers of introspection, the real struggle of the St. Elizabeths years was, as it had been at Pisa, the poet's

232

struggle with his deepest and most intimate feelings, and we find a record of this struggle in the most impressive cantos of *Rock-Drill* and *Thrones.* Before we examine these, we should first briefly consider the different types of canto that we find in these two sequences. Many of them are devoted to economic matters. Of those which are, some concentrate on civic wisdom and some amass further evidence in the case against the usurers. In the "civic wisdom" cantos, Pound works with specific texts such as the *Chou King,* the *Eparch's Book,* and *The Sacred Edict,* and these inevitably give a unity to the poetry. In the cantos and passages which deal more generally with the case against usury, Pound moves rapidly and randomly from one allusion to the next so that the result is often unfocussed and without a clear direction. The remaining cantos are "paradisal." Some of these are more generally metaphysical and deal with figures like Apollonius of Tyana and St. Anselm, while others are highly personal.

Cantos 85 and 86: *The* Chou King

Rock-Drill opens with a direct challenge to the reader. The configuration of Chinese characters and cryptic phrases in Latin, French, and English make Cantos 85 and 86 the most inscrutable in the poem and, because they open *Rock-Drill,* they force the reader to choose between investing a considerable amount of time and energy in a study of Pound's source or passing quickly by them only to be left with the feeling of having entered the later cantos by a side door. We can imagine the poet smiling to himself as, obviously aware of the dilemma with which he has confronted his readers, he leaves them to their own devices, retreating behind the deadpan footnote which informs them that he is engaged in a "somewhat detailed confirmation of Kung's view that the basic principles of government are found in the Shu, the History Classic."

In the *Pisan Cantos* he had written:

> better gift can no man make to a nation
> than the sense of Kung fu Tseu
> who was called Chung Ni
> nor in historiography nor in making anthologies
>
> [76/454]

At St. Elizabeths Pound chose to follow Kung's example and to play his part in handing on the wisdom of the *Chou* and the *Odes*. He worked on this, not only because he considered it important, but also because he enjoyed it. And he had the time to study the Chinese language much more thoroughly than he had done before. Confucius "cut 3000 odes to 300" and Pound, accepting the judgment that the 300 are indispensable, undertook to translate them all. Between 1946 and 1950 he filled thirty spiral notebooks with Chinese characters and notes on his Chinese texts. This explains, in large part, the notelike form of Cantos 85 and 86. He did not study the *Chou* so that he could write those cantos, but wrote the cantos out of his deep involvement with his source, and the characters take their dominant position in these cantos because they were the main focus of his attention. On most of the pages he runs a line of them straight down the middle so that they become a kind of "unwobbling pivot" around which are grouped the transliterations and renderings in Latin, French, and English.

These cantos are admittedly demanding, and sooner or later readers might well ask whether the demands being made on them are unreasonable. But once one has decided to take up the challenge and to work with the *Chou,* it is likely that the investment of effort will seem justified. Pound is aware that he is asking a lot of his readers, but assumes that at least a few of them will keep up with him—as he says when he is about to launch into his anatomizing of the *Eparch's Book,* in the first canto of *Thrones:* "One demands the right, now and again, to write for a few people with special interests and whose curiosity reaches into greater detail" (96/659). Yet in the *Chou* cantos and in Canto 96 it is likely that the reader will be drawn to the poetry, not by a preexisting special interest in Chinese history or Byzantine commercial law, but by curiosity about the place that his new material will take in the total pattern of the poem—by an interest in *The Cantos* themselves. We are prepared to find the new material important because we expect from previous experience that Pound's commitment to the subjects he singles out for attention will be genuine and intense. The cumulative force of the rest of the poem validates the poet's judgment about what is important as well as creating the context within which each individual passage can take on its full significance.

Yet there is an important difference between the *Chou* cantos and the canto of the *Eparch's Book.* The latter is much more accessible to readers, even if Byzantine Greek is as much of a mystery to them as Chinese, because of the direct way in which the English part of the text translates or refers to the Greek. In the *Chou* cantos the meaning or context of the Chinese characters can rarely be deduced from anything else on the page. They are the pivot of the meaning, and the phrases that surround them take their significance from them, so Pound ensures that the reader must work directly with them. Although one can use secondary materials, they have particular limitations in the case of the *Chou* cantos. In *The Cantos,* the text is often deeply rooted in a source, and to read an account of another person's findings will inevitably be less satisfying than to work with the source directly. The particular nature of the *Chou* cantos, however, poses some special problems for the critic and neither discursive explications nor annotations in tabular form can really come very close to giving an impression of the impact that the poet intends these cantos to have. In the case of a discursive explication the problem arises from the extremely cryptic nature of the cantos. Since Pound's single characters or words or brief phrases stand for whole passages from the original text, any thorough explication must quote and comment upon so much material that all sense of the conciseness and patterning of the poetry is likely to be lost. The extensiveness of the necessary annotations argues, then, for their arrangement in a convenient tabular form, and Thomas Grieve has provided a detailed and clearly organized set of annotations of this kind in *Paideuma* 4, nos. 2 and 3. Here the necessary information is easily accessible to the reader. Yet, in one sense, this very accessibility prevents the reading of these cantos from being the absorbing experience that the poet intended it to be. A great deal is lost when the reader comes to these cantos only through an intermediary. One could argue, in fact, that the process of tracking down the sources of the characters is an indispensable part of the experience of reading this part of the poem.

It turns out that even here, in the most difficult section of Pound's poem, readers can make their own way; it is possible to trace the characters back to their original contexts in the *Chou* without outside help and with no prior knowledge of Chinese. In the process one becomes familiar with the contents of the *Chou,* with something of the thoroughness that Confucius recommended. One also comes to understand some of the rudiments of the Chinese language. And in working by trial and error the reader follows Pound's original approach to the language.

In the note to Canto 85, Pound refers us to Séraphine Couvreur's edition of the *Chou King* and to R. H. Mathews's *Chinese-English Dictionary.* However, if one tries to work with these books alone—supposing one can get a copy of Couvreur, which in itself is not easy—the task becomes unnecessarily difficult. There are several disadvantages to using Mathews. First, one must know the sound of the character to be able to look it up, and Pound does not always give a transliteration. When he does, it is usually Couvreur's rendering, which rarely corresponds exactly to that in Mathews. Even when one finds the correct character, it is sometimes hard to know which of the various meanings given is appropriate for the particular instance.

For someone who knows no Chinese, Legge's edition of the *Shoo* in *The Chinese Classics* gives most help with Cantos 85 and 86, and Pound seems to have been using it concurrently with Couvreur.[1] Legge's glossary gives exact definitions of characters according to the passages in which they appear, so it is possible to find out not only the meaning of the character, but also which particular passage in the *Chou* Pound is referring to. To use the glossary it is first necessary to learn to look up characters by their radicals, but this is not as hard as might first appear. For easy

---

1. For example, "Three hundred years until P'an" (85/548) seems to be from Legge (*Shoo King,* 3: 220 n.), and Legge (*Shoo King,* 3: 233 n.) singles out and translates the sequence of five characters which Pound reproduces on 85/548. Pound writes "Liu dogs" (85/553), as in Legge, but Couvreur calls this document "Le chien de Liu," and clearly favors the idea of *one* dog: "Les habitents de Liu . . . offrirent en tribut un chien (ou des chiens) de leur pays" (Couvreur, *Chou King,* p. 210).

reference one can list the radicals and their numbers, copying from
Legge's glossary, and then, having found the main radical of each
new character in the poem, see what number it is and look it up in
the glossary. Since some of the radicals are modified when com-
bined with others in a character, it is helpful to add the modified
version to the list when it is discovered. Although at the beginning
the reader must work by trial and error, with each new character
one becomes more expert and can finally use the glossary with
ease. This is both fascinating and satisfying, since it is as though
one is sharing, in the most immediate way, Pound's own initial
excitement at his discovery of Chinese. Because Legge's glossary
locates those passages where the characters appear, it is easy to
find the episode to which Pound is referring. Couvreur's much
briefer glossary is no help in this respect. Pound chose Couvreur
for his own use because it contains both a Latin and a French
translation of the Chinese, and also because it indicates the sounds
of the characters, both pronunciation and tone, on the same page
as the Chinese text. His previous study of Chinese had left him
familiar enough with the forms of the characters that he could
concern himself with their sounds as well, but the reader of the
Chou who has no prior knowledge of Chinese must first master
the forms and can do this most easily by using Legge.

In the process of tracking down the referents for the quota-
tions or allusions that Pound gives, we are being made familiar
with the contents of the *Chou* in a surprisingly thorough way. As
we move back and forth between the times of Tching T'ang and
his counsellor I Yin of the Shang dynasty and the stories of the
kings of the Chow dynasty, we find that we must take some pains
to sort out the interrelationships and the characters of the people
referred to. This is less likely to be the case in our reading of Can-
tos 52–61, where Pound keeps to the chronological sequence of
Chinese history. Paradoxically, because these earlier cantos are
more straightforward and easier to read, they are likely to make
less impression on us and they often move too fast for us to hold
in our minds the distinctions between the various rulers. The un-
familiar names, some in dominating capitals, coerce the eye, dis-
tracting attention from the action.

Two of the characters which appear in these cantos will be particularly important later in the poem. One is *ling*[2] which opens the *Chou* Cantos and which will be discussed in connection with Canto 97, and the other is *chên.* In Canto 86 Pound writes:

> non coelum non in medio
> but man is under Fortuna
> ? that is a forced translation?
> La donna che volgo
> Man under Fortune,
>   CHÊN

[86/566]

The Latin is Couvreur's rendering of a passage from "The Prince of Lou Upon Punishments," in which the Prince as King Muh's spokesman says, "you should ever stand in awe of the punishment of Heaven. It is not Heaven [*non coelum*] that does not deal impartially [*non in medio*] with men, but men ruin themselves" (*Shoo King,* 610). Pound paraphrases this idea in "but man is under Fortuna." Although he asks whether this is a "forced translation," he is, in fact, making a very deliberate link here between the Chinese idea of divine justice at work in human affairs and the idea which he finds in Cavalcanti and Dante of Fortuna as not blind but purposeful in her actions. "La donna che volgo" comes from a stanza of Cavalcanti's "Canzone to Fortune" which Pound had long ago singled out in *The Spirit of Romance:*

> Io son la donna che volgo la ruota
> Sono colei, che tolgo e dò stato
> Ed è sempre biasmato
> A torto el modo mio da voi mortali
>
> I am the woman who turneth the wheel,
> I am who giveth and taketh away.
> And I am blamed alway
> And wrongly, for my deeds, by ye, mankind.   [*SR,* 111]

In Karlgren's *Analytic Dictionary of Chinese and Sino-Japanese,* which Pound uses to determine etymologies, the first meaning for *chên* is "shock of thunder" and, as we shall see, when Pound includes this character in Canto 91, he follows it with "timing the thunder." In the *Chou, chên,* meaning "to move or agitate," is used to refer to the impulse toward good or evil actions, to gratitude or to anger. By emphasizing "thunder" Pound focusses on the idea of retribution and one thinks of Zeus's thunderbolts. "Timing the thunder" also suggests waiting to see when and where the thunderbolt will strike, that is, when people's evil actions will catch up with them. Throughout the *Chou* we find the assumption that this will always happen and that the downfall of dynasties is a punishment for the corruption of rulers. In the first book of part 5, for example, the "cruel oppression" of Chow-sin, the King of Shang, is recounted and we are told: "Great Heaven was moved [*chên*] with indignation" and charged Wăn "to display its majesty" bu killing the tyrant and establishing the Chow dynasty (*Shoo King,* 285). In the *Chou* Cantos the emphasis is on the operation of "Fortuna" in the state, but Pound's later references will suggest that he is thinking of the way in which this goddess determines the course of individual lives, including his own.

Rock-Drill: *Cantos 90–93*

The first half of *Rock-Drill* is devoted to civic wisdom and the case against the usurers, but, with Canto 90, the mood of the sequence changes abruptly. In Cantos 90–93 we see the poet receiving a paradisal revelation and struggling to sustain it. Canto 90 celebrates the inspirational and redemptive power of Amor without reservation, but Canto 91, although it begins positively, turns to elegy and then suddenly to hatred, which the poet quickly suppresses, becoming first nostalgic and then stoic. In Canto 92, he is most vulnerable to despondency and becomes increasingly oppressed by the spectacle of "25 hundred years desensitization." In Canto 93, as in Canto 81, the poet confronts his own past limitations of feeling and thereby comes to a recognition of the power of benevolence. He is helped in this by thoughts of his daughter and by the wisdom which he finds in Dante's *Convivio,* but most of all by his own love for a particular woman to whom he says "You have stirred my mind out of dust" (93/632). This woman is the young painter Sherri Martinelli, who frequently visits him in St. Elizabeths, and, as we look back over these four cantos, we realize that it is his strong feeling for her that has led him to his celebration of the healing power of Amor.

Canto 90 has as an epigraph a passage from Richard of St. Victor which translates: "The human soul is not love, but love flows from it, and therefore it does not delight in itself, but in the love which comes from it."[2] This and the other quotations from Richard in the canto emphasize the need for the creative power of love to manifest itself in specific and tangible ways. For Richard, as for Dante, man's ability to love is a sign of his divinity, and Richard compares a person's desire to look upon the beloved to the desire of the reason to apprehend divine truth: "Where love is, there is the eye [*Ubi amor ibi oculus est*]. We are pleased to look upon that person whom we love greatly. This is undoubtedly so because he who can love invisible things, indeed steadfastly wishes to know them and to see them by means of the intelligence, and the more . . . the ability to love grows, the more strongly . . . burns . . . the eagerness to know."[3] Pound is not merely celebrating Amor, but is actively trying to put his new understanding of the relationship between love and creativity into practice. His immediate task is the writing of his poem, and, as he works on these cantos, the very lines in which he explains how the power of love is transmuted into intellectual and artistic energies supply the proof of his thesis.

The epigraph to Canto 90 prepares us for the apotheosis of AMOR at the end of the canto, but before this can take place, the poet must be raised up from "Erebus," from spiritual exhaustion and sterility. As we have seen in chapter 2, Amor's apotheosis is proclaimed by the coming of the altar to the grove and its mate-

2. Richard of St. Victor, *Quomodo Spiritus Sanctus est amor Patris et Filii, Patrologiae Latinae,* tomus 196, col. 1012 B. Translation mine.

3. Richard of St. Victor, *Benjamin Minor,* xiii, *Patrologiae Latinae,* tomus 196, col. 10. Translation mine.

rialization in carved stone, "taking form in the air" (90/608). The importance of the theme of concrete and tangible manifestation of a spiritual state of inner nature is attested to by the first two lines of the canto: " 'From the colour the nature / & by the nature the sign!' " In the natural world there is a direct and unambiguous correspondence between the inner nature and its visible form. The "oak-ness" of every oak tree is proclaimed by every leaf, by its bark, even by the grain of its wood. This is the basis of the medieval doctrine of "signatures" which Pound had encountered very early in the *Holy Guide* of John Heydon, an obscure seventeenth century astrologer and Rosicrucian whom he describes in Canto III as "Worker of miracles, dealer in levitation, / In thoughts upon pure form, in alchemy, / Seer of pretty visions ('servant of God and secretary of nature.')" Pound quotes from Heydon several times in these four cantos and we see that the poet's renewed interest in the "signatures" in nature and in "the intelligence that enables grass seed to grow grass: the cherry-stone to make cherries" (*C,* 193), is part of a new attentiveness to the patterns and processes of the natural world that persists until the end of the poem. From his experience at Pisa he associates introspection with meditation on the phenomena of nature and he has taken seriously his admonition to himself, "Learn of the green world what can be thy place / In scaled invention or true artistry" (81/521). Throughout the rest of *The Cantos* we find evidence of the inspiring and consoling effect of the poet's admiration for the perfections of "the things of earth." Hence his particular interest in Alexander Von Humboldt, Agassiz, Linnaeus, and Ambroise Paré.

The natural world has a paradisal quality to the extent that, in it, appearances are not deceptive—things are what they seem. Human society is quite otherwise, often, Pound believes, because people must rely on words to express their intentions and to codify their ideals and render them in a form in which they can go into action. This leaves society at the mercy of those unscrupulous people who, motivated by self-interest, distort the meanings of words so that the spirit of an idea or intention is perverted or lost. The paradisal state is a state beyond words where light and crystal take the place of "verbal manifestations" and where the inner nature of things and of people shines out unambiguously and infallibly. One can attain paradisal vision through the power of Amor, and works of stone often capture or manifest the paradisal. On the first page of Canto 90 we read:

> Beatific spirits welding together
>> as in one ash-tree in Ygdrasail.
>> Baucis, Philemon.
> Castalia is the name of that fount in the hill's fold,
>> the sea below,
>>> narrow beach.
> Templum aedificans, not yet marble,
>> "Amphion!"   [90/605]

The one tree, both linden and oak, into which Baucis and Philemon were metamorphosed is seen as a smaller version of Ygdrasil, the "world-ash" which holds together the whole world. Their meta-morphosis was a reward for this couple's generosity to Zeus and Hermes and was a sign of the fullness of their perfect married love which enabled them, in spite of their poverty, to show ἠγάπησεν πολύ, much affection, to strangers. Not only did Zeus grant their request that when the time came they might not be separated by death but die together; he also changed their hut into a temple of marble and gold. This manifestation in stone of their love and benevolence is like the symbolic altar which appears in the grove at the end of the canto, and before the altar can appear, the poet must be raised from his depression to a conviction of the power of love. He must be carried from Erebus to Castalia.

Castalia, in these cantos, is associated not only with poetic inspiration, but also with healing. In coming to Castalia at Delphi, the place of Apollo's oracle, Pound is like Dante who, as he begins the *Paradiso,* also calls on the god's help in his awesome under-taking: "O good Apollo, for the last labor make me such a vessel of your worth . . . that I may show forth the image of the blessed realm which is imprinted in my mind" (3. 1. 13–24). Apollo at Delphi was always beneficent, as Orestes found when he came to the oracle to learn how to escape from the torment of the Furies and cleanse himself from the guilt of the murder of his mother. It seems that Pound sees some similarity between his own situation and that of Orestes, driven to commit a crime by the demands of duty and honor. In the previous canto Pound has alluded to Orestes' final release from the curse of his house by the intercession of Athene—" Ἀθήνη swung the hung jury" (89/601)—and, at the end of Canto 90, among those freed from Erebus is Electra "the dark shade of courage / Ἠλέχτρα / bowed still with the wrongs of Aegisthus." Mary tells how in 1959, at Schloss Brunnenberg, Pound, troubled by remorse, and sensing her distress at the tensions in the household, quotes to her from *Electra:* "Οὐ ταῦτα πρὸς κακοῖσι δειλίαν ἔχει; Shall we to all our ills add cowardice?" (*Disc.*, 306).

Pound, in St. Elizabeths, often finds himself in "Erebus"—in a state of spiritual fatigue and hopelessness from which he cannot raise himself but must be rescued by some external power whom he calls "Isis Kuanon":

> from under the rubble heap
> > m'elevasti
> from the dulled edge beyond pain,
> > m'elevasti
> out of Erebus, the deep-lying
> > from the wind under the earth,
> > > m'elevasti
> from the dulled air and the dust,
> > > m'elevasti
> by the great flight,
> > m'elevasti,
> > > Isis Kuanon
> from the cusp of the moon,
> > > m'elevasti   [90/606]

"M'elevasti" refers us to canto 1 of the *Paradiso* where Dante wonders whether he was present in Paradise in body or only in soul and concludes: *"amor che 'l ciel governi, / tu'l sai, che col tuo lume mi levasti"* ["O Love that rulest the heavens, Thou knowest, who with Thy light didst lift me"] (3. 1. 74–75). Yet Pound's is not a Christian but a composite goddess, a fusion of the Egyptian Isis and the Chinese Kuanon, the Bodhisattva of Mercy—"She who hears the cry of the world"—who also appears in some of the Noh dramas. Both goddesses are particularly associated with rescue and healing and both have themselves descended into the underworld. The viper and the blue serpent suggest not only the *uraeus* or sacred serpent of Isis's headdress but also Aesculapius and the power of healing. The iconography of Isis with the child Horus and of Kuanon with a child attendant is sometimes markedly similar to that of the Virgin and the Christ child, and certainly all three are, above all, compassionate. The Virgin is alluded to here by Pound's reference to the festival of the Madonna of Montallegre, during which floating lamps are set in the water, "the sea's claw drawing them outward," an echo from Canto 47.

Through the intercession of the compassionate goddesses, the poet's inspiration returns, represented by the gushing water of the Castalian spring and by the confluence of the rivers Wei and Han "rushing together" with "bright fish and flotsam / torn bough in the flood / and the waters clear with the flowing" (90/607). "By the great flight," the poet is carried "Out of heaviness where no mind moves at all" (90/607). Finally, in stillness beside still water, the altar comes to the grove:

> and in the flat pool as Arethusa's
> a hush in papyri.
> Grove hath its altar
> under elms, in that temple, in silence
> a lone nymph by the pool   [90/607]

The fountain of Arethusa is on the Island of Ortygia in Sicily, which is sacred to Artemis and where there is also a Doric temple to Apollo, and this provides us with a much gentler and more peaceful counterpart to the fountain and temple at Delphi. The fearsome Sibyl is replaced by "a lone nymph," perhaps Arethusa herself. Where Dante's vision of paradise takes him up into the heavens, Pound's manifests itself upon the earth. To the altar of Amor come the beasts of the earth-god and goddess, Dionysus and Artemis, and also "the procession of Corpus," of οἱ χθόνιοι not of Corpus Christi but of humanity:

ac ferae, [wild animals]
> cervi, [stags]
>> the great cats approaching.
Pardus, leopardi, Bagheera
> drawn hither from woodland,
woodland ἐπὶ χθονί [upon the earth]
> the trees rise
> and there is a wide sward between them
οἱ χθόνιοι myrrh and olibanum on the altar stone
giving perfume
> and where was nothing
now is furry assemblage
> and in the boughs now are voices
grey wing, black wing, black wing shot with crimson
and the umbrella pines
>> as in Palatine
as in pincta. χϲλιδών, χϲλιδών [swallow]
For the procession of Corpus
> come now banners
comes flute tone
> οἱ χθόνιοι [those of the earth]
to new forest,
> thick smoke, purple, rising
bright flame now on the altar
> the crystal funnel of air   [90/608]

As we have seen, the paradisal pageant takes place under the elms and pine trees of Saint Elizabeths and around the small "altar-stone" on which the poet would sometimes burn olibanum. Even the "black wing shot with crimson" suggests the specifically American red-wing blackbird. This visionary moment attests to the irresistible power of Amor which can establish a *"paradiso terrestre"* even "in the halls of hell." The pines around him remind Pound of the "pineta," the pine-wood of Chiassi [Classe] near Ravenna where the last stanzas of the *Purgatorio* were written and from which Dante takes *his* description of the Earthly Paradise in which he finally sees Beatrice. Here, "the little birds among the tops . . .

greeted the morning hours with full joy among the leaves, which kept such burden to their rhymes as gathers from branch to branch through the pine forest on Chiassi's shore when Aeolus lets forth Sirocco" (2. 28. 14–21). Where Odysseus gives blood to the ghosts in Hades, Pound burns incense for them, freeing them from Erebus altogether:

> Tyro, Alcmene, free now, ascending
> e i cavalieri,
> ascending,
> no shades more,
> lights among them, enkindled,
> and the dark shade of courage
> Ἠλέχτρα   [90/608–09]

The canto ends as it began, with Richard's definition of Amor:

> Not love but that love flows from it
> ex animo
> & cannot ergo delight in itself
> but only in the love flowing from it.
> UBI AMOR IBI OCULUS EST.   [90/609]

Once we have read Canto 94, we realize that Isis-Kuanon is, in large part, Sherri Martinelli herself, and we find that she has in fact painted a picture of this composite goddess which is included in *La Martinelli,* the booklet of reproductions of her works which Pound arranges to have published for her in 1956. As she herself realizes, the poet sees her as more than an individual; she comes to represent for him the very idea of love as inspiration. Set against the bleak and stultifying reality of the asylum ward, her youth, enthusiasm, and spontaneity must seem to provide a contact with all those things in the outside world that he most minds being shut away from. She suggests that Pound loves her, "because I symbolize the spirit of Love to him."[4] This explains why, in the first part of

4. David Rattray, "Weekend with Ezra Pound," *The Nation* 185, no. 16 (Nov. 16, 1957): p. 348.

Canto 91, the poet returns to the theme of Canto 36 and the "Cavalcanti" essay and we notice that, where Pound's analyses of "Donna mi prega" had focussed rather theoretically on the operation of love, Canto 91 elevates the figure of the beloved woman and particularly considers her inspirational effect on the man who loves her and even on the events of her own times.

In this canto, the eye of the beloved becomes the dominant image. As the specific point from which the "light" of love flows to inspire the beloved, it becomes the *nous* in miniature, and Pound's description of the *nous* as a "sea crystalline and enduring" explains the recurrent imagery of sea and crystal in this canto. Together with the line of Provençal verse which tells of the sweetness that comes to the poet's heart, Pound gives at the head of Canto 91 the neumes which indicate the melody which accompanies the poetry. He is reminding the reader of his love of poetry like that of the troubadours, which is not only musical but which is actually intended to be sung. He finds a marriage of verbal and instrumental music comparable to that of Provence in the works of Thomas Campion and Henry Lawes and feels that "for 300 years," since their time, there has been no comparable "music" of this kind. For this reason, Pound has dedicated his "Cavalcanti" translation of "Donna mi prega" "To Thomas Campion his ghost, and to the ghost of Henry Lawes, as prayer for the revival of music."

The troubadour convention of the unattainable Lady, who by refusing to satisfy the lover's passion inspires his art, persists not only in the Italy of Dante and Cavalcanti, but even up to the time of Campion and Lawes. For the Elizabethans, the dominating presence of the "Virgin Queen" gives new substance to this convention of courtly love and, as Pound reminds us in this canto, Elizabeth inspires not only poets, but also men of action like Drake. In the days of Eleanor of Aquitaine and Elizabeth I, these queens personified Amor as the source of intellectual inspiration, and gave focus and currency to this idea, and Pound wishes that somehow the idea could be given new life in his own time:

> that the body of light come forth
> from the body of fire

> And that your eyes come to the surface
> > from the deep wherein they were sunken,
> Reina—for 300 years,
> > and now sunken
> That your eyes come forth from their caves
> > & light then
> > > as the holly-leaf   [91/610]

From unfulfilled passion—"the body of fire"—comes the "light" of artistic inspiration, and "Reina" is the archetype of the woman who first excites the lover's passion and then inspires his intellect. For Bernart de Ventadour she is Eleanor of Aquitaine; for Dante, Beatrice; for Simon Magus, Helen of Tyre; for Justinian, Theodora; for Drake, Elizabeth, and finally for Brutus, Diana herself. As each individual holly-leaf reproduces the same essential form, so each individual who finds inspiration through passion encounters for himself, in the person of his beloved, a manifestation of the Reina whose realm is the *nous.* The crystalline sea and the brilliance of the *nous* are the proper elements for the Reina, and the eyes of the beloved remind us of this:

> Miss Tudor moved them with galleons
> from deep eye, versus armada
> from the green deep
> > he saw it,
> in the green deep of an eye:
> . . . .
> Light & the flowing crystal
> > never gin in cut glass had such clarity
> That Drake saw the splendour and wreckage
> > in that clarity.   [91/611]

In addition to the "seas" of the *nous* and of the beloved's eye, there is the actual sea sailed by Drake and even the "sea" of the air through which sails the sun-boat of the Princess Ra-Set.

Pound's passages on the Princess are flanked by references to the *Paradiso:*

> Crystal waves weaving together toward the gt/
> > healing
>
> Light *compenetrans* of the spirits
> The Princess Ra-Set has climbed
> > to the great knees of stone,
> She enters protection,
> > the great cloud is about her,
> She has entered the protection of crystal
> > > convien che si mova
> > > la mente, amando
> > > > XXVI, 34
>
> . . . .
>
> The golden sun boat
> > by oar, not by sail
> Love moving the stars παρὰ βώμιον
> by the altar slope   [91/611-12]

Dante's Beatrice is an ideal embodiment of Pound's conception of Amor. Although her main role in the *Paradiso* is to enable the poet to apprehend the love of God, she is still the woman whom Dante had loved on earth, and the essence of the earthly love is not lost but intensified and sublimated as Dante rises with her through the nine spheres to the Empyrean. The "gt / healing" refers us to canto 26 of Dante's poem. The poet has been blinded by the brilliance of the light which shines from St. John, but is reassured by the saint that this is only a temporary blindness which can be cured by the power of Beatrice. The poet replies: "At her good pleasure, soon or late, let succor come to the eyes which were the doors when she did enter with the fire wherewith I ever burn. The good which satisfies this Court is Alpha and Omega of all the scripture which Love reads to me, either low or loud" (3. 26. 13-18).

Dante's descriptions of God as the supreme good and as light of unbearable brilliance are also appropriate as descriptions of the Neoplatonic One, and Pound intends us to think of the latter rather than of the Christian God. "Convien che si mova / la mente, amando" refers us to that passage in canto 26 in which Dante says that it is fitting that the loving mind should move toward "that

Essence wherein is such supremacy that whatsoever good be found outside of It is naught else save a beam of Its own radiance" (3. 26. 31–35). Pound invites us to substitute a Neoplatonic for a Christian cosmology by referring to Heydon, Apollonius, and Ocellus and also in his reference to the "Light *compenetrans* of the spirits." This line is echoed in the passage on Plotinus with which Canto 100 concludes, in which we read, "nous to ariston autou [intellect, the best part of himself] / as light into water compenetrans" (100/722). Pound provides a further counterweight to the Christian context of Dante by introducing the Princess Ra-Set, who seems in part to be a Beatrice-figure.[5] By making her a princess, Pound gives her a lower rank and less power than Isis or Kuanon and her ascent to "the great knees of stone" where she enters "the protection of crystal" suggests Beatrice's ascent to the third circle of the celestial Rose where she is enthroned in glory. This connection is reinforced when Pound follows his reference to Ra-Set's "golden sun-boat" with "Love moving the stars" from the final line of the *Paradiso: "l'amor che move il sole e l'altre stelle."* The eyes of the beloved enable the poet to glimpse the paradisal, but he must always return to the real world and its problems. Drake sees not only "splendour" in the Queen's eye, but also "sea-wrack," and Pound is well aware of the obstacles to his pursuit of a "paradiso terrestre."

His mind is ranging over great stretches of time and this inevitably produces an elegiac mood. He is still thinking, as he had been in the *Chou* Cantos, of the rise and fall of dynasties, only now he looks to England rather than to China and to Layamon's account in the *Brut* of the history of the Britons.[6] He moves in short space from Brutus's landing in England to the exile of Cadwalader, the last of the kings of the Britons, the end of whose power is prophesied by Merlin and the Sibyl: "So hath Sibile a boken isette." As he transcribes Brutus's prayer to Diana, we sense

5. See Boris de Rachewiltz, "Pagan and Magic Elements in Ezra Pound's Works," *New Approaches to Ezra Pound,* ed. Eva Hesse (Berkeley & Los Angeles, 1969), p. 180.

6. See Christine Brooke-Rose, *A ZBC of Ezra Pound* (Berkeley & Los Angeles, 1971), for details of Pound's use of Layamon.

that Pound is appropriating this to make his own appeal for a safe homecoming:

> Leafdi Diana, leove Diana
> Heye Diana, help me to neode
> Witte me thurh crafte
> whuder ich maei lidhan
> to wonsom londe.   [91/612-13]

Also the reference to Lear, brief as it is, sets up resonances the most significant of which are similarly personal.

> Now Lear in Janus' temple is laid
>
>   timing the thunder
>   [91/613]

Although the story of Layamon's Leir has a happy ending, we are invited to think of Shakespeare's Lear, both by the spelling of the name and by the reference to the thunder. Where *chên* in Canto 86 was associated with the operation of "Fortuna" in the affairs of the state, the association of retributive justice with Lear introduces the idea of the workings of Fortuna in the lives of individuals. In the storm, Lear associates the thunder with the power of the gods to punish crimes, calling on these "dreadful summoners" to lay bare the hidden sins of others, but his night on the heath is, of course, part of his own punishment for having foolishly rejected his daughter. Pound, like Lear, is a man who, by judging wrongly, brought suffering upon his own head, and this is surely the main reason for Pound's reference to Lear at this point.

The defeat of the Britons makes the poet think more generally of the destruction of cultures and then of the collapse of civilization in his own time. He suddenly gives in to anger—"*Democracies electing their sewage / till there is no clear thought about holiness / a dung flow from 1913 / and, in this, their kikery flourished, Marx, Freud / and the american beaneries*" (91/613-14). Here, as he had at Pisa, he turns to nostalgia to recover his self-control, and he particularly remembers Verona. Thinking of the courage of Nanni

Torquato and of Musonius, he strengthens his own resolve to continue his struggle, believing that "They who are skilled in fire / shall read . . . the dawn." At Pisa he had written, "hast'ou swum in a sea of air strip / through an aeon of nothingness, / when the raft broke and the waters went over me" (80/513), and again in Canto 91 he compares his own fate to that of Odysseus. Here, however, he has a rescuer, his Leucothea, Sherri Martinelli, who can show him how to save himself, advising him to "get rid of paraphernalia," and to rely on his powers of endurance—"TLEMOUSUNE." He knows that he must learn to conquer anger and hatred, that, if "the mind come to that High City" it will be through "charitas insuperabilis." The perfect order of the natural world suggests that there is a "road to felicity," and the poet is prepared to believe that visions are still possible, that Joan of Arc's is not "A lost kind of experience." He resolves "That the tone change from elegy," and concludes by hailing "Queen Cytherea," and by recalling Dante's address to the angels, "who by understanding move the third heaven." In the second tractate of the *Convivio* he confides to these angels the conflict between his love for the dead Beatrice and his growing love for a new lady.

In Canto 92 we see how the poet finds that he cannot sustain his paradisal vision. He reasserts his faith in the perfect harmony of the "process" and in the importance of courage and honor, but these are not enough to keep him from despondency. The canto opens positively with a reference to the Earthly Paradise at the summit of Mount Purgatory—"And from this Mount were blown / seed"—and, among his references to honorable men he includes a quotation from Guicciardini which he has translated in a note to his *Chung Yung* as, "Nothing impossible to him who holds honor in sufficient esteem" (*C,* 188). He thinks of the Heaven of Venus, both as Dante describes it in the *Paradiso,* and as a place where Venus herself is worshipped. Here Dante finds people who have been saved despite their passionate excesses. Folquet of Marseilles points out to Dante, Rahab the harlot "in questa lumera appresso," and the poet talks to another spirit who tells him, "I was called Cunizza, and I am refulgent here because the light of this star overcame me" (3. 9. 32–33). When Pound quotes this, he omits

her name—" 'fui chiamat' / e qui refulgo' " because he intends this
to apply to another woman, the one of whom he has just written:

> "And if I see her not,
>   no sight is worth the beauty of my thought."
> Then knelt with the sphere of crystal
> That she should touch with her hands,
>   Coeli Regina,
> The four altars at the four coigns of that place,
> But in the great love, bewildered
>   farfalla in tempesta   [92/619]

This passage is surely a tribute to Sherri Martinelli, and the "sphere
of crystal" that the poet holds out to her is perhaps the poetry
which she has inspired him to write. In her honor a new altar has
been added to the three altars of Canto 79. The intensity of his
feelings perplexes him and makes him feel vulnerable: "in the
great love, bewildered / farfalla in tempesta," and this recalls
Dante's reminder to the Proud in Purgatory that "we are worms,
born to form the angelic butterfly [l'angelica farfalla] that flies
into judgment without defenses" (2. 10. 124–26).

In his paradisal moments at Pisa, the poet had achieved "Ely-
sium, though it were in the halls of hell" (81/521) and the experi-
ence is repeated at St. Elizabeths:

> Le Paradis n'est pas artificiel
>   but is jagged,
> For a flash,
>   for an hour.
> Then agony,
>   then an hour,
>   then agony.   [92/620]

In the rest of Canto 92, Pound is oppressed by the extent of the
damage done by usury and by "the degradation of sacraments,"
and he contemplates the spectacle of "25 hundred years de-

sensitization" against which only a few people seem to have taken a stand.

Canto 93 is powerful and moving in the same way as Canto 81 with its vision of the eyes of the three women whom the poet has loved, and the *Rock-Drill* canto is similarly personal. Here, Pound is resolved to acknowledge the importance of benevolence and he begins with the words of the Egyptian king, Khaty, "A man's paradise is his good nature." "Panis angelicus" [the bread of angels] refers to Antef, the minister of King Khaty, and his description of himself as "food for the hungry and help for the outcast,"[7] but even more directly to the *Convivio* from which Pound quotes extensively in this canto. Here Dante speaks of man's natural desire for knowledge and aspiration toward perfection and how these are often thwarted by physical or moral defects in the individual, by the pressure of practical concerns, and by lack of facilities for learning, so that, finally, only few men are able to devote themselves to the pursuit of knowledge, and the rest must "live all their lives famished for this universal food." He continues: "Oh blessed those few who sit at the table where the bread of angels is consumed."[8]

Pound is determined to continue to aspire toward knowledge and a vision of perfection and understands the need to work on his own defects and particularly to replace his anger with benevolence. He is now feeling more self-reliant and optimistic and feels that he now has more control over his reactions—"having his own mind to stand by him." In his worst moments he must have considered suicide, but now decides that "The suicide is not serious" whose death is the result of "sheer physical depression," and that those who take their own life "from conviction" should "first bump off some nuisance." He is now also prepared to concede that the advantages of being a member of society outweigh the disadvantages,

7. Noel Stock, *Reading the Cantos* (London, 1967), p. 96.
8. Dante Alighieri, *Il Convivio, Le Opere di Dante Alighieri,* ed. E. Moore and Paget Toynbee (Oxford, 1963). I have used P. H. Wicksteed's translation, *The Convivio of Dante Alighieri* (London, 1924), treatise 1, chapter 1, lines 50–54. Subsequent quotations from the *Convivio* in English will be taken from this edition and will be identified by treatise, chapter or ode, and line numbers.

even when the society is full of corruption, and refers to Charles Martel's question to Dante, "Now say, would it be worse for man on earth if he were not a citizen [se non fosse cive]?" Dante replies (3. 8. 115–17) that this is so obviously true that it needs no proof, and Pound clearly agrees.

In this canto, the poet is interested in two main themes in the *Convivio*—Dante's contention in ode 3, that true nobility is a matter of character and personal virtue and not of rank, and his examination, in ode 2 and its treatise, of the connection between love and philosophy (see appendix 1). Ode 2 praises the virtues of the woman who has taken the place of the dead Beatrice in the poet's affections, and the treatise which follows interprets the ode allegorically so that the beloved becomes not only the woman whom the poet loves, but also the personification of Philosophy. Pound seems to have chosen to think of Sherri Martinelli in somewhat the same way. Dante claims that love is the instinctive response of the soul to "the excellences of nature and of reason," and that by contemplating the object of its love, the soul is made aware of its own inner qualities. In ode 2 he writes of his lady:

> Things are revealed in her aspect which show us of the joys of Paradise, I mean in her eyes and in her sweet smile, which love assigneth there as to their proper place. They transcend our intellect, as the sun's ray the feeble vision. . . . Her beauty rains down flamelets of fire, made living by a gentle spirit, which is the creator of every good thought. [*Convivio,* 3, ode 2, 55–56]

In treatise 4, Dante considers the true nature of gentility in men to establish that it is determined not by wealth or lineage, but by virtue. He says that nobility of character shows itself in manhood as dedication to "deeds of loyalty" and in old age as justice and generosity which takes satisfaction in the excellence of others.

The poet is now ready to examine his own shortcomings and he prays for compassion to "Lux in diafana, / Creatrix," to Saint Ursula, Ysolt, Ydone, Picarda, and "Isis-Luna." He confesses his own failure to be compassionate in the past: "J'ai eu pitié des autres. / Pas assez! Pas assez!" On the first page of the canto he had remembered with affection one afternoon in Rome with his daughter when, walking with them from a café to a carriage, the Archbishop Monsignor Pisani had handed Mary "a gilded box of Gianduja chocolates" (*Disc.,* 113–14):

> so the arcivescovo fumbled round under his
>   ample overcloaks as to what might have been
> a left-hand back pocket of civil clothing
> and produced a cornucopia from "La Tour"   [93/623]

Now he thinks of his daughter again and prays "For me nothing. But that the child / walk in peace in her basilica, / The light there almost solid" (93/628). We have seen how, in the *Pisan Cantos,* Pound has already recanted his earlier "Compleynt Against Pity," and now asserts that decisive action and kindness are not incompatible but closely allied. He uses his own translation of a passage from the *Chung Yung* to express his new conviction that "energy is near to benevolence" (*C,* 155), and will increasingly insist "that the truth is in kindness" (114/793).

We then find the poet sitting in the "sleeping wood," "Au bois dormant," where "The trees sleep, and the stags, and the grass; / The boughs sleep unmoving" (93/629). He is waiting for the arrival of Sherri Martinelli, which will awaken the wood, and as he waits he recalls the injunction which was written "in letters of gold on T'ang's bathtub": "AS THE SUN MAKES IT NEW / DAY BY DAY MAKE IT NEW / YET AGAIN MAKE IT NEW" (*C,* 36). He arms himself with this resolve as a way of insuring that he will be able to continue to preserve "his mind entire" in "the halls of Hell." Then the young woman, whom Pound here calls "Flora Castalia," arrives to "dare Persephone's threshold." It is through her agency that "petals" and "cool rain" have come to "sward Castalia"–that Pound's poetic inspiration has been quickened– and, perhaps, by choosing the name "Flora," he intends us to think specifically of this goddess as she is represented in Botticelli's "*Primavera.*" Pound's "Flora" now borrows the words of the poet Sulpicia to remind Pound/Cerinthe to put away fear, "pone metum" because "god does not harm" lovers. After the character *hsien,* Pound's "tensile light," he writes:

> nuova vita
>
> e ti fiammeggio.
>
> Such light is in sea-caves
>
> e la bella Ciprigna
>
> where copper throws back the flame
>
> from pinned eyes, the flames rise to fade
>
> in green air   [93/630–31]

The poet's new experience of love has meant a "nuova vita" just as did Dante's first love for Beatrice. "E ti fiammeggio" takes us from the *Vita Nuova* to canto 5 of the *Paradiso*. As canto 4 ends, Dante says: "Beatrice looked on me with eyes so full of the sparkling of love and so divine that my power, vanquished, took flight, and I almost lost myself with eyes downcast" (3. 4. 139–42). Canto 5 begins with Beatrice's response: "S'io ti fiammeggio nel caldo d'amore . . ." "If I flame on you in the warmth of love beyond the measure that is seen on earth and so vanquish the power of your eyes, do not marvel" (3. 5. 1–4). "La bella Ciprigna" refers us to Dante's canto 8 where "the beautiful Cyprian" is the planet which, it was believed in the ancient world, "rayed down mad love." She is also Aphrodite in the person of the poet's beloved from whose eyes "flames rise to fade / in green air," as the light of a flame is reflected from copper. (He further explores this same imagery of the reflected light from the beloved's eyes in Canto 102.) Here in Canto 93 he returns to the image of eyes as "sea-caves" and borrows from Cavalcanti's Ballata 5 when he writes:

> There must be incognita
>
> and in sea-caves
>
> un lume pien' di spiriti
>
> and of memories.   [93/631]

This "light full of spirits [of love]" and full of memories is hidden in the depths of eyes and so these seem not to be the eyes of Sherri Martinelli from which the light is thrown back so readily, but to belong to another woman, perhaps his wife, in whom this ready light is now a memory. Pound turns from these thoughts to his present situation and when he says, "Beloved, do not fall apart in my hands," he is acknowledging his reliance on his new love, but also expressing his concern that she may not have the reserves of stoicism and endurance that he has found in such large measure in his wife and in Olga Rudge. His love for the young woman has inspired him, but it has not been like the all-consuming passion of Dante for Beatrice which can not only elevate but also spiritually transform the poet. Pound acknowledges this limitation when he writes: "You are tender as a marshmallow, my Love, / I cannot use you as a fulcrum. / You have stirred my mind out of dust" (93/632). The last lines of Canto 93 also make clear that Sherri Martinelli is less a Beatrice-figure than a personification of the Spring:

> Flora Castalia, your petals drift thru the air,
> the wind is 1/2 lighted with pollen
> > diafana,
> "e Monna Vanna . . . tu mi fai rimembrar.   [93/632]

As Flora in Botticelli's *Primavera,* she is an attendant to Venus, the central figure in the painting. As "Monna Vanna," she is Cavalcanti's Giovanna who, Dante tells us in the *Vita Nuova,* was called "Primavera" for her beauty and was Beatrice's harbinger. "Tu mi fai rimembrar" are Dante's words to Matelda in canto 28 of the *Purgatorio* when he tells her that she reminds him of Persephone. Dante meets Matelda in the Earthly Paradise where she, like Giovanna, prepares the poet for the arrival of Beatrice.

This moving tribute to Sherri Martinelli with which the canto closes is even more poignant when we realize against what odds such paradisal moments are achieved. Pound has left reminders there for the reader who is ready to look, but the dignity of his words keeps the underlying anguish at a distance. He wonders if he will continue to be equal to the unremitting struggle to preserve "his mind entire," surrounded as he is by insanity on every hand: "Without guides, having nothing but courage / Shall audacity last into fortitude?" Each day is a new struggle, and for him "dawn" is probably not only sunrise but also the moment at which he can escape from the wards and corridors of the asylum—from the "Blind eyes and shadows"—out into the open air:

<pre>
    to enter the presence at sunrise
    up out of hell, from the labyrinth
            the path wide as a hair.   [93/632]
</pre>

These daily exits from his new "Hell" are an eerie reenactment of his escape from Hell in Canto 15.

Thrones: *Cantos 97, 106, and 109*

In *Thrones* only Canto 106 is wholly personal. Pound would like to be able to bring his poem to a paradisal conclusion and this would necessarily require from him a highly personal assertion, but he postpones this, partly because his sense of duty demands that he suggest some more "terrestrial" and practical alternative to the fatalism he sees around him. Before the war, he had been the prophet of doom, obsessed with the corruption of Europe and the hell of his own times, but his purpose had been to shake his contemporaries out of their complacency so that things could be changed for the better. Now, after the war, the atom bomb, and the witch-hunts, the problem is not complacency but hopelessness, and he finds himself in a new role, bound, in spite of his own confusions, to insist on a vision of order and purposeful action. He presents his position eloquently in his interview for the *Paris Review:*

> The world in twenty years had piled up hysteria—anxiety over a third war [and] bureaucratic tyranny. . . . The immense . . . loss of freedoms, as they were in 1900, is undeniable. We have seen the acceleration in efficiency of the tyrannizing factors. . . . I must find a verbal formula to combat the rise of brutality—the principle of order versus the split atom. . . . I am writing to resist the view that Europe and civilization are going to Hell. If I am being "crucified for an idea"—that is, the coherent idea around which my muddles accumulated—it is probably the idea that European culture ought to survive . . . along with whatever other cultures, in whatever univer-

sality. Against the propaganda of terror and the propaganda of luxury, have you a nice simple answer?[9]

In the same interview we find him describing the principal subject of *Thrones* when he says: "The struggle for individual rights is an epic subject, consecutive from jury trial in Athens to Anselm versus William Rufus, to the murder of Becket and to Coke and through John Adams." He compares the thrones in the *Paradiso,* which are "for the spirits of people who have been responsible for good government," to the thrones in the *Cantos* which he calls "an attempt to move out from egoism and to establish some definition of an order possible or at any rate conceivable on earth." He says that this sequence of the poem "concerns the states of mind of people responsible for something more than their personal conduct," and we realize that, at this point in the poem, Pound himself has chosen to concentrate on a general vision of order in preference to thinking too closely about his own conduct.

Although Canto 106 is the only completely personal canto in *Thrones,* one luminous passage in the middle of Canto 97 provides a prelude to it and stands both as the poet's profession of his credo and as a propitiatory rite:

親 ch'in[1]　旦 tan[4]　親 ch'in[1]

οἶνος αἰθίοψ the gloss, probably,
not the colour. So hath Sibilla a boken ysette
as the lacquer in sunlight ἀλιπόρψυρος
& shall we say: russet-gold.
　　　　　　　　　That this colour exists in the air
not flame, not carmine, orixalxo, les xaladines
lit by the torch-flare,

　　　　& from the nature the sign,
as the small lions beside San Marco. Out of ling
the benevolence

9. Donald Hall, "Ezra Pound: An Interview," *The Paris Review* 28 (Summer/Fall 1962): 22–51.

Kuanon, by the golden rail,
 Nile διϊπετέος the flames gleam in the air
and in the air <u>ἀίσσουσιν</u>
Bernice, late for a constellation, mythopoeia persisting,
 (now called folc-loristica)

. . . .

δολιγηρέτμοισι

"Ten men" said degli Uberti "who will charge a
 nest of machine guns
"for one who will put his name on a chit."   [97/675–76]

Appropriately, since it deals with the mysteries, the central revelation of the passage is simultaneously dramatized and veiled by being presented through Chinese characters. The size and central position of the character *ling* leaves no doubt of the main focus and emphasis of the passage, and we remember how this same character dominates the opening of *Rock-Drill*. There Pound had translated it as "sensibility," and it referred to the virtues of a sovereign. "Our dynasty came in because of a great sensibility," is Pound's paraphrase of the Duke of Chow's words to the nobility of Yin as, acting as the king's spokesman, he warns them to be loyal to their new rulers because it was "the will of Heaven" that the corrupt Shang dynasty be overthrown: "Ye numerous officers of Yin, the case is now this, that the sovereigns of our Chow, from their great goodness were charged with the work of God" (*Shoo King,* 458). Pound's decision to render Legge's "goodness" as "sensibility" draws attention to the three components of the character which suggest that "goodness" is the result of attentiveness to "the will of Heaven" through conscientious performance of the rites. 巫 , *wu,* means "witch," "wizard," or the ritual that these perform—"the service of spirits"; 雨 , *yu,* means "rain,"

and the shape of the raindrops falling from clouds suggests, meta-
phorically, the divinity's response to ritual invocation; and the re-

peated ⧠ , *k'ou,* "mouth," in the center of *ling,* suggests to
Pound oracular pronouncement by one who has been attentive to
the divine will. He connects *wu* with the Sibyl, as Legge inciden-
tally does in a footnote on *wu* (*Shoo King,* 196). In Canto 104
when Pound again transcribes *ling,* he "glosses" it, "Pitonessa /
The small breasts snow-soft over tripod / under the cloud / the
three voices."

Yet when he uses *ling* in Canto 97 he is thinking, not in terms
of the state, but in terms of the family—not of public virtue, but of
private sensibilities and specifically of benevolence. He thinks
of the small stone lions beside Saint Mark's as symbols of benevo-
lence and mentions Kuanon in conjunction with the Nile, recalling
the compassionate Isis-Kuanon of Canto 90. His explicit comment
on benevolence is made in the six characters which he has taken
from the *Ta Hsio,* and the three characters that stand at the head
of the passage clearly point forward to these. We recognize *tan*[4],
"the dawn," from Cantos 77 and 91, and from Legge's glossary we
learn that *ch'in*[1] can mean both "to love" and "relatives." Pound
has rearranged the six *Ta Hsio* characters so that there also *ch'in*
stands at the beginning and at the end. He has translated this pas-
sage, which he offers here as his credo,

> counting his manhood and the love of his relatives the true
> treasure. [*C,* 75]

"Manhood" here means "moral courage" which, as he remembers
degli Uberti to have said, is so much rarer a commodity than
physical courage.

Pound's tribute to benevolence and "the love of relatives"
is made against a background of sea imagery, particularly the
dazzling play of sunlight on the surface of the waves. He begins
philologically with Homer's epithet for the "wine-dark sea" and, re-
jecting what seems to him the simplistic and unimaginative assump-
tion that the color of the waves is being compared to the color of

wine, he suggests that Homer was noticing the effect of light on the sea surface—"the gloss, probably, / not the colour . . . / . . . / as the lacquer in sunlight." Under a brilliant sun the flashes of light reflected back from the moving water do seem to hover above the surface of the sea—"the flames gleam in the air." Under full sunlight this light is a brilliant white, but as the light changes so does the color of the "flames." In Canto 90 Pound had remembered the look of "the sea gone the colour of copper" (80/500), and this is picked up here in "russet-gold. / That this colour exists in the air / not flame, not carmine, orixalxo [copper], les xaladines / lit by the torch-flare." Pound is thinking both of the sea at Venice and of Egypt and the "Nile δῖπετέος." Both δῖπετέος [heaven-sent] and δολιχηρετμοισι [long-oared] are found in that section of Book 4 of the *Odyssey* which tells how Menelaus learns from Proteus that he will be unable to return home safely until he sails back to the "heaven-sent waters of the Nile" to make the correct sacrifices to Zeus and the other gods. This, in conjunction with another Egyptian allusion, the reference to the story of Berenice, suggests that, in writing this passage, Pound is himself performing a rite to ensure his own safe return across the seas to Italy. When her husband, Ptolemy III, marched into Syria to attempt to rescue his sister, Berenice dedicated a lock of her hair in the temple of Aphrodite for his safe return. When the lock disappeared, the astronomer Conon of Samos claimed that it had been taken up into the heavens to become the constellation *Coma Berenices.*

Pound follows the *Ta Hsio* passage with a meditation on Fortuna:

All neath the moon, under Fortuna,
      splendor' mondan', [worldly splendors]
beata gode, hidden as eel in sedge, [and rejoices in her bliss]
      all neath the moon, under Fortuna

hoc signo   貞   chen(*four*), hoc signo
with eyes pervanche,
      three generations, San Vio
darker than pervanche?
      Pale sea-green, I saw eyes once,

. . . .
Earth under Fortuna,
                    each sphere hath its Lord,
with ever-shifting change, sempre biasmata, [always blamed]
          gode,
. . . .
Even Aquinas could not demote her, Fortuna,
              violet, pervanche, deep iris,
                    beat' è, e gode, [she is blest, and rejoices]
the dry pod could not demote her, plenilune,
              phase over phase.
Dante had read that Canzone.   [97/676–77]

Chen[4], "to be correct or firm," emphasizes that the operations of
Fortuna are not arbitrary, but just and inevitable, and reminds us
of what Pound has said about Fortuna in the second *Chou* canto.
"Sempre biasmata" is taken from Cavalcanti, but the overall tone
of the passage is most strongly influenced by Veigil's account of
the goddess (see appendix 1) in the *Inferno*. He describes her to
Dante as one of God's ministers who lives in eternal bliss and is
impervious to the way in which she is maligned on earth by those
whose lives she rules. Yet Pound's presentation of her is much
more than an allusion to Dante. He is thinking of the influence of
Fortuna in his own life and chooses to write of her immediately
after his assertion that the love of relatives is "the true treasure."
In making the goddess's eyes "violet, pervanche, deep iris," he has
given her the violet-blue eyes of Olga Rudge, making a connection
that seems an entirely appropriate intimation of the extraordinary
influence that she has had over the course of his personal life. In
emphasizing Fortuna's dignity and vitality, he shows that he is pre-
pared to take a philosophical view of the way in which his life has
been shaped by forces that have seemed beyond his control.
     Canto 106 is to *Thrones* what Cantos 90–93 are to *Rock-Drill*.
Here again the poet can glimpse and record the paradisal, and
again it is focussed for him by a woman's eyes. This canto begins
with a reference to a woman with dark hair and eyes:

              AND was her daughter like that;
              Black as Demeter's gown,
                              eyes, hair?

> Dis' bride, Queen over Phlegethon,
> girls faint as mist about her?   [106/752]

It seems most likely that these are the same eyes that the poet cannot "enter . . . by probing" and which are the focal point of the whole canto. These eyes are mysterious and elusive but project such power that eventually the poet's surroundings are metamorphosed. They reveal their power only gradually and hesitantly: "So slow is the rose to open. / A match flares in the eyes' hearth, / then darkness" (106/752). This woman is described only by analogy with various goddesses. The poet's initial comparison of her to Persephone gives way to a description of Persephone herself, and then the poet suggests a limited resemblance between this dark-eyed woman and Circe:

> between the two pine trees, not Circe
> but Circe was like that
> coming from the house of smoothe stone
> "not know which god"
> nor could enter her eyes by probing
> the light blazed behind her
> nor was this from sunset.
> Athene Pronoia,
> in hypostasis
> Helios, Perse: Circe
> Zeus: Artemis out of Leto
> Under wildwood
> Help me to neede   [106/754]

The differences between the woman and Circe outweigh the similarities, so Pound compares her next to Athena "the Foreknowing" and finally to Artemis. The virginity of these last two is more appropriate than the claustrophobic sexuality of Circe. The light which blazes behind this woman suggests that she embodies some divine power and it also reminds us that Pound follows Plotinus in thinking of the body as inside the soul, surrounded by it as by an aura (98/685). There is also fire in the depths of this woman's eyes—not the fire of mere physical passion but the intellectually and spiritually animating fire of Amor, which clearly distinguishes her from Circe. This explains the cryptic lines: "—violet, sea green, and no name. / Circe's were not, having fire behind them," in which Pound adds to the eyes of the "tre donne" of Canto 81 this fourth pair of dark eyes.

References to Artemis come to dominate this canto and suggest that Pound sees his "dark lady" as an Artemis figure. He thinks of this goddess in connection with temples, alluding first to the temple of Diana in Layamon's *Brut* which Brutus comes upon on the island of Logice and where he prays to the goddess to "Help [him] to neede" and make known to him where he must go to settle his people in a new land. The temple which "shook with Apollo" (106/754) is probably the temple at Delphi, both because of Pound's previous references to Castalia, and because the sanctuary of Athene Pronoia is close to both spring and temple. Pound, with his habitual preference for goddesses over gods, largely transfers the inspirational power of Apollo to his sister and this is preserved in his incantation: "And in thy mind beauty, O Artemis." Pound also compares his lady to Arsinoe (see appendix 1), the queen who "rose into heaven," to Berenice, whose hair was said to have been turned into a constellation, and to the Tennin in *Hagoromo,* who, in return for her feather mantle, teaches the fisherman a "dance that can turn the palace of the moon." During her dance the chorus notices that the "pine-waste of Miwo puts on the colour of spring" (*T,* 313), and a similar change occurs at the arrival of the poet's young woman. The "bois dormant" of Canto 93, where "The trees sleep, and the stags, and the grass; / The boughs sleep unmoving" finally awakens. When she appears:

> As with leopards by mount's edge,
>   light blazed behind her;
>   trees open, their minds stand before them
> As in Carrara is whiteness:
> Xoroi [the dance] . . .   [106/754]

The grounds of St. Elizabeths are metamorphosed by her presence and its power over the poet's imagination into a temple precinct and she becomes an incarnation of Artemis/Selena herself. This same passage is echoed in the conclusion to this canto:

Selena, foam on the wave-swirl
>   Out of gold light flooding the peristyle
>   Trees open in Paros,
>   White feet as Carrara's whiteness
> in Xoroi.
>   God's eye art 'ou.
>   The columns gleam as if cloisonné,
>   The sky is leaded with elm boughs.
>   [106/755]

Paros is not only, like Carrara, famous for its white marble, but is also close to a sanctuary of Apollo and Artemis. The trees which "open" here are perhaps the columns of the sanctuary, which look like tree trunks stripped of their bark, suggesting an image similar to Pound's description of the columns rising from the Venetian canals in 17/76: "the trees growing in water, / Marble trunks out of stillness." It seems most likely that the dark-eyed and dark-haired woman of this canto is Marcella Spann, who replaces Sherri Martinelli in the poet's affections and to whom he refers both directly and indirectly in the final sequence of the poem.

Here the paradisal moment is intimately personal, but at the end of *Thrones* Pound comes as close as he can to a more generalized vision. Unlike Dante and those who want to "burst out of the universe" (102/731), Pound is content to record as much of the paradisal as can be found on earth either in the phenomena of the natural world or in the achievements of humanity.

>   Clear deep off Taormina
>   high cliff and azure beneath it
> form is cut in the lute's neck, tone is from the bowl
> Oak boughs alone over Selloi
>   This wing, colour of feldspar
>   phyllotaxis
> Over wicket gate
>   INO Ἰνώ Kadmeia
> Erigena, Anselm,
>   the fight thru Herbert and Rémusat
> Helios,

Καλλῐαστράγαλος Ino Kadmeia,
San Domenico, Santa Sabina,
Sta Maria Trastevere
in Cosmedin
Le chapeau melon de St Pierre
You in the dinghy (piccioletta) astern there!
[109/774]

We notice immediately both the dominant mood of calm and the note of resignation. The quest is unfinished, but the poet has a very clear idea of the odds against which he must continue to struggle, and he persists with a sober realization that he must no longer expect any dramatic dénouement or epiphanic resolution. The calm is established by a sequence of images that are highly charged with luminous memories. The intense blue of the deep water beneath the cliffs at Taormina is echoed in the "wing, colour of feldspar." This, in turn, looks back to the butterflies "by hundred blue-gray over their rock-pool" of 106/754 and, much farther back, to "Canzone: Of Angels," published in 1911. Here, describing the third angel he had written:

That azure feldspar hight the microcline,
Or, on its wing, the Menelaus weareth
Such subtlety of shimmering as beareth
This marvel onward through the crystalline,
A splendid calyx that about her gloweth,
Smiting the sunlight on whose ray she goeth.
[*CEP*, 140]

He had dedicated *Canzoni* "To Olivia and Dorothy Shakespear" and this particular canzone to "her whose spirit seems in sooth / Akin unto the feldspar, since it is / So clear and subtle and azure." There is a longhand version of the canzone also, copied by Dorothy Shakespear into one of her notebooks.

As we would expect, Pound also thinks of the way in which the paradisal has been captured in works of stone, in the large sweep of arches, the symmetry of columns and the intricacies of mosaic. He thinks of San Domenico in Siena and we recall "Narrow alabaster in sunlight / in Classe, in San Domenico" from 93/ 623. Within the romanesque basilica of Santa Sabina, a double line of Corinthian columns of Parian marble captures the very essence of the Greek temple—like those "in Selinunt', / in Akragas" (107/ 756)—and recreates Sicily in the heart of Rome. When he remembers Santa Maria in Trastevere, he thinks of the mosaics which, it seems to him, "recall a wisdom lost by scholasticism" (*SP,* 320) and particularly of the representation of the Virgin and Christ seated together, like a bridal couple, "trastevere with La Sposa / Sponsa Christi in mosaic till our time" (74/425).

The light in Pound's "earthly paradise" is not otherworldly, but, on one hand, the sunlight, and on the other, the light of wisdom which shines out from the writings of Erigena, Anselm, Herbert of Cherbury, and Charles de Rémusat. Throughout the canto we have been reminded of our debt to the lucid intellect of Sir Edward Coke, and in the first of the Coke cantos Pound has written:

> So that Dante's view is quite natural:
> this light
> as a river
> in Kung; in Ocellus, Coke, Agassiz
> ῥεῖ, the flowing
> this persistent awareness
> [107/762]

Dante sees and drinks from the river of light in the Empyrean, but Pound's heroes can only keep the light flowing through the strenuous exercise of their intellects on earth, usually struggling against the current of thought in their own time—"the fight thru Herbert and Rémusat."

Pound makes clear that he realizes that his poem cannot contain a definitive resolution to his own struggle because no end to the struggle is in sight. "Oak boughs alone over Selloi" reminds us that he feels a sense of kinship with Herakles in the *Trachiniae.* Sophocles' hero, dying from the poison in the blood of the long-dead Nessus, finally learns the true meaning of Zeus's assurance that he will not be killed by any living creature and of the oracle's promise that he will finally be released from his labors:

> The dead beast kills the living me.
> and that fits another odd forecast
> breathed out at the Selloi's oak—
> Those fellows rough it,
>> sleep on the ground, up in the hills there.
> I heard it and wrote it down
>> under my Father's tree.
> Time lives, and it's going on now.
> I am released from trouble.
> I thought it meant life in comfort.
> It doesn't. It means that I die.
> For amid the dead there is no work in service.
> Come at it that way, my boy, what

> SPLENDOUR,
>> IT ALL COHERES.   [*WT*, 49–50]

In his translation Pound has made Herakles' realization of his fate not just acceptance but a triumphant illumination, and in his stage directions he specifies that at this point the hero remove his mask of agony to reveal "make-up" representing "solar serenity." Like Herakles, Pound himself has arrived at the revelation that the only end to his struggle will be his death.

At the end of *Thrones,* where we might expect some conclusion to the poet's quest, we find instead allusions to new journeys about to be made. "Over wicket gate" calls up the figure of Christian at the point of beginning his difficult and dangerous journey to the Celestial City: "Then said Evangelist, pointing with his finger over a very wide field, Do you see yonder wicket-gate? The man said, No. Then said the other, Do you see yonder shining light? He said, I think I do. Then said Evangelist, Keep that light in your eye, and go up directly thereto: so shalt thou see the gate;

at which when thou knockest it shall be told thee what thou shalt do."[10]

The two other journeys that Pound alludes to are sea-voyages. His reference to Leucothea—"Ino Kadmeia"—reminds us that the poet, remembering Odysseus's reversals even toward the end of his voyages, feels that he still needs help before he can make his homecoming. Dante, about to launch into the writing of the *Paradiso,* warns his readers: "O you that are in your little bark, eager to hear, following behind my ship that singing makes her way, turn back to see again your shores. Do not commit yourselves to the open sea, for perchance, if you lost me, you would remain astray. The water which I take was never coursed before" (1. 2. 1–7). Dante, inspired by Minerva and guided by Apollo and the Muses, has no doubt that he will reach his goal, but when Pound refers us to this passage in the final line of *Thrones,* we should not assume that he is speaking with the self-assurance of Dante. Here, at the beginning of the *Paradiso,* Dante is forging confidently ahead, but Pound is on the point of ending his poem. He had hoped to be able to provide it with a paradisal conclusion, decisive enough in its own way to be comparable to Dante's, but he now sees that this will be impossible. He realizes that his poem must soon stop, with or without a ringing conclusion, and yet he has no clear idea of what the ending will be. In this sense, and perhaps in another, he is still sailing into the unknown. Not only must he end his poem, but he must also sail out beyond it, toward his own death.

Drafts and Fragments

Drafts and Fragments begins with a "quiet exultance":

> Thy quiet house
> The crozier's curve runs in the wall,
> The harl, feather-white, as a dolphin on sea-brink

10. John Bunyan, *The Pilgrim's Progress* (London, 1918), pp. 9–10.

. . . .

             —wake exultant
                  in caracole
Hast'ou seen boat's wake on sea-wall,
                how crests it?
What panache?
            paw-flap, wave-tap,
               that is gaiety,
Toba Sojo,
         toward limpidity,
                that is exultance . . .
                    [110/777]

The "panache" of the diction itself buoys up the resilient delight of the poet's mood and we see what kind of resources he will be able to rely on in the struggle with despondency and remorse which will occupy him for the rest of his life. He identifies the "quiet house" later in the canto when he writes, "Byzance a tomb, an end, / Galla's rest, and thy quiet house at Torcello," and he is addressing himself to the Virgin, since the cathedral at Torcello is both named for her as *Santa Maria Assunta* and contains a fine mosaic of her. In Canto 110 he confronts the spectacle of "time's wreckage" and his own inability to make any significant stand against the deterioration of western civilization, but he avoids fatalism. He demonstrates his faith that individuals can find the means to save themselves from despair, and for each painful fact and episode he records, he finds some force to counteract it. Yet he cannot relax into peaceful meditation. Although he could be content with "the sun and serenitas" (113/786), his conscience will not let him rest: "Out of dark, thou, Father Helios, leadest, / but the mind as Ixion, unstill, ever turning" (113/790).

Canto 110 is concerned with the quest for redemption. He is concerned about his own confusion and feeling of disorder, that "the mind jumps without building / . . . / and there is no *chih* [resting place] and no root," and his state of mind is much like that of the poet at the end of *The Waste Land:* "From time's wreckage shored, these fragments shored against ruin." Yet there is cause for hope also and he recalls King T'ang's admonition to

Figure 9. Madonna in Torcello Cathedral, Venice.
". . . and thy quiet house at Torcello" [110/780]

himself to "Make it new" each day, and remembers Leucothea, KALLIASTRAGALOS, of beautiful ankles, the rescuer. The beauty of Lake Garda uplifts him as it had back in Canto I, and when he returns in 1959 with his wife and Marcella Spann, he finds its beauty as moving as ever:

> And in thy mind beauty, O Artemis,
> > as of mountain lakes in the dawn,
> Foam and silk are thy fingers,
> > Kuanon,
> and the long suavity of her moving,
> > willow and olive reflected,
> Brook-water idles,
> > topaz against pallor of under-leaf
> The lake waves Canaletto'd
> > under blue paler than heaven,
> the rock-layers arc'd as with a compass,
> > this rock is magnesia,
> Cozzaglio, Dino Martinazzi made the road here (Gardesana)
> > > [110/778]

The mood of the Noh seems particularly in harmony with his state of mind at this time and he thinks of four Noh plays which deal with the theme of redemption. In *Sotoba Komachi,* the heroine, Ono no Komachi, once a beautiful and talented woman, is now old and crazed and reduced to begging. She remembers her past pride and beauty and explains how the spirit of her lover, Shosho, torments her with madness because of her cruel rejection of him. In the sequel to this play, *Kayoi Komachi,* which Pound refers to at the end of the canto, the spirits of Ono and Shosho are saved and reunited for eternity once they can conquer their pride.

Awoi no Uye tells the story of the exorcising of Awoi's jealousy. She can only be helped by some power outside herself and is saved by the exorcists who call upon the names of the "powerful good spirits," and by the answering "forbearance and pity" of Bosatsu. She turns from jealousy to compassion and the play ends with the words of the Chorus: "Pity has melted her heart, and she has gone into Buddha. Thanksgiving" (*T*, 331). We see from his introduction to his 1916 translation of the play that the poet was particularly interested in the psychological subtlety of the presentation of Awoi's obsession. He explained how her "passion makes her subject to the demon-possession" (*T*, 325); he now knows to his cost that hatred as well as jealousy can let in demons, and, which is even more troubling, "That love [can] be the cause of hate" (110/780).

Pound had become particularly interested in the culture of the Na-Khi people of southwest China, whose literature and customs were recorded before they passed into oblivion by the botanist and anthropologist Joseph F. Rock. Pound discovered Rock's works in 1956 and used them as a major source for Cantos 101 and 112 as well as in this canto. Rock himself became one of Pound's heroes for his courage and perseverance in the face of frustration and difficulty. Rock lost all the fruits of twenty years' research on Na-Khi culture—including eighteen 300-page notebooks and a four-volume manuscript—when the ship carrying them to America was torpedoed and sunk by the Japanese. Rock returned to the Na-Khi and began his work again, from the beginning.[11] In Canto 110, the poet refers to a Na-Khi romance which tells of a young girl, married against her will to a man she does not love, who decides to commit suicide but cannot persuade her lover to take his life too.[12] Her lover comes upon her corpse by chance and, after cremating her, is driven by her spirit to hang himself.

The fate of Na-Khi suicides is similar to that of the souls in the first circle of Dante's Hell, since they "become the constant companions of the winds and the wind-demons," and Pound recalls the spirits of Paolo and Francesca "che paion' si al vent'." Unlike Dante's spirits, those of the Na-Khi lovers can be freed from their torment if the proper rituals are performed and the most impor-

11. "The [2]Muan [1]Bpo Ceremony or the Sacrifice to Heaven as Practised by the [1]Na-[2]Khi," *Monumenta Serica* 8 (Peiping, 1948): preface.

12. For information on this romance I have used Jamila Ismail's "News of the Universe: [2]Muan [1]Bpo and *The Cantos*," *Agenda* 9, nos. 2–3 (Spring/ Summer 1971): 85–86.

tant of these is the ²Muan ¹bpo (sacrifice to Heaven) ceremony of
purification and thanksgiving which Pound refers to in:

> heaven   earth
>   in the center
>   is
>   juniper
>   The purifications
>   are snow, rain, artemisia,
>   also dew, oak and the juniper   [110/778]

By referring to this ceremony at this point, Pound suggests
that the pain of earthly love has been transcended, and he rein-
forces this idea with his cryptic reference to the Noh play *Kakitsu-
bata:* "Yellow iris in that river bed." Like the stories of Ono and
Awoi, the story of Kakitsubata is redemptive, and we can see its
importance to Pound from his concluding "Note" to his transla-
tion of the play. He explains that the spirit of Kakitsubata, whose
name means "the colors of remembrance," is partly embodied in
the flowers of the iris and can appear to those who, reflecting on
the beauty of the flowers, recall her beauty. Pound says: "It is by
memory that this spirit appears, she is able or 'bound' because of
the passing thought of these iris. That is to say, they . . . are the
outer veils of her being. Beauty is the road to salvation, and her
apparition 'to win people to the Lord' or 'to enlighten these
people' is part of the ritual, that is to say, she demonstrates the
'immortality of the soul' or the 'permanence or endurance of the
individual personality' " (*T,* 340).

The forces of disillusionment and despondency are very strong,
and the poet cannot save himself by the power of his own intellect,
which now seems no stronger than a candle flame, but he does
believe that there is a power outside himself to which he can pray
for strength:

> Falling spiders and scorpions,
> Give light against falling poison,
> A wind of darkness hurls against forest

the candle flickers
is faint
Lux enim—
versus this tempest.
The marble form in the pine wood,
The shrine seen and not seen
From the roots of sequoias

ching[4]

pray 敬 pray

There is power
Awoi or Komachi,
the oval moon.   [110/781]

Canto 113 shows particularly clearly the struggle which Pound is still undergoing in his own mind. He wants to arrive at some fair and accurate appraisal of life as he sees it, and to this end insists on confronting the full extent of the bad as well as celebrating the good. At first he posits an entirely dispassionate cosmos in which the sun and Fortuna observe human affairs unmoved:

Thru the 12 Houses of Heaven
seeing the just and the unjust,
tasting the sweet and the sorry,
Pater Helios turning.
"Mortal praise has no sound in her ears"
(Fortuna's)
[113/786]

If the gods are unconcerned with the fate of humanity, then, Pound suggests, it is an act of self-preservation to "make gods out of beauty," and when this is no longer done "this is a dying" (113/786). He then considers what he finds most inspiring and comforting in his own experience—the perfection of musical form, scientific precision in the observation of the natural world, a garden, a beloved woman, the power of the imagination and of

memory, the dedication of those who work to increase the store
of human knowledge and who demonstrate personal courage:

> Yet to walk with Mozart, Agassiz and Linnaeus
>   'neath overhanging air under sun-beat
> Here take thy mind's space
> And to this garden, Marcella, ever seeking by petal, by leaf-vein
>   out of dark, and toward half-light

> And over Li Chiang, the snow range is turquoise
> Rock's world that he saved us for memory
>   a thin trace in high air
> And with them Paré (Ambroise) and the Men against Death
>   [113/786]

The poet who before had always preferred to think less of how
things are than of how, with luck and effort, they might become,
now must come to terms with his life as it has been and look back
on it as something which will never be any more final than it is
now. To live means "to know beauty and death and despair," per-
haps without ever seeing how to reconcile them, and he realizes
that the lack of finality which he feels is part of the nature of the
universe: "and to think that what has been shall be, / flowing, ever
unstill / . . . / The hells move in cycles, / No man can see his own
end." He wonders how far he can rely on his intimations of pagan
energies in nature—"The Gods have not returned. 'They have never
left us.' / They have not returned. / Cloud's processional and the
air moves with their living" (113/787). Even now he finds it hard
to settle for perception uncompleted by action, and in spite of his
comforting faith that "there is something intelligent in the cherry-
stone," and his ability to take pleasure from the color of sunlit
buildings, he still thinks of the need to discover how "to hitch sen-
sibility to efficiency" (113/788). On one hand he sees the intract-
able negative, and on the other, compensatory virtue, but the two
are merely opposed and virtue cannot lessen human folly, only
strengthen one in the face of it: "Error of chaos. Justification is
from kindness of heart / and from her hands floweth mercy." He
may well be thinking of Eliot when he talks of those "who de-

mand belief rather than justice," since he has already borrowed Eliot's "fragments shored against ruin" and will make another "Waste Land" allusion in Canto 115.

Pound is still not ready to substitute faith for his desire for social justice—and insists that "to know interest from usura / . . . In this sphere is Giustizia" (113/789). In the mind of Artemis there is beauty, and the poet's mind can rise to apprehensions of perfect order and harmony, but he must still return to the irritations and inadequacies of day-by-day reality and of strained personal relationships which have made "Pride, jealousy and possessiveness" seem "3 pains of hell." On one hand he concedes that "There remains grumpiness, / malvagità," but he also knows that "in every woman, somewhere in the snarl is a tenderness" (113/ 789). He chafes at the lack of "magnanimity" in the world around him, and in "scala altrui" regrets not only his exile but also his dependence on others. The quotation is from Cacciaguida's speech to Dante in the *Paradiso* (3. 17. 58–60), where he warns the poet that "You shall come to know how salt is the taste of another's bread, and how hard the path to descend and mount by another man's stairs." The poet restates his poetic creed, from which he has never deviated and which has sustained him through all his trials: "God's eye art'ou, do not surrender perception" (113/790).

The poet slips into an elegiac mood when he quotes from *Homage to Sextus Propertius,* "When the Syrian onyx is broken." In Canto 110 he has included "Quos ego Persephonae [maxima dona feram]," from the same elegy, so it would seem that Propertius's mood in this poem bears some correspondence to Pound's state of mind in these cantos. Propertius, considering the prospect of his death, tells Cynthia that there will be no grand funeral rites for him but

> A small plebeian procession.
>   Enough, enough and in plenty
> There will be three books at my obsequies
> Which I take, my not unworthy gift, to Persephone.
>
> You will follow the bare scarified breast
> Nor will you be weary of calling my name, nor too
>   weary

> To place the last kiss on my lips
> When the Syrian onyx is broken. [*P,* 219]

What could become a maudlin frame of mind is interrupted by a call to the things of this world as "Out of dark, thou, Father Helios, leadest," but the sun does not always bring "serenitas" and the poet's struggle continues, "the mind as Ixion, unstill, ever turning."

Canto 114 is a celebration of kindness and begins appropriately with Voltaire as an old man turning his back on his earlier love of vituperative attack and refusing to hate even his arch-enemy, Jean Fréron.[13] Pound as an old man finds himself thinking about his ancestors as he had done in *Indiscretions.* At that time he had made a point of his dislike of the "encroachment of one personality upon another in the sty of the family" (*PD,* 11), but now, thinking perhaps of how he himself will take his place as an ancestor before too many more years, he finds himself moved by a feeling of family pride:

> This is not vanity, to have good guys in the family
> or feminine gaiety—quick on the uptake
> "All the same in a hundred years."
> "Harve was like that" (the old cat-head
> re a question of conduct.)
> "the appointed when nothing can stop it—
> unappointed when nothing can kill you."
> Even old Sarah,
> quick on the uptake
> snobism—niente—
> the *tribù.*
> Armes et blasons!
> me foot!!
> Al's conversations—reputed. [114/792]

"Old Sarah" is the poet's grandmother, Sarah Angevine Loomis, wife of Thaddeus Pound, and her comment about "Harve" is the

13. Richard Sieburth, "Ideas into Action: Pound and Voltaire," *Paideuma* 6, no. 3 (Winter 1977): 387.

only remark of hers that Pound remembers. "Al" is Thaddeus's brother, Albert, and the poet particularly remembers him for his approval of the fact that the Episcopal Church interfered "neither with a man's politics nor his religion" (*Life,* 2).

In the passages on kindness, the poet approaches the mood of the more meditative passages of the *Pisan Cantos:*

> Tanagra mia, Ambracia,
>   for the delicacy
>   for the kindness,
> The grass flower clings to its stalk under Zephyrus.
>
> [114/793]

and again:

> The kindness, infinite, of her hands.
>   Sea, blue under cliffs, or
> William murmuring: "Sligo in heaven" when the mist came
>   to Tigullio. And that the truth is in kindness.
>
> [114/793]

In his references to the Greek towns Tanagra and Ambracia, the modern Arta, the poet may have in mind some personal experiences which have made him associate these places with kindness and delicacy, but he may well be thinking more of places than of people and perhaps of the Byzantine Church of Our Lady of Consolation, *Panagria Parigoritissa,* at Arta, in which case this reference would carry forward from "Byzance, a tomb, an end," and echo "thy quiet house at Torcello." The hands of infinite kindness may well belong to Olga Rudge, who was to care tirelessly for the poet from 1961 until the end of his life and to whom *Drafts and Fragments* is dedicated.

Canto 115 begins with the chaos of his own times when "The scientists are in terror / and the European mind stops," and he sets against this the courage of Wyndham Lewis in his last years, the beauty of flowers, and the precision of Mozart's music and Linnaeus's botanical observations. The chaos has intruded into personal relationships also and threatens the security of one of the poet's last strongholds—his faith in personal kindness. He asks: "When one's friends hate each other / how can there be peace in the world?" He feels old and weary and describes himself as "A blown husk that is finished," but this is not wholly despairing, as we see when he adds "but the light sings eternal / a pale flare over marshes / where the salt hay whispers to tide's change." In his reference to himself as a "blown husk," Pound seems to have in mind the ending of *Kakitsubata,* and this further limits the negative connotations. Here, the spirit of Kakitsubata describes herself as "A light that does not lead on to darkness," reminding us of "A little light, like a rushlight / to lead back to splendour" (116/797). When the Chorus recites her lover's lament: "My body / Is not my body, / But only a body grown old," she makes clear the separation between the ephemeral earthly body and the immortal spirit. She performs a dance which recreates her youthful beauty, but then her spirit goes, "leaving its apparition, which fades as it returns to the aether," of which the Spirit says: "It is only the cracked husk of the locust." The Chorus closes the play by saying: "Day comes, the purple flower / Opens its heart of wisdom, / It fades out of sight by its thought. / The flower soul melts into Buddha" (*T,* 340).

For the poet still trying to arrive at some conclusion about life on earth, there is no certainty: "Time, space, / neither life nor death is the answer." He still struggles with the central enigma of his own life, "of man seeking good, / doing evil." When he writes: "In meiner Heimat / where the dead walked / and the living were made of cardboard," he is accusing America of the kind of torpor and lethargy that he had found in London and Paris and condemned in Canto 7. The echo of *The Waste Land* in "Heimat" also seems to suggest that Pound feels that there has been little progress beyond the spiritual sterility that Eliot had described in his poem.

Canto 116 begins with the personification of the *nous* as Neptune, whose mind "leaping like dolphins" represents the exhilaration of the play of the intellect on ultimate questions: "These concepts the human mind has attained. / To make Cosmos— / To achieve the possible—." His own poetry now appears to Pound as a "palimpsest," offering only "a little light / in great darkness." He sees the light himself, but cannot get it into his poem:

> I have brought the great ball of crystal;
> who can lift it?

> Can you enter the great acorn of light?
> But the beauty is not the madness
> Tho' my errors and wrecks lie about me.
> And I am not a demigod,
> I cannot make it cohere.   [116/795-96]

To present his vision is of great importance, but it is not enough; the poet has a duty to concern himself with the immediate problems of mankind in society, with "The voice of famine unheard." He again insists that "If love be not in the house there is nothing," and remembers how he was saved from despair in St. Elizabeths by the affection of Sherri Martinelli and Marcella Spann: "How came beauty against this blackness, / Twice beauty under the elms—" (116/796). Again he shows that even in moments of transcendence he cannot be entirely free of his underlying awareness of social chaos: even that state of mind which corresponds to the "Heaven of Venus" is "a nice quiet paradise / over the shambles." He then suggests that he may be wrong to want to reconcile the two; that a vision is something to be seen, not to be lived in, and that its limited accessibility does not make it less authentic: "the verb is 'see' [videre], not 'walk on' / i.e. it coheres all right / even if my notes do not cohere." He acknowledges that he has made "many errors" in his judgments but he had propounded his idea of a conspiracy of usurers as a way of explaining the chaos of his own times. If he is wrong, perhaps there is no clear cause of the problem and life is intended to be a "hell"; perhaps his ideal of a "paradiso terrestre" is mocked by the impossibility of ever improving society. His intentions at least had been admirable—he had tried to set up an alternative to fatalism even if he has only, finally, achieved "Many errors, / a little rightness" in his attempt "to excuse his hell / and my paradiso" (116/797). He knows of course that his impulse *was* the right one; that it is necessary "to affirm the gold thread in the pattern." He will not give in to despair, nor go back on his assertion that "it coheres all right," and he realizes that self-knowledge which is self-destructive has no value; that it is important "To confess wrong without losing rightness."

Ultimately he judges his poem according to its accuracy as a diagnosis of the social ills of his own time and as an attempt to point to some solution to these ills or at least give some reassur-

ance that such a solution may be possible. Judged by these criteria
the poem is clearly a failure, and hence he writes:

> That I lost my center
> fighting the world.
> The dreams clash
> and are shattered—
> and that I tried to make a paradiso
> terrestre.   [117/802]

His own judgments of his poem toward the end of his life—that he
was "Ninety-per-cent wrong," that he had "blundered always,"
that his writing was "stupidity and ignorance all the way through"[14]
are similarly disclaimers of his previous insistence on "usury" as
the root cause of social decline. In his self-deprecating foreword
to *Selected Prose,* dated 1972, he writes "re USURY: I was out of
focus, taking a symptom for a cause. The cause is AVARICE," and
he describes the contents of this anthology as "the scrapings from
the cracker-barrel." In his anxiety to recant opinions he is now
ashamed of, he is ready at times to deny any value to his poem, as
though there were nothing more in it than his condemnation of
Usura. His sense of his past blindness aggravates his sense of failure
and he blames himself for being unable to supply a definitive
conclusion for his poem. Not only has the vision of an earthly
paradise eluded him, but he has also been unable to produce a con-
clusion to his poem which would in any way be comparable to
Dante's unifying vision in the *Paradiso.* Where he blames himself
for this, the reader is likely to be surprised not that he failed to
arrive at such a vision, but that he ever expected to do so.

   It was very important to Pound that his poem conclude de-
cisively. For all his commitment to "ideogrammic" presentation,
with its fidelity to the fragmentariness of consciousness and its
usefulness in mirroring the social dislocations of his own time,
Pound seemed to believe that his poem should conclude with a

---

14. Heymann, p. 312. Grazia Livi, interview with Pound, *Epoca,* March
24, 1963, reprinted in Ezra Pound, vol. 2, *Les Cahiers de L'Herne* (Paris,
1965), p. 223. Pound to Allen Ginsberg, quoted in Heymann, p. 297.

finality sufficient to stand as a counterweight to the flux and disorder which he had been documenting. His readiness to deny value to the whole poem when he realized that he could not conclude it to his satisfaction suggests that he may consider his ideogrammic method a kind of "poetic licence" which is only allowable on the condition of a final, unequivocal assertion of significant order. His failure to meet this condition provokes his description of *The Cantos* as "a botch" and his comment: "I picked out this and that thing that interested me, and then jumbled them into a bag."[15] He cannot see, as the reader can, that as a "record of struggle" his poem has a unity which is in no way compromised by his failure to arrive at the kind of conclusion which he has hoped for.

The essential struggle documented and dramatized by *The Cantos* is not, as Pound believes, the struggle which he loses—his fight against the economic and social corruption of his own times. The more fundamental struggle of which he is only partly aware is the one that he finally wins when he overcomes his self-evasiveness and rediscovers and acknowledges the value and power of personal benevolence and of love. This acknowledgment, important as it is, does not however bring peace of mind, and he is oppressed by the consequences of having for so long chosen anger over benevolence. He blames himself for not having seen more clearly in the past, and looking back at his errors of judgment, he cannot free himself from the idea that his life's work has been a monumental failure. He also blames himself for the suffering that he has caused those closest to him. It would have been possible for him to have abandoned this struggle with remorse, at the last, by giving in to fatalism and despair, or by deciding that "belief" without "justice" can be sufficient, or even by taking refuge in his hard-won faith in the value of love and kindness. He accepts none of these escapes from his severe self-accusation, nor does he indulge in self-pity. He never loses his tenacity or his integrity; but despite moments of serenity, there is little certitude. He seems unable to see his final, unflinching self-scrutiny for the act of courage which it undoubtedly is.

In his sensitive and illuminating description of Pound as he was in March 1960, Donald Hall gives valuable insights into the poet's

---

15. Pound to Daniel Cory in conversation, quoted in Stock's *Life,* pp. 457–58.

state of mind at that time.[16] Pound felt homesick for America and out of place in Italy, but the main cause of his distress was his increasing difficulty in marshalling and developing his ideas to his satisfaction. He had trouble answering Hall's questions for the *Paris Review* interview, and Hall tells how Pound's pride made these failures "torture" to him. "Wyndham Lewis chose blindness / rather than have his mind stop," but what if one were to be given no choice—no alternative? His great fear was that he would never be able to write again. Hall describes the devastating waves of fatigue that would sweep over Pound with no warning, totally incapacitating him and plunging him, for as long as they lasted, into despair.

After the summer of 1961, the poet chose silence. Not the years in St. Elizabeths but the last eleven years of his life were to be his atonement for his "many errors," and this self-imposed penance must have been far more painful than his long imprisonment in the asylum. It was inevitable that someone who was by nature so reticent about his emotions should choose to make this most painful episode of his self-confrontation a wholly private matter, and his silence allowed him no relief from his remorse. Eliot had found peace in his submission to the Church, but Pound, as always, doing things the hard way, chose contrition without promise of pardon—it would be hard to say which of the two showed more humility.

The poet's daughter believes that the silence was like the mystic's "dark night of the soul." Donald Hall thinks of it as a descent into a "personal inferno," remembering that the poet was to say of it later, "I did not enter the silence; silence captured me."[17] Yet we should take this last as a comment on the inevitability of the choice rather than an indication that there was no choice. In entering the silence the poet was making a decision that was not only deliberate, but also premeditated, as we see from a remark of Pound's that Hall himself reports. Hall describes how Pound, having

16. Donald Hall, *Remembering Poets*, "Fragments of Ezra Pound" (New York, 1979), pp. 111–94.

17. Ibid., p. 183.

shown him the manuscripts that would later be *Drafts and Fragments,* was delighted by the younger man's enormous enthusiasm for them only to be suddenly overwhelmed by fatigue and hopelessness. As he recovered, Pound observed, "There can be such—communication—in silence."

Within the silence, although the struggle continued, the poetry ceased, and the fragmentary nature of the final cantos and parts of cantos points forward to the phase of the struggle which was not to be put into poetry or into words at all. The lines which presently stand as the conclusion to the poem, for all their beauty and pathos, suggest too much finality to make them the best possible ending:

> I have tried to write Paradise
>
> Do not move
>   Let the wind speak
>   that is paradise.
>
> Let the Gods forgive what I
>   have made
> Let those I love try to forgive
>   what I have made.   [120/803]

Although in the current *New Directions* edition of the poem these lines are entitled "Canto CXX," they were not chosen by the poet as the conclusion to his poem, nor were they originally written as a separate canto. They first appeared as part of the fragment from Canto 115 and it is likely that in future editions they will not be printed as Canto 120.[18] Perhaps the best conclusion to *The Cantos* will prove to be the last of the dated fragments.[19] In

18. I am indebted to Christine Froula for providing me with information about the publication history of "Canto CXX."

19. This fragment in the Pound Archive of the Beinecke Library at Yale is part of the Norman Holmes Pearson bequest and was shown to me by Mary de Rachewiltz.

these few lines we see the stoicism and tenacity with which the poet will move forward toward death through silence and through the "lowest depths of dark night." His boat will move "by oar, not by sail" and he will find strength for the journey because the journey has to be made:

28 Sept
1960

for a long pull
& a
long
wane
ima vada
noctis
obscurae

Appendix 1
Further Readings of *The Cantos*

Canto 4

"The pine at Takasago." In the spring of 1916, Pound was work-
ing concurrently on translations of Noh plays and on *The Cantos*
and wrote to Harriet Monroe of his first three cantos that their
"theme is roughly the theme of 'Takasago,' which story I hope to
incorporate more explicitly in a later part of the poem,"[1] an in-
tention which he soon abandoned. In the play, a priest and his
attendants come to Takasago to see the famous pine tree which,
according to legend, is the twin of a pine that grows in Sumiyoshi.
They find there an old man and old woman sweeping away the
fallen pine needles who tell them the story of the pines and reveal
that they are the spirits of the trees in human form. The priest
then sails to Sumiyoshi and there meets Myōjin, God of the shrine,
who performs a god-dance. The two pines, linked together despite
the distance between them, represent the ideal of married love.
When the priest is surprised to hear that the old man lives in
Sumiyoshi and travels each day to Takasago, he is told: "Though
miles of land and sea may part them, / The hearts of man and wife
are joined by love; / Naught do they reck of distance." The couple
explain how the trees further symbolize the reigns of great em-

1. Myles Slatin, "A History of Pound's *Cantos I–XVI*, 1915–1925,"
American Literature 35 (May 1963): 186.

perors and how "the unfading greenery of the Pines / Stands for the art of poetry flourishing as of old."[2]

Canto 5

"John Borgia is bathed at last." Burchard gives the following version of Schiavone's account of the disposal of Borgia's body:

> a man came, mounted on a white horse, having behind him a dead body, the head and arms of which hung on one side, and the feet on the other side of the horse; the two persons on foot supporting the body, to prevent its falling. They thus proceeded towards that part, where the filth of the city is usually discharged into the river; and turning the horse, with his tail toward the water, the two persons took the dead body by the arms and feet, and with all their strength flung it into the river. The person on horseback then asked if they had thrown it in, to which they replied, *Signor, si* (yes, sir). He then looked towards the river, and seeing a mantle floating on the stream, he inquired what it was that appeared black, to which they answered it was a mantle; and one of them threw stones upon it, in consequence of which it sunk.[3]

"where Barabello / Prods the Pope's elephant, and gets no crown." Roscoe describes Baraballo as "one of that unfortunate, but numerous class, who, without the talent, possess[es] the inclination for writing poetry [and] . . . thought himself another Petrarca, and, like him, aspired to the honour of being crowned in the Capitol. The Pope and his attendants encouraged him in this for their own amusement and "to add to the ridicule, it was resolved that the elephant, which had lately been presented to the pontiff by

2. *The Noh Drama: 10 Plays from the Japanese,* Japanese Classics Translation Committee (Rutland, Vt. and Tokyo, 1960), pp. 9–10.

3. William Roscoe, *The Life and Pontificate of Leo X,* 4 vols. (Liverpool, 1805), 1: 266–68. Subsequent references to *Leo* will be to volume and page number in this edition.

the king of Portugal, should be brought out and splendidly deco-
rated, and that Baraballo, arrayed in the triumphal habit of a
Roman conqueror, should mount it, and be conveyed in triumph
to the Capitol." The ceremony was abruptly halted, though, when
"arriving at the bridge of S. Angelo, the sagacious quadruped re-
fused to contribute any longer to the ungenerous mirth of the
crowd, and the hero of the day was glad to descend in safety from
his exalted station" (*Leo,* 3. 334–36).

"Sanazarro / "Alone out of all the court was faithful to him."
Giacopo Sanazzaro was "distinguished by the excellence of his
Latin and Italian compositions" and Ferdinand of Naples, recog-
nizing his talent, extended his patronage to him. To the king and
his sons, Alfonso and Federigo, Sanazzaro "throughout all their
calamities . . . maintained an unshaken attachment." He continued
loyal to Alfonso when Charles VIII of France was marching on
Naples. Alfonso had fled the city, abdicating in favor of his young
son, and to ingratiate themselves with Charles "those distinguished
scholars, who had celebrated [Alfonso's] triumphs, and immortal-
ized his name in their works, endeavoured to expiate their error,
and prove their abhorrence of his misconduct, by the severest
reprehensions." When Alfonso's brother Federigo was deprived of
his kingdom by a papal bull, he retired to France where he lived
quietly until his death. Sanazzaro accompanied him and "sold the
remainder of his hereditary possessions to relieve the necessities of
his sovereign, and remained with him to the time of his death"
(*Leo,* 1. 57–58, 200–01, 316 n.).

"Frascator (lightning was midwife)." Roscoe writes of the "awful
event which occurred in the infancy of Frascatoro [which] has
also been considered as a presage of his future eminence. Whilst his
mother was carrying him in her arms, she was struck dead by light-
ning, but her child received not the slightest injury" (*Leo,* 3. 283).

Pound's spellings of the proper names in Roscoe are very inaccu-
rate: he gives Barabello for Baraballo, Mozarello for Mozzarello,
Navighero for Navagero, and Sanazarro for Sanazzaro.

Canto 6

The original version of this canto concentrated on the rivalry between Louis VII and Henry II, Eleanor's first and second husbands, and between their heirs, Philippe-Auguste and Richard, in their dealings with Tancred, King of Sicily. Frederick II the Holy Roman Emperor was praised for his shrewd and honorable dealings with the Saracens and Conrad de Montferrat for his courage in defending Tyre against Saladin.[4] It is important to notice how in the final version of this canto the emphasis has radically shifted from the political problems and intrigues of these men to the presence of the two powerful and passionate women, Eleanor of Aquitaine and Cunizza da Romano.

Both women were the inspiration of troubadours and the canto concentrates on Sordello's love for Cunizza and Eleanor's patronage of Bernart de Venta, who asks her to intercede for him with Eblis II of Venta to persuade him to free his wife Alice, whom he has kept in confinement because of her love for Bernart. "Guillaume," Eleanor's grandfather, is one of the earliest of the troubadours. Eleanor is first married to Louis, but, after fifteen years, is divorced and marries Henry, Duke of Normandy and Count of Anjou, who becomes Henry II of England. Louis is not passionate enough to please her, as Pound suggests in his comment about her "uncle" in Acre, and the two become estranged when Eleanor accompanies her husband on the second crusade. Louis is naturally angry at her second marriage, which adds Aquitaine to Henry's lands, meaning that the King of England owns more of France than the French king himself. Henry's father had earlier won Normandy for him, making him heir of "Gisors, and Vexis, [and] Neufchastel." Richard, Henry's son, had been betrothed to "Alix," second daughter of Louis VII, but he repudiated her because of his animosity toward Philip II, her brother.

Pound is interested in Eleanor not only as a patron of troubadours and the inspiration of much love poetry and courtly literature, but also as a strong and efficient ruler, who had great influ-

4. See Ronald Bush, *The Genesis of Ezra Pound's Cantos* (Princeton, 1976), pp. 214–20, and Appendix B, the text of the original Canto 6.

ence over the political events of her time. She took her sons' part when they joined Louis against their father and supported Richard against John, his brother, and at the age of eighty, she held the town of Mirabeau against her grandson's forces until John could relieve her. The continuing loyalty to England of her ancestral lands in Aquitaine is in large part a cause of the Hundred Years War and makes her also something of a Helen-figure.

Cunizza is a great favorite with Pound. She is the inspiration for Sordello's best poetry and Dante places her in the Heaven of Venus as a generous giver. In 1265 she freed her slaves in the house of the Cavalcanti where Dante could possibly have met her. She was over eighty when she died. Pound imagines Dante hearing from Guido Cavalcanti about her:

> . . . of beauty incarnate, or, if the beauty can by any possibility be brought into doubt, at least and with utter certainty, charm and imperial bearing, grace that stopped not an instant in sweeping over the most violent authority of her time [her brother, the notoriously cruel Ezzolino da Romano] and, from the known fact, that vigour which is a grace in itself. There was nothing in Chréstien de Troyes' narratives, nothing in Rimini or in the tales of the antients to surpass the facts of Cunizza, with, in her old age, great kindness, thought for her slaves. [*GK,* 107–08]

"And Cairels was of Sarlat. . . ." Pound includes his brief life-story in "Troubadours . . .": "Elias Cairels 'was of Sarlat; ill he sang, ill he composed, ill he played the fiddle and worse he spoke, but he was good at writing out words and tunes. And he was a long time wandering, and when he quitted it, he returned to Sarlat and died there' " (*LE,* 98).

Canto 20

"Shelf of the lotophagoi, / Aerial, cut in the aether." In his engraving and painting, "The Circle of the Lustful: Francesca da Rimini," upon which Pound is basing his description, Blake shows his pairs of lovers drawn up from sea waves into a great current which carries them first to the left and upward and then loops around and sweeps them upward again so that, as Pound remarks, they are "Shot from stream into spiral." For the most part, the figures are studies in voluptuous ease rather than in torment, although some of those just drawn up from the waves show some distress and one figure in the center of the painting has crashed head-first into the ledge of rock upon which Dante lies, unconscious. This figure's companion looks in horror at his fate, but otherwise the spirits within the spiral itself do seem, as Pound says, "Swift, as if joyous," and most of them are embracing their partners. Pound's description of the painting captures the relaxed voluptuousness of the figures perfectly, and also shows that he had been studying the engraving as well as the painting. Only in the former do we find "The left hand like a calyx, / Thumb held against finger, the third, / The first finger petal'd up, the hand as a lamp, / A calyx." This hand belongs to one of the two most striking female figures and she is shown with "Head in arm's curve, reclining" just at the point at which the current sweeps around to the right to begin the spiral. The second woman occupies the most central position in the spiral and it seems very likely that she is Helen and that Pound is looking at her when he writes "cosi Elena vedi."[5]

Canto 50

Here Pound follows the history of Tuscany from the time of the Medici to the reign of Leopold II after which Tuscany becomes a part of the kingdom of Italy. The Medici, under whom state debt increased from five million to fourteen million scudi, are contrasted to Leopold I, whose reforms Pound has already written on in Canto 44. On the death of his brother, in 1790, Leopold becomes Holy Roman Emperor and must leave for "hell's bog, in the slough of Vienna," the center of power of Metternich, the devil incarnate of "Mitteleuropa," who is dedicated to the overthrow of Napoleon. Of Napoleon's defeat of the Austrians at Marengo

5. For further details see my "Pound's Blake and Blake's Dante: 'The Circle of the Lustful' and Canto 20," *Paideuma* 6, no. 2 (Fall 1977): 155–65.

Pound writes, "Mars meaning, in that case, order / That day was Right with the Victor / mass weight against wrong." Under French occupation, Tuscany had at least not been run into debt, but, after the Congress of Vienna, Tuscany is given to Austria and under Count Rospigliosi, the Austrian regent, the Tuscans are treated like serfs. Pound claims that Napoleon's defeat, by strengthening England and Austria, increases the power of the usurers. When Napoleon leaves Elba on the *Incostante* there is a glimmer of hope for Europe, but it lasts only for the "Hundred Days." Pound preserves Bonaparte's dignity by seeing him as more the victim of his own misjudgments than of England and Austria: " 'Not' / said Napoleon 'because of that league of lice, / but for opposing the Zeitgeist! That was my ruin.' "

Pound's main source in this canto is Antonio Zobi's *Storia Civile della Toscana.* "But Genoa took our trade and Livorno / kept treaty with England to the loss of Livorno . . ." refers to the flourishing of Genoese trade as a result of their dealings with America, comparing this to the restrictions on Livorno's trade with America that were imposed by a treaty with England which meant that Livorno's cargoes could only be sent to America in Genoese vessels.[6]

"Te, admirabile, O VashinnnTTonn!" is an allusion to Zobi's eulogy on the virtues of Washington, his officers, and the whole American people, who have provided Tuscany with the perfect blueprint for improving its own conditions. We understand the reason for Zobi's impassioned digression when we see that this history is published in 1850 as the revolutionary phase of the *Risorgimento* draws to a close and Italy must still wait eleven years for unification. Zobi's digression ends:

> Bless you, o illustrious land of America, daughter of Italy, who have received so many unfortunate Italian exiles! To the favor of your hospitality add, for them, the instruction

6. Antonio Zobi, *Storia Civile della Toscana,* 5 vols. (Firenze, 1850–52), 2: 385–90. Translation mine.

through which they may grow in power, dignity and greatness; and thus a day will come which will put the lie to those words of the greatest poet:

> 'Ahi serva Italia, di dolore ostello,
> 'Nave senza nocchiero in gran tempesta
> 'Non donna di provincie, ma bordello.

The reader will excuse this brief digression, which has such a close bearing on our current problems.[7]

"And so on the 30th of October Lord Minto / was in Arezzo . . ." The episode from Lord Minto's visit to Italy in 1847 is taken from Zobi's *Storia* (5. 236–37), where we read that, when the crowd in Arezzo cheers for the friends of Italian independence, for free trade, for the National Customs Union, for Cobden and the English Parliament, Minto responds with "*evviva a Leopoldo II, ed all' independenza italiana.*" This, reported in the newspapers, stirs up much speculation about England's intentions toward Italy. Minto had only intended to be politely ambiguous.

Canto 51

In this canto Pound's emphasis is on man the "artifex." The second section deals with the details of making fishing flies and suggests that the fly-fisherman is, in his own way, an "artifex." He makes flies with skill and precision and according to an established tradition based, in turn, on a minute observation of the natural world and with an eye to what will achieve a positive result. It can be said of him as of the great artist and even of the Creator himself that the creation of each "hath the light of the doer, as it were / a form cleaving to it," and this explains the point of the first lines of the canto: "Shines / in the mind of heaven God / who made it / more than the sun / in our eye." The creative power of God permeates the whole of creation, and Pound, who expresses this infinite creativity by analogy with light, sees it reproduced on a minute scale in man's creation of artifacts. Precision of perception must

7. Ibid., 2: 390. Translation mine.

precede creativity and the canto ends with the *Ching ming* ideo-graph which Pound uses with the meaning of "precise definition."

"Deo similis quodam modo / hic intellectus adeptus [This attain-ing intellect is like God, in a certain way]." Pound finds this in a passage from Albertus Magnus's *De apprehensione* that is cited in Ernest Renan's *Averroes et l'Averroisme,* and shows the Christian theologian's debt to Arabic philosophy in his adoption of the con-cepts of the *intellectus agens, intellectus possibilis,* and *intellectus adeptus.* The "agent intellect" is the supreme Intellect which can manifest itself to the *intellectus possibilis* of the individual through the latter's disposition to receive intelligible forms. When these two function together, the individual attains to the *intellectus adeptus,* the state of having made contact with the *nous.* In "Cavalcanti" Pound quotes from Albertus: *"Ex possibili et agente compositus est intellectus adeptus, et divinis dicitur, et tunc homo perfectus est. Et fit per hunc intellectum homo Deo quodam modo similis . . .* [From the union of the *possibilis* and the *agens* the *intellectus adeptus* is formed and is said to be divine: then a man is made perfect. And by this intellect man is made similar in a certain way to God]" (*LE,* 186).

Canto 78

"Thiy." It seems most likely that Pound chooses to call Bride Scratton by this name after Tiy, the chief wife of Amenhotep III, "the Magnificent," by the ruins of whose funerary temple stand the Colossi of Memnon. Pound compares himself to Amenhotep when he writes of Gaudier's bust of him: "Oh well, *mon pauvre caractère,* the good Gaudier has stiffened it up quite a lot, and added so much of wisdom, so much of resolution. I should have had the firmness of Hotep-hotep, the strength of the gods of Egypt" (*GB,* 50).

Canto 79

"Cimbica servant of Helios" (79/492). In "Hudson: Poet Strayed into Science," published in *The Little Review,* May–June 1920 (*SP,* 431), Pound writes of Hudson's *The Naturalist in La Plata:*

"He would lead us to South America; despite the gnats and mos-
quitoes we would all perform the voyage for the sake of meeting
a puma, Chimbicá, friend of man, the most loyal of wildcats."

Canto 81

"Aoi! / a leaf in the current." Mary de Rachewiltz writes that
"the cry of AOI is an outburst more personal than any other in
the Cantos and expresses the stress of almost two years when
[Pound] was pent up with two women who loved him, whom he
loved, and who coldly hated each other" (*Disc.,* 258). This cry of
distress is not, I think, related to the "Aoi" which divides the sec-
tions of the *Chanson de Roland,* but is borrowed from the Noh. In
Pound's translation of *Kinuta,* for example, this cry is spoken first
by the wife, then by her ghost, and then by the Chorus, lamenting
her fate. She dies from grief when her husband, who went to the
capital "for a casual visit" stayed on there for three years "en
tangled in many litigations" without either returning to her or
sending a message. The wife's suffering at the husband's selfish
preoccupation and lack of consideration for her feelings bears
some resemblance to the suffering which Pound feels that he has
caused.

Canto 93

Quotations on 93/625–27 from treatises 3 and 4 of the *Convivio.*
Pound isolates several passages from the treatise on ode 2. His
" 'quest' unire / 'quale è dentro l'anima / veggendo di fuori quelli
che ama' " refers to the union between the human soul and "the
excellences of nature and of reason" of which Dante writes: "this
union it is which we call love, whereby the inner quality of the
soul may be recognized by examining outwardly the things which
it loves."[8] In *Convivio* 3. 13 Dante says of the "Lady Philosophy"
that "the folk who are enamoured here, to wit in this life, perceive
her in their thoughts, not always [*non sempre*], but when love

8. *The Convivio of Dante Alighieri,* trans. Philip H. Wicksteed (London,
1924) treatise 3, chapter 2, lines 66–70.

makes them feel of his peace" (26–30), and later observes that
"love is the form of philosophy [*è forma di Filosofia*] and there-
fore here it is called her soul" (109–10). In *Convivio* 3. 15, Dante
explains that "the beauty of wisdom . . . results from the order of
the moral virtues, which enable her to give pleasure that may be
perceived by the senses. And therefore I say that her beauty, to
wit, morality [*cioè moralitade*], *rains down flamelets of fire*, that
is to say right appetite, which is begotten by the pleasantness of
moral teaching" (119–26). The other allusions are from the ode
and commentary of treatise 4. In the seventh part of ode 3, Dante
describes the characteristic behavior of a man of true gentility:
"The soul whom this excellence adorns [*cui adorna esta bontade*]
holds it not concealed . . . [but] shows it forth till death" (121–
24). In manhood the soul of each man "delights only in deeds of
loyalty [*solo in lealtà far si diletta*]" and in old age is just, gener-
ous, and gratified "to hear and to discourse of others' excellence
[*D'udire e ragionar dell'altrui prode*]" (131–35). *Bontade*—the
moral excellence which is the root of gentility—comes, Dante says,
from God alone, hence Pound's "Dio, la prima bontade," which he
equates with the Chinese character *i*⁴, meaning morality or righ-
teousness. In the commentary on *"L'anima cui adorna esta bon-
tate,"* Dante writes: "this nobleness openly shines [*risplende*] and
glows through the whole life of the noble one" and Pound seems
to be referring to this passage in "onestade risplende," even though
he substitutes "honesty" for "nobility." Dante "mentions distribu-
tive justice" in *Convivio* (4. 17. 62) as the eleventh moral virtue.

Canto 97

" 'splendor' mondan', / beata gode / . . . / beat' è, e gode" (97/676–
78). In the *Inferno* (7. 73–96), Dante has Vergil say of Fortuna:

> He whose wisdom transcends all, made the heavens and gave
> them guides. . . . In like manner, for worldly splendors [*li
> splendor mondani*] He ordained a general minister and guide
> who should in due time transfer the vain goods from race to
> race, and from one to another blood, beyond the prevention
> of human wit, so that one race rules and another languishes,

pursuant to her judgment, which is hidden like the snake in the grass. . . . This is she who is much reviled even by those who ought to praise her, but do wrongfully blame her and defame her. But she is blest [*s'è beata*] and does not hear it. Happy with the other primal creatures she turns her sphere and rejoices in her bliss [*e beata si gode*].

Canto 106

"Selena Arsinoe / So late did queens rise into heaven. / . . . / Arsinoe Kupris" (106/755). The queen who "rose into heaven" is Arsinoe herself, sister and then second wife of Ptolemy II, who deified both her and himself. "Arsinoe Kupris" links her to Aphrodite and probably also refers to the fact that Famagusta in Cyprus was called Arsinoe in her honor. Her stepson married Berenice III, whose hair, said to have been turned into a constellation, also "rose into heaven."

Appendix 2
Pound and T. E. Hulme

Pound's disclaimer of any debt to Hulme is not entirely reliable. Hulme's self-assurance and impressiveness, together with his claim to having "discovered" the French neoclassicists first, was somewhat annoying to trailblazers like Lewis and Pound. For all Lewis's condescension in *Blasting and Bombardiering* he was really very concerned with Hulme's opinion of him. The story of how Hulme suspended him upside down by his turn-ups on the railings of Soho Square is often repeated, but the less well-known prelude to this incident, if Kate Lechmere's account is reliable, is very revealing of Lewis. Lewis was upset at the intimacy between her and Hulme, and, as Hulme's biographer, Alun Jones, retells the story: "Lewis was desperate. He took her out to an A. B. C. teashop and wagging his finger over the marble table kept repeating 'Remember Hulme is Epstein and Epstein is Hulme.' Perhaps he thought it was a plot to drive him out of the Rebel Art Center and install Epstein as its leader. Finally, Lewis said he would have to kill Hulme, and Miss Lechmere tells how she ran all the way down Piccadilly after him shouting, 'Please don't kill him, please don't.' "[1] Jones's conclusion about Hulme's feelings toward Pound helps to explain why Pound would have wanted to deny any debt to Hulme: "Hulme's attitude toward Ezra Pound, always vaguely patronizing and con-

1. Alun Jones, *The Life and Opinions of T. E. Hulme* (London, 1960), p. 123.

temptuous, developed into open hostility when Pound joined Lewis against him. Hulme from this time on began, as it were, to cultivate a private life while Lewis and Pound went on living their lives as publicly as possible."[2]

Pound claims in "This Hulme Business"[3] that "the critical LIGHT during the years immediately pre-war in London shone not from Hulme but from Ford (Madox etc.) in so far as it fell on writing at all," but this has rightly been contested. When he goes on to say that Hulme's "evenings were diluted with crap like Bergson," he is simply parroting Lewis. As Sam Hynes, an editor of Hulme's writings, has shown: "the originator of Imagism was clearly Hulme. By discrediting thought as the source and logic as the method of the poetry, he reinstated physical experience as the core of the poem and imagery as the texture.[4] Hulme's Imagism is the result of his application of Bergson's principles to the practice of writing poetry[5] and this presents a problem for Pound, since he accepts Lewis's criticisms of Bergson. K. K. Ruthven takes up Hulme's "case" in *A Guide to Ezra Pound's Personae,* and points out that Pound found in de Gourmont the same basic ideas that Hulme found in Bergson. He bases his case for Pound's debt to Hulme rather than to Gourmont on one comment of Pound's in his 1914 essay "Vorticism": "The point of Imagisme is that it does not use images *as ornaments.* The image itself is the speech. The image is the word beyond formulated language." The source of this, as Ruthven shows, is not Gourmont but must be either Bergson or Hulme paraphrasing Bergson in a *New Age* article of 1909: "Images in verse are not mere decoration, but the very essence of an intuitive language." Gourmont does not make this point.[6]

This article of Hulme's, "Searchers after Reality, II, Haldane," was published just four months after Pound joined Hulme's group

2. Ibid., p. 124.

3. Ezra Pound, "This Hulme Business," *The Townsman* 2, no. 5 (Jan. 1939): 15.

4. T. E. Hulme, *Further Speculations,* ed. Sam Hynes (Minneapolis, 1955), p. xix.

5. Explained by Hynes, p. xvii.

6. K. K. Ruthven, *A Guide to Ezra Pound's Personae* (Berkeley and Los Angeles, 1969), pp. 12–13.

of poets. Nor was Pound at that time of the opinion that Bergson was "crap." In December 1911, he wrote to his mother that he was impressed with Hulme's lectures on Bergson which he had attended, which were probably "Bergson's Theory of Art" and "The Philosophy of Intensive Manifolds." In another letter home, on February 21, 1912, he described Hulme as a "very good sort" and said, in addition, that Flint had recommended to him some very good French authors, among them Gourmont. In April of that year, Pound's "The Wisdom of Poetry" was published in *Forum* and was a translation of Hulme's material into his own terms (*Life,* 113). In the *Egoist* of May 1, 1915, Flint describes how Hulme and F. W. Tancred spent hours each day looking for the exact phrase, for "absolute accurate presentation and no verbiage." Pound's desire to give Ford Madox Ford his due was understandable, but he was certainly not the only searcher after *le mot juste.* Also, he was not interested in poetic theory.

Clearly the personal and professional frictions between Hulme, Lewis, and Pound account in part for Pound's and Lewis's anxiousness to minimize Hulme's role. Pound's eulogizing of Gourmont seems, at least initially, to have been part of an attempt to push Bergson into the background and thereby avoid bringing down upon himself the scorn of Lewis—a fate, incidentally, which Pound proved no better than anyone else at escaping.

Index